LL ___ _ _____

CONFESSIONS OF AN AFRICAN SAFARI GUIDE

TRUTHS, TALES AND TABOOS OF THE SAFARI LIFE

LLOYD CAMP CONSULTING
AFRICA

Every story is a gift, and everyone takes what they need from it. All that matters is some starting point in the story that allows it to become someone else's, to take on a new truth.

A friend

Almost all of what I say is usually true. Sometimes.

The same friend

Front cover image credit: Claudia Vogelbach

First Printing, 2020

ISBN: 9781674064307

Published by Lloyd Camp Consulting Africa,
in association with Mudd Buffalo Moments.
Richmond-upon-Thames
Surrey, UK

www.lloydcamp.co.za

For my parents, Kelson and Moira Camp,
with the greatest love.

Distances and weights

1 metre = 1.1 yards
1 kilometre = 0.6 miles
1 mile = 1.6 kilometres
1 kilogram = 2.2 pounds
1 pound = 0.45 kilograms
0 Celsius = 32 F (an extremely chilly morning game drive)
18 Celsius = 64 F (the temperature at which red wine should be served)
38 Celsius = 100 F (an extremely hot afternoon game drive)

The abbreviations 'm', 'km', 'kg' and 'ml' are sometimes used for metre, kilometre, kilogram and millilitre.

CONTENTS

Acknowledgements.. IX
Maps X
Ever Thus (A Poem For Sunrise)...................................XII
Introduction... XIII

1. That One Thing..17
2. Don't Go Commando 22
3. Pain Has A Colour.. 30
4. Apocryphalia 37
5. Game Of Secrets.. 69
6. Just Say A Number.. 79
7. Africa's A Big Country 86
8. Steve, And The Modern Novel 92
9. Fool's Garden 97
10. The Actress And The Giraffe 106
11. I Can Never Speak Of This....................................... 112
12. Malaria Dreams 117
13. Mary 28 123
14. She Never Saw That Coming.................................... 131
15. Investigated 138
16. Picture Man 145
17. No Laughing Matter... 154
18. Cookie Cutter 163
19. I Never Went For The School 171
20. Hi, I'm From HQ, I'm Here To Help 193
21. Don't Mention The Monkey..................................... 202
22. Bad Chemistry 210
23. First World Problems.. 215
24. The Sand Samaritan 223
25. Take Off, Take Two 231
26. Glyssps, Or Marthambles?.. 238
27. Sudden Justice 248

28. Hard Choices 253

29. Dead Weight 261

30. Mountain Of Fire 270

31. Meat Loaf On A Saturday 276

32. Body Bag 284

33. Another Kind Of Normal 290

34. Diminishing Returns 296

35. Vanilla Guiding 302

36. VVVIP 313

37. Except When It Isn't 321

38. Fifty Shades Of Khaki 327

39. Misnames 339

Epilogue 341

Paying Attention (A Poem For Sunset) 343

Glossary 345

About The Author 351

ACKNOWLEDGEMENTS

It would be a gratifying literary flourish to thank all the many people who have helped me through hard and desperate times, so I tried to remember some character-forming personal disasters to exaggerate and I have to admit that they've been disappointingly scarce. Never underestimate luck as a life strategy! As a result, you will be relieved to hear that I shall not be writing an autobiography: it would be total rubbish.

Even so, there are several folk who I'd like to tip my hat to:

Perry Rendell. Again.

Shelley Evans and Sally Frost for turning this book into something vastly better.

Malcolm "Foxtrot" Ainscough. And his mate, Hymie.

Liz Ellway and Jos Evans.

Kate Thompson for the book title.

Rob Simmons for the story title, '*Fifty Shades Of Khaki*'. And for our house in Hertzinger Strasse.

62 Tony for the story title, '*Pain Has A Colour*'.

Braam van Wyk for the story title, '*One Thing That's Not Two*'. And for saving a drowning seagull.

Nils Kure for the quotation, '*I Never Went For The School*'.

Peter Allison for coining the expression, '*Vanilla Guiding*'.

All you lovely people who bought *Africa Bites*. Some of you wrote to tell me that it made you laugh. Several said that it made you yearn for Africa, and many said that my stories actually made you come on safari. That's a win-win. Mission accomplished.

The countless safari travel clients and colleagues everywhere who continue to provide the food for my thought.

Sue. Always.

And my continent, which keeps us all guessing: *ex Africa semper aliquid novi.*

Africa

TANZANIA

Vamizi

NAMIBIA   ZIMBABWE

MOZAMBIQUE

BOTSWANA

ATLANTIC
OCEAN

INDIAN
OCEAN

SOUTH
AFRICA

The countries in which these stories take place

Southern Africa

Shakawe

Selinda Game Reserve

DumaTau
Zibalianja

Duba

Mombo

Chitabe

Maun

Okavango Delta

Serra Cafema Camp

Owamboland

Victoria Falls

Purros

Mushara

Kasane

ZIMBABWE

Desert Rhino Camp

Ongava
Palmwag Lodge

Damaraland Camp

Brandberg

Ghanzi

Pafuri

BOTSWANA

Windhoek

Gaborone

Mala Mala Game Reserve

Sossusvlei

NAMIBIA

Tswalu

iMfolozi

Pietermaritzburg

ATLANTIC
OCEAN

SOUTH
AFRICA

Durban

Cape Town

INDIAN
OCEAN

EVER THUS
(A Poem For Sunrise)

Tonight I am a sweated-up *vaquero*
Sitting a slat-ribbed horse on a slaty ridge
Pointed into a hard wind
A torn hat hiding the look in my eyes
And the horse unwilling.
Too much time for thinking, and too little.
Contemplating the nature of all things.
As the red sun leavens the outer edge of the earth
I find that the leaving brings a hard-earned understanding
Eventually
That all you know
All whom you love
Are always yours, and you theirs.
I put the horse at the sun.

INTRODUCTION

The Bezos swift-shopping forum throws up an abundance of choice if you want to read African safari stories. Many guides write books, and quite right too: we are fortunate to work in the wilds (people keep telling me that I have the 'ideal job', and I don't disagree) and we have smashing stories to tell, stories that thrill, stories that touch people, stories of love, stories that evoke images of a way our wilderness world can be. Stories, importantly, that kindle a desire to meet Africans, in Africa. Stories are the grease of life and they need to be shared. One of the best compliments anyone gave me was that he was so engrossed while reading one of my stories on the bus home from work that he missed his stop. (Thanks Stebu!)

The thing is, though, that there is a sameness to all these books, a style that is predicated by a target audience that wants stories along two main themes: guides getting a fright and running away from wild animals (see my first book, *Africa Bites*), and the romance of the African sunset and a bitterly cold gin and tonic (again, see *Africa Bites*).

But *Confessions* is different. It's time for some honest revelations and a bit of under-belly. Something just a little grittier, edgier, sometimes darker, certainly more personal; what goes on at the back of house, that staff quarter hidden away from view behind the high split-pole fence. The sign reads 'Staff only' and you always wonder, don't you: who and what makes this sublime safari experience happen? What are we not allowed to see, or hear? Every business has its public facade, its little secrets, its back-stories, its scandals and gossip. They're usually no big deal, just stuff that's always going to happen, little disasters that are rapidly managed, like ducks paddling on water, frantic below the surface, yet hoping they look like swans a-gliding, and the client is never the wiser. But you just know that some funny things go on behind the scenes, things that the staff aren't telling you about because they don't want to shatter the illusion of tranquillity and order. But what Michelin-rated restaurant chef never dropped a steak onto a greasy kitchen floor and put it straight back into the pan?

I gave an early transcript of *Confessions* to some people in the safari industry whose judgement I value and they said some of the sins and secrets in the book are a bit too close to the bone. Too forthright. A guilty conscience will do that. Their discomfort and wincing was all the encouragement I needed to go ahead.

These stories are mostly funny incidents (well, in retrospect), the great little inside truths that guides remind each other of when they meet up, the stories that usually finish with, "I can't believe we got away with that!", the insights into the pragmatic workings of the safari life and a memory-dive into the realities that are concealed just below the magical veneer of the safari experience.

But it's not all gasp and shock and "Oh, really!" Many of these tales are gentler, warmer, more sentimental. Some are more tender confessions to vulnerability, and wonder. 'Little baby impala' moments rather than the gory thrill of the kill. They are vignettes of contemplation, and love, recognition of the moments that make shifts in our lives. Different kinds of confessions.

Safari guides sometimes get placed on a pedestal by adoring clients. That's not an over-statement. The love-affair with wilderness and wild animals that a safari induces make that understandable. It's a holiday, after all, a new and stimulating experience, and the guest is in the safe hands of a guide who is the key to unlocking the experience. Guests almost always lead safe and predictable lives so they thrill to the relative unpredictability of ours. They usually do not actually *want* our lives but they do want to live them through us for a short while.

I get that, but even so I still find it a bit odd. Because guides are just normal folk like you, actually, doing what they love to do. They too are people of many parts with their own insecurities, fears and private agendas. They laugh and they cry and they dissemble. Often, unfortunately, they take themselves far too seriously. They have a good time, but they also sometimes get sad. They gossip about clients, colleagues and the competition. Some guides are sensitive, some are brash and actually believe their own bullshit, and some don't even really know why they're there. They simply fell into guiding because they didn't know what else to do; a gap year that became a living.

Don't you always want to know: who *is* your guide when he's not wearing the work-mask? How did he get into this game? Why is he *still* in this game? Does he ever grow bored with it, maybe with *us*, and is he fibbing when he says he doesn't? What thoughts, doubts, joys and little white lies lurk behind his Ray-Bans? What yarns do safari guides tell in private, what stories do they slap their thighs about, when they meet at Joe's Beerhouse in Windhoek, or at trade fairs in London, Berlin and Marrakech? When they tell tales about the time before the industry turned to marshmallow and guides could really, really play, and say sorry later? When guides were young... and naughty.

This book may answer some of those questions. If you think you recognise yourself in these stories, well then, yup, it *is* you. ("I bet you think this song is about you, don't you?"). Don't worry, names have been changed to protect the guilty. A few of these stories are slightly tangential to safari but they were inspired by amazing people that I have guided in Africa, people I sat with around a fire, that perfect forum for the telling of tales and the polishing of fables.

So then, this time round, fewer sunsets, more diesel and dust. And tenderness. It's time we had a laugh at ourselves, a glance in the mirror, and a rueful shake of the head.

You're going to like this.

(By the way, there are many colloquialisms and plentiful use of slang in this book. You'll be needing the glossary).

(And a disclaimer. I refer to guides as 'he' in this book, just because it's simpler. There are plenty of female guides these days, happily).

1

THAT ONE THING

There was nothing I wanted more, and I was nervous. I wasn't a confident kid and the interview process with the Area Director of the Pietermaritzburg Boy Scouts was nerve-wracking, but looking at the other two candidates gave me some hope. One youngster was lounging in a chair, bored, his eyes half closed and his feet on the coffee table, and the other was chewing gum and looking sulky. Obviously, his parents thought this was a good idea, and he did not. My parents thought this was a good idea too, but I was in unabridged agreement with them. They knew what this meant to me. My dad had already been on one, and when he got back he told of being treed by a charging White rhino (yes, white, not black, a bit unusual), of a massive *dhaga* boy buffalo that abruptly thrust its great hook-horned head at them through a curtain of tall reeds, of lions calling close at hand as they patrolled the White iMfolozi river at dawn, and of a mahogany-wood fire that burned slowly with a deep yellow flame all through the night. I wanted that experience more than I could say.

The iMfolozi Wilderness Trail. It is as legendary as it is iconic.

It was the first of the walking trails run by the old Natal Parks Board, in the oldest proclaimed conservation area in Africa, and has been successfully replicated by South African National Parks in places such as the Kruger. In the early days, when it was a new concept, the trails were led by hard-bitten rangers whose real focus was on conservation, not tourists. The NPB harboured a lot of contemptuous people who believed that their only concern was looking after wildlife and that the tourists who visited the game reserves were a damned nuisance, at best a necessary inconvenience. They wanted to save the White rhinoceros, burn fire-breaks, do game counts and keep the hungry and rapacious neighbouring villagers on the far side of the game fence. Proper conservation work. Not leading bloody townies on foot through lion country. But someone had to do it; some bright spark in HQ at Queen Elizabeth Park said so. ("Conservation needs the money! And it's the right thing to do. The parks are for the people.") Bloody HQ.

Despite their unapologetic disdain for the bright-eyed folk that followed them apprehensively through *Acacia* thorn thickets and along the myriad game trails, the concept of walking and sleeping wild quickly caught on. My family went to the Zululand game reserves every winter, a highlight of our year, and we were accustomed to driving ourselves around in our own low-slung saloon car, keeping to the gravel roads and sitting in hushed expectation at the game viewing hides, making sure that we were back in camp by nightfall, and never venturing beyond the perimeter of the camp at any time. The reserve officials were fierce and authoritative about it, driving their olive green NPB *bakkies* around and barking bluntly at any tourists who breached the rules. But the wilderness trail was very different to that. It was edgy and exciting, because we were out there *on foot*, not a road in sight, sleeping on the ground around a heap of glowing coals, sitting up through the inky night in hourly shifts to keep watch, while nocturnal creatures shuffled in the leaf-litter and snorted in the gloom, and little Scops owls and Fierynecked nightjars called comfortingly in the galleries of the cathedral fig under which we were camped. I tremble even now to think how wonderful it was. How wonderful it *is!*

I was chosen, one of a group of six Scouts from across Natal

Province. A free iMfolozi Wilderness Trail, sponsored by the Rotary Club. Gods, the week-long wait for the judges' decision was agonising. Why do they do that to kids? It's like being told you can't open your presents on Christmas morning, even though you and your cousins and siblings have been gathered at the base of the tree since before dawn, all because Aunty Sue wants, indeed, insists, on being there for the event, but she's gone to the mid-morning Christmas church service first. Child abuse in the first degree!

But the Area Director chose well: that wilderness trail was the most intoxicating event of my fourteen years-old life. How I'd always envied and admired those gruff trails rangers I'd seen in the Zululand game reserves. I didn't set out there and then to become one, because it all seemed somehow impossible; I didn't know people who did that sort of thing for a living, and I had no clue how to start, but a seed found fertile ground that July in 1977, and an unconscious path was set. Consequently, many years later and rather to my astonishment, after having had a go at being a history teacher for a while, I found myself at Mala Mala Game Reserve, and later, leading walking trails in Namibia, Zimbabwe, Botswana and Mozambique. Just like my iMfolozi wilderness trail hero. Adam.

By rights, I shouldn't have liked Adam at all. He was useless with kids. Well, most kids. Forbidding, impatient, grumpy, non-communicative, brooding. Yet he insisted from the outset that we call him Adam. First names only, no Mister or Sir, no silly formalities, he commanded. I'd never called an adult by their first name, and I was too much in awe of him to do it now, so I hardly spoke to him at all. He wore a tatty reddish beard, only because he was too idle to shave it, his hair jutted out from under his floppy bush hat in an ill-looking straight thatch, his tight NPB-issue shorts rode way too high up into his crotch to be acceptable in any society, he never once changed his stained uniform shirt, its once green and yellow shoulder epaulettes sun-faded and barely legible, and he smelled of pipe tobacco and ancient sweat. He scoffed at our brand new boots that took ages to unlace at every river crossing, eye-chiding us without comment, then simply wading through the stream in his town shoes, no socks, the sand spilling into them at no apparent inconvenience to him. While we fussed with burrs in our socks and flapped at flies around our heads, Adam strode steadily along in his low-cut fake-leather Hush Puppys, paying no heed to the manifold inconveniences of the terrain, the hooked thorns that tugged and the rocks that gouged. I never once in five days saw him take those cheap brogues off. He spurned sunglasses, he rejected gloves in the chilly winter morning, he declined to use effete handkerchiefs (he blew his nose with his fingers), and without any doubt, he never wore underwear. As he walked the trail, he rested his Brno .375 rifle across his shoulders, sometimes looping his arms over the stock and barrel, striding through the rising heat as if crucified upon his weapon. His nose was burnished red by the unrelenting southern sun, his manner was austere, even surly, and his gravitas was deeply impressive. But it was very obvious that he was devoted to the wilderness, and when he talked of it, of all the complexities and intricacies of the wild, he was transformed. He suddenly became animated, anxious that we should understand what moved him, and I was transfixed by his passion. He seemed to know so *much*. He slung a pair of Leicas around his neck, the best binoculars money could buy. He was Achilles. I wanted to be just like him.

I have led so many safaris, been on so many game drives, sat around so many fires in the bush, yet I remember with total clarity those four days of dramatic theatre. How I noticed that Adam never slept in his tent but always around the fire and somehow he understood that I really wanted to do that too, and he simply pointed to where I should unroll my sleeping bag. The day up on Nqabaneni hill at the bushman paintings when a tawny eagle flew straight and fast down river below us, only it wasn't a light-brown colour but almost white in the glare of the noonday sun, and when he asked me what it was I identified it straight away. A moment of intense pleasure when Adam walked us out from under the Sycamore fig into the moon-glow on the open sands of the White iMfolozi and I hesitantly pointed out my own constellation, Scorpius, the great heavenly arachnid curling towards Libra, by far the largest and most commanding set of stars in the southern sky, and Adam nodded at me, pleased. And how he always spoke quietly and with respect in fluent *isiZulu* to John, our Zulu game guard, who walked silently behind us by day, armed with a 12-bore double barrelled shotgun, minding our backs. The way Adam sat alone in the shade in the heat of the day and smoked his pipe, his blackened thumb tamping down on the hot tobacco, staring out towards the horizon where the grey trees and cobalt sky blended into an undefined opaque haze, with no desire to speak, contemplating... what exactly? Do adults always understand the profound influence, the potent effect, they can have on children? Some small gesture, a word of acknowledgment, an unexpected act of kindness that can suddenly change *everything*.

The iMfolozi Wilderness Trail was the longest continuous amount of time I had hitherto spent on one game reserve. Years later, at Mala Mala, even though I was only serving an apprenticeship at first, learning the ropes, checking guest rooms and pouring drinks and clearing roads of elephant-shoved trees, I counted the nights and when it reached the magical number of five, I had finally broken my record. It was a milestone, a landmark in a career in guiding and nature conservation, a private celebration.

I heard quite recently that Adam was eventually severely gored by a buffalo, but he survived. I'm not surprised. He was the kind of guy that, if bitten by a venomous snake, would only lie down for a while with a headache while the serpent died of septicaemia and deep regret at having targeted the wrong man.

The Scouts, the Rotary Club, and Adam himself, perhaps not altogether unwittingly, bestowed upon me an opportunity to foster beyond measure a love of wild places and its denizens, without ever fully understanding, I think, the gift they had given me. Walking in the wilderness and getting the dust of Africa on your boots. Or on your Hush Puppys. It is just so sublime to be there. Uncomplicated. There's a tranquility to it, a halcyon serenity, and sometimes, thrillingly, a sudden burst of electricity. You're always paying attention when you're on foot. You're in touch with the raw, far side of yourself and it makes your skin tingle. It's how people used to live all the time.

For me, it is, still, that one thing.

2

DON'T GO COMMANDO

I've been safari guiding for a long time now and I was probably always destined to make a living from the wonders of the wilderness, but I used to do something else. I used to *be* someone else.

Craig pushed me. Best thing he could have done, but it was odd; it was a sort of bitter-sweet favour, coming from him.

In that previous life I taught History at a high school in Durban in order to work off my government university loan, wondering what to do about my itinerant girlfriend and whether to pay any heed to that old Geography curmudgeon who kept telling me to get the hell out of the profession – "There's no money in it and the bloody kids these days are a nightmare; no respect." But I loved teaching. I didn't love being penniless by the 20th of every month (maybe that's why the girl I was smitten with was itinerant) but I have always been thoroughly intrigued by history from any era, and some of the kids really responded to my enthusiasm. Many didn't, but then they didn't seem to respond to anything at all except girls, great piles of white bread sandwiches and the opportunity to sleep at a moment's notice. Teenagers, eh?

It was my first job and a pretty good (albeit pauperish) life so I wasn't really thinking much beyond the next meagre pay cheque and each coming weekend. But there was always a nagging doubt about staying in teaching: was this what I wanted to do? And how would I go about doing something else?

Then fate stepped in.

How do people become wildlife guides? These days there are plenty of colleges sanctioned by some obscure government acronym that churn out a succession of binoculared graduates in *veldskoene*, brandishing a rolled scroll that proclaims them as experts in animal behaviour and guest management. No such requirement when I started. We just pitched up in the game reserve full of vim, and we came from all walks of life. Some of us just fell into it because we knew someone else who was doing it and it seemed like a romantic option, a stopgap until we got 'real' jobs. Some were sent into the bush by exasperated parents trying to forge a career for their ne'er-do-well offspring, a kind of extended summer camp where they got the kids out from under for at least one blessed year. Some bush guides were just escaping from a dizzyingly wide range of things: relationships gone sour, failed businesses, over-prescriptive parents, soul-numbing Monday to Friday jobs, drugs, divorces (and maybe divorcees). Some had connections in the industry and were serving a brief (sometimes reluctant) apprenticeship before strategically moving into marketing and management (where they conceived the real money to be). Some came and went so fast I barely had the opportunity to learn their names; they discovered that guiding is hard work for long hours, and they were simply never in love with the bush. Some just wanted to take pictures for a photographic essay they intended to publish, almost always about leopards, that prince of the wilderness, the animal that everyone wants more and more of (and who can blame them?). Some guides, I think, were actively looking for wives, hoping that a rich Californian might show interest. Sometimes those relationships actually prospered. Not often, though.

Me? Three things, I think. Firstly, quite simply, I just wanted to live in a game reserve and be surrounded by wildlife. I cherished any time I spent in the wilds and had always loved our annual family forays to iMkuze Game Reserve. I used to tremble with excitement on the day we all rose in the pre-dawn and my father headed that old red Ford Anglia north towards Zululand. I had never thought it was possible to actually work in a game reserve until a long-serving guide that I knew at Mala Mala Game Reserve assured me that I had the right accent, university, knowledge and enthusiasm to do the job. Lucky credentials, but that's how it worked back then. They wanted obviously trainable and reliable people who spoke a version of English that guests would easily understand. Secondly, my now-and-then girlfriend had dumped me again, and it seemed like a change was necessary. If you think this sounds like I was sulking, you're right, but I was pretty sure she'd be back. It was partly a revenge thing. ("Fine, drop me, but you'll be sorry. I'm off to be a guide, anyway. Don't call.") Hoping desperately that she would call. And thirdly, I needed to travel, to remove myself from the little hollow I had grown up in, studied in, fallen in love in: I had always dreamed about getting out of there, and it seemed to me that by meeting foreign guests I could do that. This apple wanted to fall far from the tree. And, oh yes, there was a fourth thing: money. As trainee guides, we were paid so little that I had to pay *in* at the end of every month just to cover my bar bill, but the compensation was the tips: greenbacks made a big difference to someone working on a minimum wage.

So, one cash-impoverished day towards the end of my third September at the school, whilst busy grinding through a tall pile of hopelessly mediocre matriculation trials History essay papers, and with the dazzling Durban sun soaking the beaches outside, I spoke to my Mala Mala guy. "Get yourself to an interview with the Reserve owner, here's his number," he said. I did. I called immediately. Repeatedly. All weekend. It was a hard-earned and unusual interview. But that's another story. This story is about Craig.

Craig taught Speech and Drama, and English, in an adjoining classroom. I told him about the interview and he made a funny face but immediately backed me to the hilt. He wasn't a happy teacher. He needed to escape the conservative environment of the halls. He thought I needed to, too, though he was kind enough to admit that he would miss me. He was the most unlikely of friends, the most *interesting* of my friends.

Craig was lithe and slim but his father, so different to him, was a bluff and brawny man who I think owned an import/export company, whatever that meant, and had a very nicely appointed sea view property up on the Durban Berea when that was still considered a lofty place to live. His mother mostly seemed to play bridge (or was it tennis?) and spend a lot of time drinking Earl Grey while knitting birthday jumpers for her only son. In the matter of nature versus nurture, Craig would have made an interesting case study. He appeared to tolerate, rather than love his father, who seemed permanently (though not vocally) coldly disappointed in Craig. Disapproving, actually, which was worse.

I was always aware of Craig's hands; he used them a lot when talking. They were fine and long-fingered, and they were mirrors to his soul. They were his very tongue. Oh, when Craig played a piano my spirit began to soar! How sounds like that, music that *moving*, could be produced by the simple tapping of a series of keys was beyond me. When he told me that he was playing his own compositions, I was enthralled. And he had exotic, flamboyant friends who all played music, who sang, who were actors and dancers, who seemed to be always traveling to the capitals of the world. They were from another universe and they fascinated me. Arty people who met at the bar above the Durban Playhouse, and went dancing and drinking (and doing drugs and dope, I supposed) in dodgy places down at the docks in Point Road. I tagged along once, a little nervous, feeling out of place, intrigued. They were all very welcoming, but I never went again. It was a foreign world to me, and I was completely out of my depth.

In the staff room during tea and lunch, I used to divide my time between the circle of men who discussed rugby and cricket, and Craig's group, the Art and English teachers, mostly women, who spoke of more refined things. I was comfortable in both environments.

Craig was gay, and it took me ages to recognise it. He wasn't flamboyantly so, and never affected. The rugby circle was perfectly tolerant of him, appreciative of his skills and his sharp wit. There were the usual casual jokes about needing to "watch out for Eric" when he had been drinking: then, he would become rather too familiar for some of the guys, and it made them uncomfortable. But Craig had their respect (he could out drink any of them, for one thing) and he took any innuendo in his stride; with his intellect he could dish it out, too. He would walk over to the rugby circle sometimes, and cheekily sit down in the First Team Coach's chair. "Talking about balls, boys?" he would ask.

He used to direct the school musicals and I was always staggered at the quality of performance he managed to dredge up, or inspire, out of the young actors. Boys who could barely murmur "Onward Christian Soldiers" at school assembly were often transformed into stars, given the licence and encouragement to perform. Suddenly it was cool to sing: beautiful girls from the College up the road played the female roles, and rehearsals were seldom a chore for the lucky ones chosen for the parts. Craig sometimes wrote the entire musical, lyrics, music, everything, and he would stroke the keys of the old school stage piano, singing along in his high, clear voice, nodding and winking encouragement to his cast, and smiling broadly. Music was his domain, his reason. I used to sneak into the rehearsals and watch from the back of the hall. Sometimes, if he felt aggrieved by a lack of effort, he would suddenly explode in a rage, hurling a torrent of abuse at some poor wretch who would dissolve in tears (not only the girls), at which point Craig would scream, "Yes! Yes darling! Feel it! I *want* you to *feel* it! That's how I want you to SING!" And on the night, it would be beautiful. Just magnificent. The curtains would sway up, and a whole new dimension would be revealed: top hats and canes, fishnet stockings (of course), rouged faces and the voices of angels. And the music transported us all. His music.

Yes, music and theatre was his world, and through him, briefly and tangentially, it was mine. God, he was an inspiration, so wonderfully alternate to my other friends. But Craig was a complex man, and lonely, I think. We spoke about so many things, even eventually about his lovers and his dreams. He was good enough for Broadway, he thought, and felt frustrated that he was wasting his talents in Durban. In his deepest confessions, after a number of whiskies, he spoke about failed love affairs, about how he felt obliged to remain in Durban for the sake of his parents, and the tedium and difficulties of being gay in the deeply conservative South African society of that time. He made us all happy with his music, but he wasn't that happy himself. He felt trapped. And he thought I was too.

One evening a group of us teachers had gathered at a colleague's home, and Craig, ever the social animal, was there. We were all drinking and Craig more than most. Several guys were sitting on each side of him on the long couch, and looking a bit uncomfortable: Craig was getting playfully amorous, just teasing and being silly. As the house party grew quieter and our hosts began to stare meaningfully at their watches, he suggested we go down to the Playhouse where a new musical was showing. I think Craig had written the score for it. We bundled into several cars and drove straight down there; Craig's productions were always a hit with the staff. We were so *proud* of him.

I found myself seated next to Craig at a restaurant table. It was pretty dark in there, and suddenly his small hand was resting on my leg under the table. I left it there. He had been mock flirting with everyone all evening so I didn't think much of it. Afterwards, because of what happened, I often wished I had been firm with him, and rejected his advance, pushed his hand away. But because we were friends, because he was drunk, because no one could see, because it was a bit awkward, because, oh, I don't know, just because I admired Craig and didn't want to hurt him, I left it there. I had never felt any physical attraction to him but I loved his energy, his intellect, his irreverence, his wit. No, I was in awe of it. I loved being friends with that music man, so I left his hand there. I thought it was just in alcohol-fuelled fun.

It wasn't though. Like all of us, Craig needed to be loved, and that night he assumed that I had allowed him to take our friendship to the next level. After a while I went to the toilets, and when I emerged, Craig was there, waiting, leaning against the ballustrading, in the half-dark. In my naiveté, amazingly, I had failed to recognise that I had led him on. He literally leaped at me and grabbed me in an embrace shockingly powerful for such a smallboned man, forcing me up against the railing. He hugged me, hard, and tried to kiss me. I was stunned, shocked rigid, embarrassed, and afraid. I pushed him roughly away, crying out, and fled. I made some mumbled excuse at the table to the others and went straight home, contemplating my culpability. I felt guilty, and innocent. Innocent, yet guilty. And both angry and distraught: I knew I did not have the maturity or wisdom to handle this situation. This was all new.

The next morning when I went into my classroom, a bottle of wine awaited me on the desk. It was a good bottle, too, and it bore a note. "Sorry. Craig." An act of contrition.

Nevertheless, I avoided him all day. All week, in fact, until he finally cornered me in the passage after school one afternoon. Craig understood what I was dealing with better than I did. Of course he did. He was so much more worldly than I.

"Come on, let's have tea," he invited me in a kind voice.

It was that awful government-issue school tea, too, boiled all day in a stainless-steel urn. Never mind: it went untasted that day anyway. We spoke. He apologised again, and explained that he had (not surprisingly) misread me that night.

"I have a *girlfriend*, Craig, you *know* that."

"Phhht." Dismissively. "It doesn't mean a thing."

He didn't really know her (I flattered myself that he was jealous). He said that I was behaving like a rabbit in the headlights, and that I should grow with it, move on, be friends, stay friends. That there would be no more funny business.

"Relax," he said, "it's just me."

I tried, but it was never the same afterwards, never quite as free and fun, our friendship. I wasn't yet grown up enough for that.

It became September and I went up to the Mala Mala interview. I was utterly enchanted by the experience: relaxed leopards lounging in Sausage trees, a lion killing a tsessebe antelope before my eyes, birds I had been hoping to see all my life, porcupines in the day time, things I had never seen at iMkuze. And I loved sitting around the *boma* fire and meeting interesting foreigners. I cited car trouble to the school and spent an extra day at Mala Mala, delaying my departure for Durban until the last possible moment. When I got back, Craig sensed something was up. I told him about the interview, and he was delighted for me. It was a dream I had often spoken about with him, and he had supported me, advising me to follow my heart. "Don't get trapped like me." He joked about me wearing khakis and leopard skin underwear, "The proper attire for the well-dressed game ranger."

"You've got to do it," he said. "Follow the Yellow Brick Road. Just go!"

He gave me the push. I resigned from the school.

The staff collected money for my leaving present as they do, and I requested a pair of hardy leather boots, the T-5's with the red laces, instead of the usual ill-chosen book. I made some trite speech of thanks at the year-end Christmas function, and while I spoke I was conscious of Craig's eyes boring into me, steel rods that made me flinch, and the fact that he applauded only diffidently with the rest of the staff afterwards. It was odd, unexpected. He was wearing a tightlipped smile, and I had the strange feeling that he was angry with me. It was confusing and upsetting.

But now I know: he was only sad. I think he was reflecting on his own future. I think he wanted to be the one making the goodbye speech.

Because, after the party, he found me in the car park. I was quite emotional, leaning against my car, a little drunk, contemplating this big move. A new bold step into the unknown, moving away from the girl that I loved; several species of fear all at once. Apart from everything else, I have always been bad at goodbyes: the right words just don't arrive on time. I heard his light footsteps, and knew it was him immediately. I looked at him warily, and he smiled, but this smile was the old one I knew, the one that always made me laugh.

"Aah, Campo. Never mind me. What a life, eh? When do we get to *keep* love? Here, these will be useful."

He put a small bag in my hand and laughed in anticipation while I opened it. Inside the bag was a pair of leopard print briefs, and a note in his familiar, tiny scrawl:

"For the well-dressed game ranger. Don't go commando. Good luck, my friend. Find me on Broadway. Fondest love. Craig."

I wonder what became of him. I wonder when he made his own farewell speech. I hope he reads this. I did good, Craig.

Hey, I got that girl, too!

3

PAIN HAS A COLOUR

Lots of us have done it. I've done it myself, I'm afraid. Running the electric lawnmower across the power cable. You stand aghast because you've been so careful to avoid doing exactly that. You have this lurid vision, this chilling expectation that a huge power surge will course through your body, leaving your nails blackened and your hair smoking and standing on end. Actually, all that really happens is that the machine suddenly stops working and you're left standing there feeling extremely foolish, looking about you to see who has noticed, and wondering how you're going to explain all this to the neighbour from whom you've borrowed the mower.

I'm not sure what Tony told the boss when he mangled the mower cord.

As I say, it could happen to anybody. But in this case, it was the start of a comical pattern of bad luck and poor judgement with electricity. In the end, we just started to call him 'Sparky.' I had lunch with him recently, and we reminisced about his electrical misadventures.

"Have you ever had the taste of a battery in your mouth? It's bloody horrible, china. Hey, do you know, every type of pain has its own colour," he stated, wincing and rubbing his forehead. He'd know.

We had only been at Mala Mala Game Reserve a short while when we were issued our one million candle power spotlights, brand new and signed for. These lamps were used by our trackers to find animals at night as we drove home on game drive after sundowners and they were state-of-the-art back then; powerful beams that momentarily turned the bush white and yellow and threw manic shadows across the two-track road. They plugged into the twelve-volt electrical circuit of the Land Rover, and needed to be used sparingly when the engine was switched off for fear that they might drain the battery. Twelve volts, *comprende*?

Sparky wasn't called Sparky when we arrived at Mala Mala. We were FNG's, fresh and keen, and naïve. Sparky and I took our new spotlights up to Rams, the rangers' accommodation, and he tried his out immediately. He plugged it into the wall socket. The 220-volt wall socket. BANG! There was an instant flash of brilliant white light, the sound of glass splintering as the front cover starred across its diameter, a small thick cloud of whitish smoke, and there sat Sparky on his backside, quite astonished, staring numbly at his brand new and now recently destroyed spotlight. First the lawnmower and now this. Sparky had more explaining to do. Twelve doesn't easily divide by 220, you see.

Do things really happen in threes? Apparently they do.

Came the day that Sparky acquired his nickname. The French luggage company, Delsey, had a large incentive group coming to Mala Mala: all their top salespeople on a reward trip to South Africa's most famous private game reserve, and Sparky was appointed 'ranger in charge' of a posse of us lesser mortals – mere common rangers who would guide the group for a few days. We all drove out in Land Rover 110's to the Kingston gate where we were to meet the clients, bussed in from Johannesburg. Sparky was a little nervous, and who wouldn't be, put in charge of a bunch of irreverents like us, perfectly willing to see him mildly discomfited? Just boy's stuff, naturally. We were all good mates.

The travel agent who had arranged the Delsey trip to Mala Mala had sent a large plastic banner ahead: 'Welcome to Mala Mala' it proclaimed in huge letters, with the Delsey logo prominently displayed. Now, we need to speak about luggage. We humans worry a lot about our stuff when we travel. It's only replaceable clothing, really, and trinkets purchased at the last guilty moment for families back home, but we all wait anxiously for it at the end of a flight. We get through Immigration after an interminable wait while the Border Nazis glare suspiciously at our passports, and we eventually reach the luggage retrieval belt. We scan the rainbow of luggage scraping slowly one by one under that black rubber flap and watch other people's cases go by, time and again the same damned bags belonging to other people (where do they go, these other people, there's nothing to do between Immigration and here, why haven't they collected their luggage?). Why is our bag always the last to emerge? We wonder if it *will* emerge. And then at last there *it is!* We leap at it, wrestle it triumphantly onto the dodgy trolley with the juddering front jockey wheel and head smugly towards Arrivals while dozens of jealous fellow passengers wait impatiently for their own bags, glancing every so often towards the 'Lost Luggage' counter to see how long the queue is.

Guides hate luggage. The clever fellow, bless him for ever, who first added little wheels to large suitcases hadn't yet come up with that plan when Sparky and I started guiding so we had to drag, carry, roll and generally mishandle huge coffin-like cases off planes, into trailers, onto trolleys, up stairs, along gravel paths. It was awkward and hateful work. Luggage hurts. It is sharp-edged and heavy and annoying. It's painful to carry these things on your shoulders and the handles are always in the wrong places... but it's part of the job. Why people needed such large amounts of clothing was beyond us: the lodge did complimentary laundry every single day. Into the wash basket in the morning, dried and ironed beautifully and neatly folded on your bed that night. You really don't need much kit on safari. Well do I remember a lady who came on a trip to Uganda and whose shoes suitcase (just shoes) had gone missing en route in Amsterdam. A suitcase just for her shoes, and this on a trip where one's entire luggage (as in 'single suitcase') was supposed to be no more than 20 kg. Her trip had suddenly become utterly derailed, she was sobbing in the hotel lobby in despair, her boyfriend was deeply stressed, and several trips were made to Entebbe airport in an attempt to persuade, bribe and bully *somebody* into doing *something*. The suitcase eventually did catch us up within a few days, and I must admit she did have some very nice shoes. Shoes for every occasion, actually. Except the ones she really needed the most, the ones for walking through mud and stinging nettles and jungle streams to locate Mountain gorillas. Her fur-lined knee boots and evening heels just didn't work for that. And the rest of the clients resented her for occupying twice as much luggage space in the Land Rover as they themselves were allowed. Awkward.

A Land Rover Defender is a great vehicle. It can do anything. I've even heard that they can be used to extract Toyota Land Cruisers out of the mud, but people sometimes get that all back-to-front. But when it is modified as a game-viewing car, with three banks of seats, and the last row is high above the rear axle where it is the most bumpy, it is perfectly useless for transporting luggage. But usually that's all the transport you have as a guide, and needs must. So the hefty luggage, far too large to fit properly, is wedged behind the seats, or precariously perched in the rear row, vulnerable to sudden ejection at the merest lump in the road. And wilderness roads are always lumpy. Not infrequently, the precious suitcase is not there when you reach camp. Not to worry however; these suitcases are always bright pink, with colourful ribbons and large identification tags that flap in the breeze. All the guide has to do is retrace his route, and the bag will be found, sometimes wide open from the impact, with knickers festooned on adjacent *Acacia* trees and Chacma baboons scratching with concentrated interest through the make-up bag. I particularly recall a hard-case purple Samsonite making a very audible splash as it pitched into the stream outside Xigera Camp in the Okavango Delta as I rumbled over a gum-pole bridge. The camp assistant driving behind me with the extra luggage was quick to react, and plunging into the shallow river he rescued the offensive thing, caught me up as I deliberately delayed to point out a Pied hornbill, and tossed it deftly and without being noticed back onto the car. The client was mystified as to the bag's state of dampness when she opened it. "Humidity from the airplane hold, probably," I said. "These bags are not as waterproof as the makers suggest. Should have bought a Delsey."

Pilots detest luggage too. It's not too bad these days because most safari clients are flown on Cessna Grand Caravans that have deep luggage pods that accommodate large bags quite easily. But you will still see pilots cursing, their uniform shirts slick upon their backs, sitting on their backsides in the airstrip dust and kicking vengefully at bags that won't fit into the shallow luggage pods beneath a little six-seater Cessna, thinking, "This isn't what I chose as a career, this is horrible, why do people need so much stuff, I *hate* this!"

So Delsey and their ilk have much to answer for. And that day, under the leadership of Sparky, we were there to welcome them and pretend we liked their product. Sparky affixed the banner to the fence. The electric fence. The Sabi Sands Game Reserve is separated from the surrounding community area by a robust wire fence that includes a heavy-gauge electrified cable designed to prevent elephants from exiting the reserve and wandering about in the villages, scaring people and eating the hard-won crops that the tribeswomen scratch from the tired and unresponsive soil. The cable is about five feet from the ground, just the right height to deter an elephant, and powerfully charged so that even a thick-skinned mammal will think twice about touching it again. No problem for Sparky, though: he simply ducked under the cable and tied the banner to the non-electrified outer fence. All set.

We rangers had arrived at the gate early, and were chatting in the shade, telling lies and exaggerating bush stories. After a while, the sound of an approaching bus became apparent. Sparky paused, halfway through rolling another vile cigarette, and rose to his feet.

"Right, chaps," he said, "action stations."

Almost immediately, Sparky's day began to deteriorate. An eager Frenchman, obviously the group leader, elegantly dressed in 'safari Gucci', animatedly gesturing to his charges and ignoring all our entreaties to be careful, gashed his head on a short iron stake that projected from the fence. He sank comically and with great drama to the earth, holding his head and groaning, while his people patted ineffectually at his scalp with white handkerchiefs. Sparky dashed for the First Aid kit in his Land Rover, looking pale, while the Shangaan gate guard clapped his hand to his mouth, saying, "Hau, hau, hau!" As more of the tourists filed through the narrow pedestrian gate, the place began to resemble a fish market just after the boats come in, with people rushing about and shouting, while we rangers tried to shepherd them into the Land Rovers and struggled with their bloody great suitcases. It was mayhem. After an interval, the clamour died down and Gucci Man, a large and bloodied bandage theatrically clasped to his forehead, and still muttering muted appeals to the Virgin, was finally ensconced in the front passenger seat of Sparky's Landy.

We revved our engines, the clients fumbled about for cameras and binoculars, when suddenly:

"But the banner! It is still on the fence!" exclaimed the bloodied tour leader.

"Bugger," said Sparky vehemently, and leaving the car in neutral with the engine idling, bounded from the Landy, watched impatiently by the keen French tourists.

In his haste, Sparky completely forgot about the elephant cable, and as he reached past it to the fence, struck it firmly with his forehead. There was a loud crack and a funny smell, and Sparky staggered six feet backwards and landed, to general amazement, flat upon his back. But Sparky had a job to do, and was up in a trice. To his immense credit, he snatched the banner from the fence, spat again and again into the dust (that repugnant taste of battery acid) and regained his vehicle, following a comical semi-circular route, dragging a dead leg and wobbling about like an inebriate, the banner trailing in the settling dust. This was too much for us rangers. We howled with mirth, resting our heads on the steering wheels of our cars, pointing weakly at Sparky as he stumble-hopped towards his vehicle. The gate guard was in hysterics too, literally slapping his thigh and wheezing asthmatically. Gucci Man had completely forgotten about his head wound. His mouth hung open, his thunder now quite stolen, and he gaped as Sparky valiantly attempted to regain both his car and his dignity.

Unlike automatic urban Land Rover Discoverys that are primarily employed by wealthy ladies to do their grocery shopping in and for dropping the kids at ballet and violin lessons, Land Rovers in the bush use a manual transmission. You need your clutch foot to be in perfect working order. Sparky's wasn't. He brushed away the attempted sympathy of Gucci Man and tried to pull away but his left leg wasn't his own. The vehicle leaped forward and stalled, throwing the passengers first backwards and then forwards as their massive suitcases rattled about behind. We rangers were by now helpless. This was the stuff of legend. The tears streamed down our cheeks as Sparky fiercely jammed his cap back on his head, re-started the engine and attempted to get his foot to do his bidding. The car lurched forward again with a nasty grinding bellow and jerked away in entirely the wrong gear, black smoke belching voluminously from the exhaust, with the passengers holding on in grim and silent astonishment. Slowly the vehicle gathered momentum, Sparky opting to stay in the accidental gear he had found, determinedly headed for home and never mind the damned clutch. We rangers followed in a small train of green Landys, swerving to the right and left on the gravel road for a better forward view so that we could watch the comedy ahead as our doughty leader manfully wrestled his car over drainage humps and across shallow streams, never once changing gear now that he had the car *in one* at last.

They make Land Rovers tough. Even Sparky couldn't break it. That electric wire nearly broke *him*, though: to this day, 25 years later, he still bears the tell-tale sign, a small red scar right in the centre of his forehead. I wonder what he tells people when they ask him how he acquired it. Voldemort?

Not the truth, I'll bet. Just like I didn't tell my neighbour that I'd run over his lawnmower's power cable. Confessions come in many colours, too.

4

APOCRYPHALIA

Apocryphal: a story or statement of doubtful authenticity, although widely circulated as being true.

I was sitting around a camp fire in a lodge in Botswana one evening and a guide I had never met before told his guests one of my stories from *Africa Bites*, as if it were his own. He told it well, too, although I thought he rushed the punchline a bit.

I got a kick out of that, actually. But safari guides need to be careful if they're going to plagiarise: their integrity is at stake. I can't count the number of times that I have heard the same spurious accounts told by different guides as if they were actually there themselves and you see the guests looking sideways at each other and coughing politely but desisting from embarrassing the guide by saying, "Really? That's funny because the guide in the last camp also told us that story, and he said it happened to *him*."

The same anecdotes keep coming up, again and again. They're good ones too, and certainly worth telling, but just shouldn't be passed off as original. They're apocryphal. Urban legends. Actually, in these cases, safari legends. Some of them probably really did happen once, long ago, and now they have been passed down by generations of guides, growing, indeed, improving, in the telling of them. Others are blatantly untrue but make a colourful and entertaining story. And some are pure myth but told as unquestionable fact. The oral tradition is alive and well in the industry, I'm happy to say. But here's a hint to my colleagues: everyone loves a good yarn, fellas, and if you've been guiding for long enough, you'll end up being the hero or the villain in your very own stories. Until then, start your fireside tales with something like, "Here's a great story I heard. There's this guide who... "

Ready to hear some lies, exaggerations and half-truths? Right, here we go, you're going to love these... in fact, I'll bet you've heard some of them already.

Legend 1

It's definitely pissed itself!

It's my very first night working in Botswana, sitting at a fire under a giant Sycamore fig at Chobe Chilwero lodge, the last of the February sun fizzing as it smothers itself into the Chobe river, and Andre, the camp manager, begins to tell a story in that gravelly voice of his.

"We had Americans in camp. You know how they don't really know what a hot water bottle is?"

I don't know that yet, but it seems that in the USA, electric blankets long ago replaced this more old-fashioned technique of warming a cold bed. They are flat rubber bottles covered in soft felt and filled with near-boiling water. My mother uses them religiously to this day, one for the feet and one to cuddle closely to the chest, and they provide wonderful succour to a safari client who has retreated from the comforting fire to a bed yet to be body-heated.

"*Ja*, anyway, *bru*, this elderly American gentleman goes to bed, but in ten minutes he's back at the campfire in a hurry, hellava agitated, saying that there's an animal in his room. So I calm him down and after a while he says that it's not so urgent, actually, the animal is still in the bed, but he thinks he's killed it."

Wow. That's self-reliant. The story is intriguing and I lean forward. Andre continues:

"So I cruise down to the room with him, and I notice that he's got a walking stick, you know those lightweight telescopic aluminium alpine poles the guests like to carry these days, the ones with a sharp point on the end?"

Again, I don't know. I'm new at this game, so Andre fills me in. Apparently it's become a thing. Many of the guests have two of these sticks. They're damned useful, and easy to pack in the checked luggage now that Osama bin Laden has ensured that airport security is so pedantic. No potential weapons in the passenger cabin allowed, even nail-clippers.

"*Ja*, the guy is quite chuffed with himself. He tells me that he got into the bed and he felt a furry animal in there, warm and living. He says he got a hellava fright and leaped out of bed and grabbed his stick and he beat the crap out of that creature, man!"

I'm laughing helplessly by now. This is the first time I've heard this most famous of safari fables and I'm loving it. Andre goes on:

"So we get to the room and I see the sheets are all over the place, the blankets are tangled, the pillows are in disarray but the weird thing is that the whole bed is soaking wet. I'm thinking the water bottle has sprung a leak under the barrage. And I ask the guy, what happened here? And he says, after I beat the animal up, I stabbed it a few times with the sharp end of my stick, and I don't know if it's dead yet but it's definitely pissed itself!"

Legend 2

Okay, now, you chase it off the bed!

Ongava Game Reserve in Namibia is on the southern border of Etosha National Park, and you can go out rhino tracking there if you fancy it but the best activity on the property is to sit on the lodge deck overlooking the waterhole as the sun's brutal attack peters out and allow the animals to come to you. Giraffes, hesitant herds of endemic Blackfaced impalas, flocks of Spotted sandgrouse in their many hundreds, and at the very edge of night, perhaps lions and the sought after Black rhinoceros might wander down. A casual wave of the hand to the watchful bartender will bring a very cold Tafel lager. Quite the most civilised wildlife experience one can imagine.

"*Juslaaik, ou maat,*" says Lenny the camp manager to me as he settles into a chair on the deck and lights a cigarette, "you should have been here yesterday. A hell of a story. Listen to this."

Mmh… which one is it going to be, I think. Not the hot water bottle again, I hope. I look around but there are no guests on deck yet. The cigarette can stay.

"This guest comes to me after lunch in a bit of a fluster," he continues, "and she says hey, there's a lizard on my bed, what should I do about it, and I tell her, *ag*, don't worry madam, it's just one of those geckos, they're common here, they're completely harmless."

Oh, it's the lizard story. Okay, let's hear how he tells it.

"So the lady, a single traveler, goes back to her room, room ten, you know that one there," he says, pointing to add authority, "but in fifteen minutes she's back and she says, Lenny, I can't sleep, the lizard is lying on the other bed and it's watching me, it's sort of freaking me out, please come and remove it. So I say, no, listen, they're nice those little geckos, plus they eat mosquitoes, don't worry about it, there are

41

lots of them around in these hills, just chase it off the bed with a towel."

He's grinning widely, enjoying telling the story, gesticulating and wreathing the place in tendrils of tobacco smoke. It adds to the atmosphere and I'm watching him instead of the waterhole now. He's recounting it with relish. The old ones are the good ones. He goes on.

"So I say, okay no problem, let's sort this out, and we walk down to room ten. We get to the door and she sort of pushes me inside first which makes me think a bit but anyway, I go through to the bedroom. Flipping hell *ou maat*, it's not a gecko on the bed, it's a bloody *leguaan*, just chilling there on the bed, it's tongue flicking in and out, I swear the thing was a metre and a half long, one of the biggest I've ever seen!"

"No way, Lenny!" I say, playing along. These are giant lizards, rock monitors, that usually shelter by day among the broken grey dolomite boulders and fissured rocks of the Ongava hills.

"*Ja*," he says, laughing hard and spilling cigarette ash everywhere, his eyes squeezed into narrow slits, "and the lady says to me, okay Lenny, you try sleeping next to that! Now, here's a towel, *you* chase it off the bed!"

Legend 3

That oke was on jelly and custard for a year afterwards!

When I first started working at Mala Mala in 1992 the guides were telling this story, and I have heard it again in the Lower Zambezi, Zambia and on the Serengeti in Tanzania. Naturally, it happened to the actual guide or at least one of his colleagues on every occasion. The story is best told by beginning with an old joke, one of those time-honoured ones that can be fitted to most occupations. A plumber friend of mine in London, for example, tells it thus:

"I'm called to a person's house in Chiswick to fix a leak and the owner comes into the bathroom dressed in workman's overalls. Blue. I ask him what the overalls are for and he says to me, I'm going to help you so you can charge me less. Well, I didn't need help, obviously, and clearly not from him. What's this repair going to cost me? he asks. Fifty quid, mate, I tell him, but it's seventy if you watch and a hundred if you try to help."

In guiding terms, the joke goes about replacing a flat tyre. I've written elsewhere in this book about the little thrill of fear that many folk get when that giant snake starts hissing under your car, sss, ssss, sssss, the sound of a heavy-duty tyre going flat, fast. First world cars don't even have spare tyres anymore, you just call the AA, so it's a novelty for many guests to experience a puncture, and it can feel a little scary to them. Everyone gets off the car and gathers around the offending wheel, and the men immediately start to offer advice. It's dirty work, manipulating the spare tyre off the rack, dragging out a rusty hi-lift jack, ferreting about behind the Land Rover seat for the 4-way wheel-lug spanner, squatting with the spare wheel on your lap and trying to make it fit the drum pins. It's all heavy metal, and I'm not talking about music.

"Stand back from the jack, please," you command firmly, "it's a dangerous piece of kit and when I lever the car up the hi-lift is going to be under a lot of weight, so stand over there."

But this is man's work, or that's how the male guests see it, and they just cannot help themselves. It's a bit like men finding their way; every guy has a route, and it's the best route, and he will give a hundred reasons why it's the best route, and "no, no, no, you don't want to go that way, good grief no," but actually every route is about as good as every other. Funny creatures, men, they just need to be right about certain stuff. Especially if they suspect they might be wrong.

So they gather around the jack in muted excitement, offering advice, wanting to help, needing to help, but I've changed hundreds of tyres and I'd prefer that the guests stay nice and clean and far from the centre of operations. And this is where that joke comes in.

"How long is it going to take to replace the tyre?" one will ask.

"Oh, about ten minutes, I'd guess. But fifteen if you watch and twenty if you try to help. Please stand away from the jack!"

Because why? Because it is under severe tension, it's holding up half a flipping Land Rover in the air, and the long handle is sticking out towards you, the long handle that provides leverage, the long handle that, if the locking pin in the ratchet suddenly gives under the strain, will flip up and down at such speed that it will resemble a manic mechanical scythe in a horror movie called "Nightmare on Safari Street." Ugly. Exceedingly ugly.

The guide tells the story as he swaps tyres and the men try to crowd in.

"Please stand back. Don't touch the jack! I know this guide who was doing exactly this, changing a flat tyre, and one of his guests got too close. The guy leaned down on the jack handle while the guide was re-fitting the lug-nuts. Well, the jack let go, it just let go, man, and as the Landy started to drop, the handle started to flail, and the guest caught the handle flush under the chin on the upward stroke. It picked him up and hurled him backwards and that guy was out cold long before he hit the ground. His jaw was completely shattered, he bit through his tongue and his teeth came out like dominoes. Blood all over the place, shit, what a mess."

The guests are suitably awed, and the guide continues:

"*Ja*, we got him to hospital and they wired up his jaw. I swear, that *oke* was on jelly and custard for a year afterwards!"

Legend 4

I could have lost my bloody nuts!

Harry swears blind this really happened to him, but so did Prognosis at Mana Pools in Zimbabwe. (Some Africans have rather surprising names. I knew a Motswana woman called Surprise, and in Namibia there lives a young Himba man known as Mistake. Don't ask!) Perhaps it happened to both Harry *and* Prognosis. All I know is that every time I pass an area like that on foot, I observe a simple rule of behaviour. Walk behind it, not in front. Watch out for the Kalahari Ferrari.

There are a couple of stories about Harry, actually. I guided with him at Mala Mala, a place that inculcated the discipline of being on time (actually, not being on time, being *early*) and of giving maximum, every-waking-moment attention to our guests. They were invaluable lessons for a life in the guiding industry but at the time made for arduous working circumstances: we got very little sleep. Admittedly, there were many times when we could have gone to bed but stayed up instead with our fellow rangers, drinking at the *boma* fire and telling outrageous lies of conquest and adventure. We were young. Well, younger. But the point is that we were too often drowsy during the day.

Which is why Harry, badly hungover one morning on game drive, told his guests that the leopard tracks he was pointing out were fresh and worth following up. His tracker, Justice, could clearly see that they were yesterday's paw-prints and he chuckled to himself as Harry told his guests in Titus Oatsian fashion that he was going to follow them on foot and "might be some time." Not very far from the car, yet out of sight of the guests, on a sloping river bank and in the warmth of the gentle sun, Harry had a little lie-down. He awoke in a panic half an hour later, dashed back to the car to the visibly agitated guests, proclaimed that nothing had come of the tracks, and drove away. The woman sitting behind Harry leaned forward and brushed the dried leaves and grass from his back and hair.

"Looking for the leopard in the trees, were you?" she asked.

But back to the main story. Many bush guides claim that one of the highlights of their morning is the *boskak*. Literally, a bush shit. We're a simple lot, it seems, and take delight in the moment. Be that as it may, to enjoy it there are some basics that need to be in place. Firstly, pick your spot well. Find a place that is discreet, yet relatively open. You don't want tourists passing by and taking pictures. At a critical point in the process, after all, there can be no running away. This happened to me once in the Zambezi National Park near Victoria Falls. I had no idea that the tourist road was so close and as I went about my business two women came by in a lime green VW Beetle. They didn't stop for long once they had identified the creature marking his territory but I'm sure I saw them take some surreptitious photos. This was in the days before Facebook, fortunately, otherwise that could have been compromising. But you don't want the toilet spot to be too hidden either; far, far better while at your ablutions for you to spot an old *dhaga* boy buffalo wandering down the game trail towards you before he sees you. They're easily offended, *dhaga* boys. Secondly, remove your pants entirely. Trousers puddled around one's ankles will not do when there is running away to be done. And anyway there is the issue of grass seeds, burrs and insects to consider. Imagine what the rest of your day would hold with those alien nuisances amongst your nether regions. No, hang your pants from a nearby branch. Thirdly, remember the TP, the White Gold, the loo paper (unless you're all eco-friendly and use leaves or smooth stones. Some guides do. They really do.) and make sure the stuff is within reach. Lastly, the squat. Are you spry enough to hold the position? If not, get a grip on a handy tree or rocky outcrop. You may be there for a while. This is not the time to be reading the newspaper, however; keep a sharp lookout. It's a "loo with a view" but keep your wits about you.

Harry did not. Urgently in need of a morning constitutional one day, he once again bade his guests a brief farewell and set off to 'find elephants', following days-old *spoor*, his usual ruse. He chose to settle in a nice open sandy area that allowed some privacy, with a little hillock lightly vegetated by Woolly caper bush behind him for protection, and a grand view before. Perfect. He hung his khaki shorts on a useful twig, and settled down. Almost immediately, he noticed a disturbance behind him, an echoing, shuffling, grunting, rustling kind of noise. Strange, he thought, there's only this little hill, what on earth... and a horrible realisation dawned. Oh, man! This is a termite mound and the lovely, soft, sandy patch I'm on is freshly excavated. It has been dug out by... and with a sudden rush the terrified warthog bulleted out of its burrow, its gleaming tusks foremost, its razor-sharp, viciously hooked tusks, thrusting aside the frail screen of overhanging vegetation that masked its burrow entrance and charging straight at Harry's exposed backside in a mad, horrified bid to escape.

Harry did the only thing he could do. He stood up fast and bowed his legs. And the pig, in a cascade of red sand and furious snorts, barrelled straight through between them. Straight through, and onwards, never touching Harry, the tusks narrowly missing his legs and other sundries by a whisker and by pure dumb luck.

All thought of a comfortable *boskak* had disappeared now. Mute and pale, Harry gathered his clothing and his senses, and walked swiftly back to the car. Justice was in stitches, slapping his leg like a cartoon character, laughing in a high-pitched creak, and a guest said:

"Jesus, Harry, this massive warthog just came screaming past the car at a hell of a rate, I don't know what was chasing it, it looked terrified! And why is Justice laughing so hard?"

When Harry tells that story, he chain-smokes and affects a sardonic expression.

"*Jussus, okes*, luckiest day of my life! Everyone talks about the warthog, but I could have lost my bloody nuts."

Legend 5

You should have been here yesterday!

"You should have been here yesterday. Unbelievable!" proclaims Theuns, the camp manager, chuckling.

It's a recurrent line, usually employed by a guide who is struggling to locate your safari heart's desire: Painted dogs, a leopard languishing in a tree, a scaly pangolin shuffling in the night, the elusive Cinderella waxbill. Actually, I'm really good at this, the guide is saying, we're just a bit unlucky today, if only you'd been here yesterday.

A small group of us are training to become camp managers and we've splashed through the watery road crossings from Vumbura to Duba Camp to see how they do the job over there. Part of the learning is delightfully practical: drinking sundowners on the raised wooden deck that overlooks the short-cropped flood plain that leads on to the shining pool of Okavango water beyond.

Theuns points across the grass sward with his pipe.

"I was sitting here yesterday having coffee and rusks with the guests before morning game drive and, suddenly, all hell broke loose. We've been hoping for dogs lately, we heard they were in the area, you never know where they'll pitch up, those animals, and out of the blue, there they were! Flipping sprinting across the floodplain, man, twelve of them, I think, just as the sun was coming up, straight at that herd of lechwe."

He indicates a bachelor herd of the red antelopes, contentedly grazing near the water, white egrets trailing them and beak-snapping at small grasshoppers disturbed into flight by the lechwes' hooves.

"Right in front of our eyes, those dogs took down a lechwe. A big one too, massive set of horns. It was so quick we hardly had a chance to say anything, and most of the guests completely forgot to take photos.

The lechwe tried to run into the water, you know how they do, but one dog grabbed the lechwe by the nose and the rest just started tearing it apart from behind. The rest of the lechwes fled into the pond and just stood there, alarm whistling, but the dogs carried on in a frenzy, ripping into that ram."

Theuns now points with the stem of his pipe at Old Moses, a camp worker, who is quietly mopping the teak deck close by, glancing sometimes at Theuns and obviously listening.

"And then this *skabenga...* "

And suddenly I recognise that I am in the middle of yet another safari legend. Except this time I know it's real because once at Mombo Camp on Chief's Island, it happened to me. Painted dogs chased an impala right into the camp office and slayed it on the floor, splattering bright blood across the metal filing cupboards and scaring the living daylights out of the duty manager, a Swedish volunteer who had only just arrived in camp. Quite an introduction to the safari life for her. But now I find that the familiar tale has taken on a surprising twist.

Theuns nods at Moses and grins fondly.

"We're all watching this spectacle, it's been going on for ten minutes, and then suddenly this *skabenga*, Old Moses, comes running out of camp, straight at the dogs, and he's waving a bloody *panga* above his head and I thought, *magtig*, he's trying to protect the lechwe. Moses is shouting at the top of his voice but the dogs are in their kill mode and they don't hear him at first, they just keep tugging and tearing at their prey. At the last moment one dog spots him and it barks just like an Alsatian, you know those police dogs. I've never heard one do that before, and that gets the attention of the rest of the pack and they bomb-shell, flip, it was funny to see. And I'm still thinking Old Moses is trying to save the lechwe, you know, but then he starts to hack a leg off the ram with his *panga* and I thought, *what the hell?*"

Aah, this is a good version of the story, I think to myself. Some dramatic tension here, an unexpected twist. What's going on and how will it end? This is not just the classic and oft related 'dog kill right here in camp' tale.

"*Ja*, so Old Moses finishes chopping off a haunch and I'm so gob-smacked I can't speak and the dogs are milling about and gruff-barking in amazement, and Moses just swings that lechwe meat onto his shoulder and starts trudging back to camp, and eventually I realise, oh shit, he's flipping stolen the kill from the dogs! Right in front of the guests, as brazen as you like! I tell you, I just stood there gaping at him."

Theuns is shaking with mirth now, and we're all stunned by this news. Not the done thing in a national park. Nature is supposed to be allowed to take its course. Still, it's a bit of a relief: for a horrible moment I thought Theuns was going to tell us that Old Moses had attacked the dogs! Moses has his ear cocked and is smiling at us, leaning on his mop.

"So I went over to Moses when he got back into the camp and I said, hey, Moses, no man, you can't do that, *meneer*, you've got to take it back. And he couldn't believe it. He said the dogs had *horbors* of meat, how's one leg going to make a difference? And I said, *ja* but still, the guests were watching, man, this is a conservation area, it's not allowed. *Jussus*, Moses was pissed off, hey. He wouldn't do it until I promised him extra ration meat and even then he took his time. He probably sliced a few nice pieces off first, I don't blame him, lechwe make hellava *lekker biltong*, but in the end he carried the leg back and chucked it down next to the carcass."

He laughs again and wags a friendly finger at Moses who feigns indifference and starts mopping again. Old Moses has been at Duba for years and years. He'll outlast all these managers that come and go. He harks back to the days before guns came, when men competed directly with lions, dogs and hyaenas for meat, when force of numbers, ingenuity and outright pluck was paramount for survival. This isn't the first time he's nicked meat from a predator, I reckon, and I doubt it will be the last. I mention this to Theuns.

"*Ja*, I know, who knows what goes on in the staff village and where all that *biltong* comes from but I can tell you, man, this time it was a bit blatant. Old Moses was properly pissed off with me."

Moses smiles a little secret smile, and keeps mopping.

Legend 6

Celebrate the digital age

Everyone carries a camera at all times these days. It's in your pocket. In fact, many current adverts for smart phones talk about the high resolution of the pictures they take, and the fact that you can also make a call to someone seems to be incidental. I was on safari recently at Hoanib Skeleton Coast Camp in Namibia and an elderly gentleman was remarking about the poor quality of the pictures he was getting. To be fair to the phone, the light was iffy, he was taking pictures from a moving Land Cruiser through a fog-smeared window and he kept jabbing so hard with an arthritic finger at the white photo button that the phone moved every time he stabbed it. I reminded him affably that in fact his device was actually a phone and he grinned and told me that he would kick my arse for being cheeky.

Pre-digital, in the days when we used to load a succession of expensive 36-shot Fuji Velvia colour film rolls into the back of an SLR and anxiously watch the exposure counter, making carefully weighed decisions about whether to take the photo or not, the old joke used to go thus:

"So, Bob, how was your safari holiday?"

"Dunno, haven't got the pictures back yet."

This reflected upon two things: primarily, that there was always an agonising wait until we got home before we could have the photos developed and secondly, that far too many folk spent their holidays experiencing it through the lens of the camera instead of actually looking about and taking it all in. They were too desperate not to miss the shot, that perfect sunset, the leopards mating, the Lilacbreasted roller on take-off... that dream picture... and then they might never look at the pictures again anyway, as one vacation replaced another.

More latterly, we get the instant feedback that our short attention spans crave. We edit or delete immediately, and we're all in our own pictures. That magnificent Sable antelope bull is often secondary to the main subject: us, in the foreground, grinning inanely, making funny faces or assuming a silly lip-pouting, hands-on-hips pose. Somewhere behind us in the distance is the grainy image of the animal. Or a waterfall. Or today's lunch.

But I love my iPhone, and I go nowhere without it.

So where's the apocryphal story? Getting there, folks, hang on. In the old days at Mala Mala before camera-phones... but I've heard this story told elsewhere, too. Of course!

Let's call him Eddie. He was a vindictive bastard, a highly unpleasant inward-looking fellow whose sole purpose in guiding was to make tips. I discerned no love of the bush in him, and that upset my idealistic vision of what we there to do: have a lot of fun in a wild place and enthuse our guests about conservation and the wonders of the wilderness. Eddie was moody and brittle, and he knew that quite often his guests read him all too well. This made him highly sensitive to criticism and, boy, did he reflect attitude back. He didn't last long on the game reserve, naturally, once the negative feedback started arriving. Because he had a spiteful little trick.

If Eddie wasn't getting on with his guests, he would offer to take pictures for them.

"Here," he would say at sundowner drinks, a pink sky fading to purple behind the low cloud, "Here, give me your cameras, let me take a group picture for you. Stand together on that termite mound, that's it, actually, left a bit so I can get the sky in, good, good, now, everyone say 'moneeeey!' Excellent."

Or he'd drop them off at the airstrip at the end of the safari and take the final family picture as they posed in front of the Cessna that had arrived to fetch them. They'd crowd together in their safari hats and Columbia shirts, proudly displaying the Big Five certificates that Eddie had signed and made great play of presenting to them, the aircraft behind them, and Eddie would crouch and try different angles and make them laugh and shoot off half a roll of precious Velvia.

And back home, when the pictures were finally developed, the clan would eagerly gather round the dining room table, spread all the photos out to relive the wonderful trip they'd had, look at the family gathered happily on the termite mound... and without exception, the top of every picture ended at the shoulders. No faces.

Eddie had cut their heads off.

Legend 7

Because it is known

Of course, Sunday does have a traditional Oshiwambo name but it is long and complicated and damn nigh unpronounceable to *shirumbus*, the safari guests, the white people, so he prefers to call himself Sunday because, he says, he was born on the last day of the week. Very sensible. He has several children, all named after other days of the week, and I'm not sure what his plan is when he gets past the seventh child. Tuesday Two? Months, maybe?

He's a huge presence, Sunday. A tall uplifting man with a booming, ready laugh, always in good humour and wonderful with guests, a natural host and raconteur. I always feel great while in his company: he's a tonic for the soul. He has his flaws, mind you: he's an avid Liverpool football fan. They've come right now after a long drought, Liverpool, but for a long time Sunday really did have to walk alone.

Also, he has some doubtful stories. Doubtful, but my goodness, he tells them with verve, his voice echoing through the dining room of the lodge and out across the bushveld, leaving the guests laughing and bemused and totally captivated by his energy. Any story well told is always worth the listen and veracity, in the case of Sunday's stories, is a side issue. Suspend belief and become involved in the narrative because, the thing is, he really believes his own stories. His own truth.

Take the one about the rooster, for example. There are plenty of francolins at Ongava Game Reserve, beautiful little wild chickens that wing-flap and crow from the tops of termite mounds in the mornings and scratch energetically among the leaf litter looking for seeds and crawling insects. Sunday speaks enthusiastically about them – like many guides, he likes to call them Owambo Chickens, a rather over-used joke – and he says that they breed prolifically, like the kraal chickens in his village at home in "the North." They make a nest on the ground, he tells guests, a shallow scrape lined with grass and leaves, and the females lay about six or seven eggs there, lovely little pale eggs, just like the hens' eggs you buy from the supermarket, the same shape, but a bit smaller. But sometimes, says Sunday, you'll find something different in the nest: a spherical egg, smaller than the rest, white and perfectly round, like a ping pong ball. And that one is laid by the rooster, the male chicken, he asserts.

What? Roosters don't lay eggs! No male birds lay eggs, ever. But Sunday is sure of this when I question him.

"I know you've slaughtered scores of chickens at home, Sunday," I say. "So you know what they look like inside. And you know that when you cut them up for cooking, the females look different to the males, right? I mean, you can see their apparatus for making eggs, and the roosters don't have that. Right? So roosters can't lay eggs."

"They can. They do," he says firmly. "I have seen the eggs."

"I think what you're seeing are the first-lay eggs of young pullets," I say. "I've seen those. Quite often the first few eggs of a young chicken are sort of lumpy, or funny shaped, sometimes small and round."

"No, no, I know those," he says. "I'm talking about rooster's eggs." He's resolute.

"How do you know this?" I ask him. The guests lean in. This is intriguing.

"Everyone at home knows this. We all know."

Well, what can you answer to that? Some of the guests raise a bewildered eyebrow but the discussion ends. I check this with Israel, another Owambo guide who works there.

"Oh yes," confirms Israel, "it is well known."

Okay then, news to me. Best I pay better attention in future! And I do, because on our next game drive with Sunday, I learn another startling revelation.

"You see these *Mopane* trees?" asks Sunday.

We all nod. You can't miss them, they're prolific. Where's this going?

"In some seasons, just after the rains, there is a great hatching of eggs, eggs that are laid on the underside of the leaf by the Emperor moth, and millions of *Mopane* worms emerge. Millions. Actually, they are caterpillars. And they begin to feed upon the leaves until eventually they spin a cocoon and pupate and later they hatch into the moth. We eat them, my people. The worms, not the moths."

He roars with laughter at the disgusted faces of his guests.

"And frogs. Bull frogs. We eat them also. But you also eat frogs. French people do."

Very true. But not worms. Everyone laughs with Sunday. It's impossible not to. And by the way, great job, Sunday. Metamorphosis. Not many guides talk readily about it because it's a pretty difficult process to explain, and while there are very many guests who struggle to grasp the concept, there are in fact some African guides who flatly refuse to believe it is true at all. Whose truth do you choose to believe? Metamorphosis is science. It is known. Observed. We all had silkworms in a shoebox as kids, we all saw what happens. Everyone knows! It's obvious. Perhaps. If that's the truth you are seeking.

"Yes," says Sunday, "We love them, we collect them in big sacks and dry them and sell them at the market. But it is not only people who eat *Mopane* worms. Many birds also eat them. And *leguaans*. Monitor Lizards. Have you seen one? Huge lizards, like this," he explains, spreading his arms. "Massive."

This makes sense but I've never thought about it before. Yes, *leguaans* would feed on *Mopane* worms, I reason. Ready protein would never be declined, and *leguaans* are excellent tree climbers and real food opportunists.

"What they do," explains Sunday, "they see the tree is full of worms, and they climb up the trunk. But the worms see the lizard coming so they crawl to the very tip of the branches. The thinnest branches. And that branch is too thin to support the weight of the *leguaan*."

Oh, brilliant, here we go again, another Sunday story unfolding. Let's see how this one plays out. The guests are eager, smiling to each other in anticipation, already enraptured by the style and intrigue of the story, and Sunday is in full flow. I look at him to see if I can tell if he is kidding but he doesn't seem to be. On the contrary, he is happily beguiled by his own story, relishing it, his eyes alight and his long fingers curling and uncurling as he depicts the inchworm-like progress of the intended victims as they escape towards the uttermost parts of the tree. They don't really move like that but it doesn't matter, the visual image is what counts.

"The *leguaan* is very hungry but it realises that the slender branches cannot keep it up. So it stops. But the worms keep going. So the *leguaan* starts to shake the branch as hard as it can, and all the worms fall off the branch, onto the ground. But the branch is too thin, and the *leguaan* shakes it so hard that it too falls out of the tree, onto the ground. And it knocks itself subconcious. (That's the word Sunday uses: subconcious). And it lies on the ground like it is dead and all the worms go like this" – he makes the inchworm motion with his fingers again – "and crawl back up into the tree!"

Sunday roars with laughter. We are all falling about, as much at his antics and gestures as the unlikely story. He goes on:

"And then the *leguaan* wakes up and he looks up into the tree and he sees the worms up there and he thinks, hey, food! You know, they're not very clever, these lizards. So he starts to climb the tree again... "

Sunday can barely contain himself. The lucky listener gets all of Sunday when he relates a story. I'm almost crying with hilarity. Eventually I gather myself and I have to know. I ask:

"So have you seen this, Sunday? I haven't heard of this before."

"No, not me, I haven't seen it."

"Oh. Okay. So how do you know this is true?"

His face darkens a bit and the change is unnerving. I immediately regret my question. Sunday gives me a long and pitying look, and shakes his head just slightly.

"Lloyd. Because it is *known*."

Legend 8

What other kinds of lamb do you get?

At dinner at a swanky game lodge in the Kalahari with some well-heeled guests, an American lady said she would 'try the lamb'. Now the Kiwis may say what they like about their lamb but I'll have the South African Karoo lamb every day of the week, and I told her so. I was taken aback when she informed me that she'd never eaten lamb before. Perhaps the Atlantic Cousins choose beef, chicken (or turkey) and pork for preference, but surely there is lamb on the menu in the USA? She hadn't heard of it. She liked it though, chewed thoughtfully, and then perplexed me by asking, "What other kinds of lamb do you get?"

What on earth did she mean? Was she jesting with me? Mind your flippant tongue, I thought to myself, one only knows what one knows. Be kind.

"Well," I replied carefully, "there's New Zealand lamb, and I really love the stuff you get in the Lake District in England, the Herdwicks... "

"No," she interjected, "I mean, which part of the animal does it come from?"

Now I was truly at sea. Respectfully, I explained:

"Um, well, that's the shank you're eating there, you know, the lower part of the sheep's leg, that's why there's a bone, and then you get... "

"Sheep? You said this is lamb!" she said, crossly.

"*Ja*, we usually eat lamb but you can also get mutton if the sheep is slaughtered later than one or two years. But I'm not sure what you mean exactly."

It turned out that she thought she was eating beef, but that this particular cut was called 'lamb'. It was all very confusing for both of us. But it reminded me of something. Or rather, someone.

I was running a training programme for new guides at Palmwag Lodge in Namibia, and all sorts of hopefuls had pitched up at the recruitment day, including Arnaud, a pleasant young fellow with an interesting back-story. He was a war refugee who had walked, *walked*, from the Democratic Republic of Congo, through jungle and desert, across war zones, probably evading borders, police roadblocks and army patrols, and ended up in Namibia. He spoke French, a much sought after skill in Namibia because so much of the county's income is derived from European tourists. Hello, I thought, here's an opportunity to do good: let's give the chap a chance.

He seemed willing enough, too. His own country had failed him by never giving him an education, so he struggled to read and write, but he was cheerful, keen and well-presented. Sometimes that's all it takes. The guiding profession is about relationships, not certificates. (Or should be. It's changing.)

One afternoon I took the trainees for a stroll along the high craggy bank of a small river tributary, practising safety procedures for walking safaris and talking about whatever natural phenomenon we chanced upon. A family herd of elephants was feeding in the stream below us, pushing into the depths of the Mustard bushes and head-butting the tall Fan palms until the golden-yellow fruits cascaded down upon their backs. It was a peaceful scene and a rare thing to be on foot in the presence of these giants. The small group of trainees settled comfortably on the red basaltic ridge, the perfect classroom, and we discussed elephants.

Arnuad was fascinated. He'd never seen an elephant before but he assured me that he knew a lot about them. Go ahead, Arnaud, I encouraged him, here we learn from each other.

"My grandmother in the forest at home used to see them. She knew these animals," he announced. "She told me everything about them. Very nice to eat."

Dammit. Always food. In many African languages the generic word for animals, *nyama*, is basically the same word for food. Okay, I thought, let's move the conversation from consumption towards conservation. But Arnaud was adamant. He went on:

"Yes, you get many kinds of meat from an elephant."

"One kind, surely?" I said. "Elephant meat."

"No, no," he said, "many kinds. From the back you get beef. From the shoulders, you get chicken. From the legs it is goat meat. Different places, different meat."

My mouth opened to contradict the patent absurdity of this but to my utter astonishment I saw a few of the other candidates nodding in agreement. Dismayed, I said:

"Why do you have to think about eating every animal you see? Why can't you just look at these wonderful animals and enjoy them as they are, alive, rare, trusting, magnificent? And where do you get this 'different meats' nonsense from? It's complete rubbish!"

Several of the trainees shifted uncomfortably on their rocks, and looked away. They needed employment: this was a gratis training opportunity for them, and they weren't about to gainsay me, but it was clear that I had offended them. 'Rubbish' is a tough word in southern Africa, far more provocative than its usual conversational meaning.

"Who else believes this story?" I demanded irritably.

A few hands rose hesitantly. Brave souls.

"Where do get this information? Who has actually eaten elephant?"

No response. Shifty looks. Watch out, we've made Mister Lloyd angry. No volunteers here, thanks; no-one was going to admit to eating elephant; that's tantamount to admission of guilt for poaching. The irony was that in fact I *had* eaten elephant, some meat from a culled bull in Botswana in the days when trophy hunting was allowed and the meat was distributed to the ravening community that neighboured the hunting concession. Waste not, want not. Do you want to know what that meat tasted like? Elephant.

"My grandmother told me," repeated Arnaud. "She knew."

"Okay, listen, guys," I said, calming down, "if you're going to be guides you need to understand your guests. It's the most important thing. And they do not want to hear about eating the bloody animals. Okay? So let's talk about something else. Arnaud, how do elephants breed? What did your grandmother tell you about that?"

"Ah, it is very interesting," he said, happy to move onto a new topic. "When a bull elephant wants to make a baby, he looks for the females and when he finds them he stands at the top of a hill."

So far, so good, we were on more certain ground now, I thought. But I should have known better.

"Yes, then he chooses one of the females, and he charges at full speed down the hill and he mates with her, bang, he just hits into her – here, Arnaud makes an obscene gesture with one index finger and the circled digits of his other hand – and immediately, right there, the new baby is born!"

I looked at him in stony silence. He was pleased with himself, he reckoned he'd just come top of the class, new job as a guide guaranteed. The other trainees looked nervously at me. Here goes Mister Lloyd again, they thought, watch out, Vesuvius time!

Heavily, slowly, deliberately, I said:

"So, Arnaud, this is all true, right? You have not seen this happen but you believe it."

He nodded eagerly and started to speak but I stopped him with an upraised hand.

"I know, I know, because your grandmother told you. Because it is known."

Legend 9

One thing that's not two

The Himba up on the Kunene river in Namibia hold this legend to be true, but I was also told this story by a guide in Mozambique, and yet another guide, in Kenya, confirmed it. It's an amazingly widespread belief. As a test, I asked a Namibian guide to show it to me in a book once. Of course, it wasn't there but the guide's reaction was interesting. He thought the authors were pretty slack for leaving it out; after all, everyone knows about it. It is known.

The story goes about a snake. A huge great snake. No-one I've spoken to has actually seen it, except for its lights at night. Yes, lights. I'll explain shortly. But pretty much everyone's grandmother has seen it. Those old girls are the fount of all wisdom, it seems. My theory is that these fairy tales are of the ilk of the scary monster stories of the Brothers Grimm. Told by grandmas around the world, as the kids gather at their knee, they are moralistic, cautionary tales that define the difference between good and evil, and they are designed to scare the crap out of you and keep you in line. In the case of the Giant Snake of Africa, the lesson is this: do not go out in the dark!

The story varies a little in details from region to region but the Himba man was the first to tell it to me, balancing on his thin *Grewia* stick with a small metal scratching spear stuck into his hair above an ear and his tatty robes flapping in the Kunene breeze.

"There is a massive snake, not an African Rock python, no, no, we know what those are, no, this snake is much, much bigger, thick like your waist and twice as long as a python. Huge. You never see it in the daytime. It lives up in the hills in caves but it comes to the villages at night. It has a red crest on its head, like a rooster. And it will eat you like that if it finds you outside at night."

"So it comes to the village to hunt?" I asked.

"Not really, it comes to gather dung from the goat kraal. It takes the dung up to the cave and it collects it there in its nest, and that is where it lays its eggs."

"How does it carry the dung?"

"I don't know, maybe in its mouth."

"Have you ever seen its cave?"

"There are many caves in the hills. Many. The snake moves. But we know where it is sometimes because you can see its light at night."

"Light?"

"Yes, it has lights. They shine in the dark, and you can see the snake moving."

There has been speculation that the lights are actually sparks caused by rocks grating against each other as a result of earth tremors, a not uncommon phenomenon in Namibia. It's just plausible, I suppose. But the concept of earth tectonics would find little traction amongst Himbas who have never had the science-based education that I did. They'd call that a ridiculous myth without foundation and shake their heads at the tommyrot that I am prepared to believe.

No, I reckon I'll go with The Great Snake. And I'll tell you one thing that's not two, mate, you won't find me going out after dark into those hills!

Legend 10

Who's your Drongo?

"They're very clever birds," Blessing, our guide from Little Makololo camp, told us. "Very clever. And bad, also. We don't like these birds. They make a lot of problems for us."

This avian prodigy was blithely perched on the outer edge of a Zambezi teak tree in Hwange National Park, Zimbabwe, grating away in a mixture of whistles and shrill notes, quite unaware of its own genius, its dark-red eyes scanning for unsuspecting flying insects.

"Mate," drawled Mark, an Australian tourist, "That's news to me. Where I come from, a 'drongo' is an idiot; a bloody moron. And they make a lot of problems for *us*, too."

"Oh, you have also drongos there in New Zealand?" asked Blessing, surprised.

"The sheep-shaggers? They're *all* bloody drongos, mate. But I'm an Aussie. Completely different. Especially the accent," he said, grinning.

Blessing raised a sceptical eyebrow. I knew what he was thinking: "You all sound the same to me."

"Ask an Aussie and a Kiwi to say the number 'six' and listen to the result, Blessing," I volunteered. "You'll soon tell the difference. But listen: this bird, this Forktailed drongo, is one of the African species. There are 29 different kinds of drongos across the Old World – Africa, southern Asia and Australasia. Almost always glossy black."

"But why do Australians think they are stupid? Here in Zimbabwe they are too clever," asked Blessing.

"Mate," said Mark, "I'll tell you. I dunno about the birds – if Lloyd says we have them in Oz, then I reckon he's right – but back home, 'drongo' is used as an insult to describe someone who is a loser. Like our current Prime Minister. And I happen to know why, too. Because sometime in the 1920's or thereabouts, there was a famous racehorse, a black one, like this drongo of yours, that never ever won a race. Came close a few times but never actually came first. And it was called 'Drongo.' And the name stuck."

Amazing what you learn on safari. Blessing and I would undoubtedly be using that information on future game drives. But Blessing wasn't about to allow our African drongo's name be besmirched by association with a mere dumb equid.

"Okay, but that was a horse, and this is a bird. And it is *very* clever," he insisted.

"Funny thing," I added. "I looked this up, once. The name 'drongo' comes from the Malagasy language, apparently, but it is used in Africa, India and Australia. But the early people of Madagascar ostensibly sailed over the ocean from south-east Asia at some point. So the question is, where does the name 'drongo' come from? Maybe it actually started in Indonesia or Malaya."

Blessing listened with interest. The drongo cocked its head with casual indifference and continued to survey the blue sky in search of lunch.

Mark said: "Yeah, anyway, Blessing, never mind the bloody history lesson, so tell us why this drongo of yours is so clever, then."

"Because what they do, they wait for the veld fires, you know, when the grass is long and dry at the end of winter, and it burns, and all the animals run before it. And these birds perch high above the flames, in tall trees, like that teak tree there, and they wait. And then, when the fire gets to a firebreak, like a river or a road or those wide corridors that we grade around the safari lodges, when the fire is going to die out because it cannot advance, then the drongo is very naughty."

Blessing is a natural story-teller, and he had us in anticipation now. I'd never heard this particular story but I realised that I was engrossed in yet another safari legend. It was great entertainment.

"Yes," continued Blessing, gesticulating indignantly towards the perched drongo. "They learn bad tricks from each other, these birds. That one! It is like the rotten tomato in the box. If one goes bad, then all of them are infected. Like *tsotis* – you know, those township youths that walk around in gangs, stealing and making trouble."

"They do tricks with fire? What do you mean, Blessing?" I asked.

Blessing took off his sunglasses and placed then carefully and deliberately on the dashboard. His eyes were dark with exasperation at the brazen knavery of these birds.

"Just when you think the fire is stopped and your crops and your cattle and your house are saved from the fire, these birds fly up into the smoke and they catch some burning grass that is floating in the hot air up there, they grab it in their beaks, still burning with flames, and they fly with it to the other side of the firebreak, and they drop it in the dry grass there, and then it all catches alight, and you are in trouble. They are trouble-makers!"

"Mate," said the Aussie, grinning, "That sounds *exactly* like our Prime Minister! You should shoot the buggers!"

"Eish, but there are too many!" agreed Blessing. It was obvious that his land and chattels had suffered at the wings of this bird in the past. Or... had they?

This is a legend I have actually seen myself. I don't need an aged grandmother, who *knows*, to assure me of this truth. Except what Blessing is telling us just *ain't* true. Drongos are sally-hunters; hawking birds: they perch and wait and watch, and then dash out, snatch a passing butterfly or beetle or wasp with an audible snap of the beak, then return to their perch to smash it to death before swallowing it, head foremost.

And when the wild fires sweep across the parched land, the drongos gather in dozens, hundreds even, to feed. It's a bonanza: the flames and heat scare the insects out of the grass as their refuges are consumed by the leaping fire, and as they scatter into the smoke and carnage of the conflagration, the drongos are waiting to strike. The birds swirl in a crazy feeding frenzy, like Spitfires darting at Luftwaffe Dorniers in the 1940 summer skies above Kent, snaring aerial insects as well as descending upon the charred remains of ground reptiles that could not escape the furnace: chameleons, lizards, small snakes, ground-nesting birds. The drongos are up amidst the burning embers, capturing scorched prey, then flying off to consume it away from harm's way, usually in a tree where the fire hasn't yet reached. Usually on the far side of the river, or the road, or the graded break.

The fire crosses, all right. The wind carries combusting material across the break. The *wind* does that, not the drongo. Why on earth would they?

"You're right, Blessing," I said. "Drongos *are* very clever. For example, they are excellent mimics. They make the sound of the Pearlspotted owlet, and even domestic cats, to scare other birds into dropping their prey. And they aren't afraid to harass large raptors like Tawny eagles. They fly above and behind them and peck at their backs and their heads until the big birds leave the area. Unlike the people that Mark is talking about, these drongos are very sharp indeed."

Blessing nodded.

"Yes," he agreed, "They do that. They are too clever. That's why they know about making fire."

"But why would they transfer the fire?" asked Mark. "What's in it for them? I don't understand."

"It is not for us to know," cautioned Blessing. "It is how things are. God decides these things."

5

GAME OF SECRETS

The two-way radio clicked, catching my attention, there was a short hissing pause in my ear-piece and then a ranger's voice said excitedly: "Stations, the mkulu nhlambe nyati have balega'd from the hlatini into the mfuleni. I think there may be ngonyams about."

What? What had he just said? It was my debut game drive in the Mala Mala Game Reserve and the first ten days of my employment there had been spent learning to be a barman, road-clearer, roof fixer and toilet inspector. I had yet to learn this mishmash of a language. There was certainly some English in there but the remaining words were what some guides at Mala Mala (known as 'rangers' in the Sabi Sands Game Reserve) fancied was Shangaan, the language of the local tribal people. In reality, the lingo was an effort at *Fanakolo*, a pidgin-English lingua-franca employed across South Africa between whites and blacks, especially in the mines, on farms and in game reserves such as this one.

So that morning as a FNG ('Fucking New Guy') when I heard on the radio that, "the large herd of buffalos had run from the bush into the river" I thought, well, that sounds quite clever but why not just say it in plain English? The answer was soon to become obvious: it's all part of the game, the game that guides play with their guests. A game of secrets.

At Mala Mala we rangers operated with head-sets, private earpieces, instead of open channel sound, and we used the Shangaan names for animals, places, intentions and actions so that we could keep secrets from the guests. The guests couldn't hear the radio and they couldn't understand what we said to each other when we replied to a transmission. *Fanakalo* was fun to use, and I discovered that I wanted to learn it fast. I wanted to be part of the brotherhood. Guides who used *Fanakalo* fluently achieved a certain status amongst their peers, and probably also amongst the local Shangaan staff: making the effort to speak the language (albeit a bastardised version of it) was appreciated. It was useful too. The guests on board the Land Rover usually had absolutely no idea what was going on: where we were, where we were going, what we were talking about. We could drive the same road twice, show them the same lion twice in the same place, but it all looked the same to them. They were always astounded when we rounded a bend in the road at the end of a game drive and the lodge came into view. "What camp is that?" they would ask. For some of them, especially Americans, even our South African accents and idiom were enough to confuse them; never mind *Fanakalo*, we might just as well have communicated in our version of English. So you can imagine how easy it was to take advantage of the guests' naiveté; and we did. But it wasn't malicious; there was a good reason to do so. It was called 'surprise and delight.' Why play the Joker when you still have good cards in your hand?

So, in order to make ourselves look like great guides, to make it appear that we were finding everything ourselves, we new guys collaborated. We employed several ruses. Speaking *Fanakolo* was one. Secondly, where possible, we would try to time our arrival at a sighting carefully so that we were the only car there. This created the impression that we had discovered the animal on our own. The guests on board never seemed to notice all the fresh tyre tracks, flattened grass and broken shrubbery created by vehicles that had been there only minutes before. It was always amusing later at brunch when my guests would tell another guide how we had "found the lions hunting" when in fact we were perhaps the fourth or fifth vehicle to see those lions that morning.

"Yes, we saw those," the guide might reply.

"I thought *we* had tracked those lions, Lloyd?" my guests would ask.

"Um, *ja*, different lions, there are several prides here," I'd say, looking meaningfully at my artless colleague.

More secrets. Just harmless fun, and all designed to enhance the guests' experience. What we were doing was creating mystery, making the guests feel special. It wasn't so much about secrets, actually, as illusion. Magic requires technique, but it must be done well: don't drop the cards on the table, and always keep the 'Reveal' to the end.

"Look, a cheetah, out there on the open plain!" I'd point out.

"Wow, how did you spot it, Lloyd? Gosh, what luck! Our first cheetah!"

The guests seldom noticed the tell-tale little dust cloud as the previous Land Rover vacated the sighting, its tracker merrily waving a battered hat towards the cheetah as his vehicle swept out of sight on a quest to the family herd of elephants down at the waterhole, already spotted by some other ranger. Naturally.

But there was another aspect to this game, this harbouring of information: we were young then, and we were competitive young buggers, typically with fairly fragile egos, and desperate to be the first at a sighting. We wanted respect from our guests, our peers, our trackers, from management, and the best way to get that was simple: find things! Find them first! Track animals through sign – their *spoor*, their vocalisations, by understanding their habits and idiosyncrasies – and then call the sighting (in barely muted triumph) on the radio. We wanted to be the ranger that found the leopard, and we wanted to give our guests the best and most private viewing we could. Phase one was the finding. Phase two was the keeping. How long could you enjoy the sighting, just you and your guests, before you felt obliged to call it in? Before you had to share it with other vehicles? There was no question that you *would* let the other rangers know, but when? As you were leaving? More secrets! Woe betide the ranger that sat on a great sighting without calling it and was then spotted by another vehicle. Acutely embarrassing, and selfish. You had to play the game of secrets carefully, and as equitably as possible.

The game drive radio. I loved it back then, but I have come to hate it now. It is noisy and disruptive, an alien clamour in a gentle, peaceful, wild environment, and many guides spend so much time listening to it and talking nonsense to their colleagues that they ignore their guests. They have become radio-controlled robots, dashing around the reserve, racing from one sighting to the next, ticking off the Big Five (a concept borrowed from the Great White Hunter era, now unfortunately morphed into a marketing tool), never bothering to find anything for themselves, never slowing to feel the heartbeat of the wilderness or listen to its song. Never being content that safari is sometimes a matter of chance and that perhaps today you could just have a peaceful amble about the reserve instead of seeking out the large, the horned, the tusked and the toothed. New guides, or older ones without confidence, depend upon the radio; I certainly did at first. It made me look good, but crucially it also ensured that my guests saw what they came to see. It was a necessary game.

Most lodges use open-speaker radios, horrible, crackling intrusive tools, but in our section of the Sabi Sands the ear-piece cut out the incoming radio noise. This allowed us to hold secrets, of course, but some of them were necessary. If a caracal cat, for instance, was spotted briefly and then immediately lost, with no hope of being relocated, the other guests would simply never know about it. Why foster disappointment? If leopards were mating in a distant part of the reserve and it was too far to get to, we wouldn't create despondency by letting on. This approach can work well if there is strict radio discipline with brief, accurate messages that do not need to be repeated, and some guides are really good at this, but the problem is that the guide tends to be distracted by the radio conversations, and often will cut off a guest conversation in mid-sentence to turn his attention to a radio-colleague instead because he is terrified of missing an important transmission.

Some guests find this extremely annoying. What is gained is that there is no audible radiobabble; what is lost is that the guests become secondary to the tracking and finding process. They have no idea what has been found, so when they arrive at a hyaena den or a rhino with a calf, they can easily be led to believe that their guide is the first at the sighting that day. Sometimes the guests, the *mlungus*, figure it out though, and demand to be told what is going on. The game of "look how amazing I am, understand how lucky you are to have me as your guide, see what I have tracked/spotted/chanced upon by blind luck for you" is chancy. And since you never really know who you have on board, you have to be careful not to patronise your guests. Most guides are of course highly competent at their jobs: enthusiastic, knowledgeable, personable, and skilled in tracking and spotting. And many operate chiefly independently of their colleagues while on game drive, depending on their own skills to locate wildlife and to entertain their guests without resort to that dreadful two-way radio.

Don't for a moment think that I believe we do not need radios in the game drive cars. Properly used, they are invaluable; they vastly improve the guest's chances of seeing the stuff they hoped for. It is a long way from Castres, California and Canberra, and if a guest hears at brunch that the other tourists saw leopard cubs but you didn't get them there (because there was no radio in the car), they are going to be at least extremely disappointed but more probably furious. The safari business can't afford that, and nor can one's career as a guide. Furthermore, the radio is useful in the event of an emergency, or for relaying pertinent information about matters such as aircraft arrival and departure times. There are a dozen good reasons that radios should be installed, but they do facilitate a level of cunning that is in total disregard for the intelligence of many guests.

It doesn't have to be that way. Experienced guides, those who long ago got past their egos, deal very comfortably with this situation. They abandon the silly use of Shangaan (or Zulu or Shona or Afrikaans) animal names, and speak openly in plain English on the radio. They tell their guests what is going on at all times, what they are hearing on the radio, and their conversations are open and honest. They set realistic expectations, and involve their guests in the tracking and spotting process.

"Folks, Frank has found a pack of Painted dogs down at Rosie's Pools. They are very active, hunting it sounds like, and he's struggling to keep up with them. We are miles away, at least an hour's drive. Let's keep looking for lions in this area, and then head down to where Frank is this afternoon. We may be lucky. Okay?"

Or: "Okay, I have something you are really going to enjoy. It's about twenty minutes from here, and the animal is very relaxed. There are other cars there right now so we will amble along and take our turn."

A perfectly acceptable little secret: build the anticipation.

Very confident guides listen to the radio message, acknowledge it, switch the radio off, drive at a moderate pace in the direction of the sighting, look out for things of interest – and sometimes find something even better along the way – and when they are fairly close, tune in again, check with the guide in charge of the sighting, and slowly approach the sighting, the guests eager with anticipation, all leaning forward in their seats and trembling. Job done. No hiding of facts, no false expectations, and no secrets.

On the eastern side of Etosha Game Reserve in Namibia, the skulduggery is taken to a higher level. There are many independent lodges in the area, all operating on a common game drive radio channel, and because the guides all live in different places they use the radio as a telephone, exchanging lengthy greetings and indulging in general gossip and laughter that has nothing to do with the job at hand. The open-speaker radio just never stops blaring, and it is maddening. In this case the languages are local – Oshiwambo, Oshiherero, Damara-Nama, Afrikaans – so the guests are entirely excluded from the conversations. But these guides have an extra trick. Because many of the guests have now learned the local names of the Big Five, the guides have given the animals code numbers instead. In their own language they will tell all and sundry that, "There is a number three at Klein Namutoni waterhole". The dust cloud as perhaps ten cars converge on the spot to view the lion is horrifying, and then when they arrive the guides keep jabbering to one another, often ignoring the guests completely.

This is an area where finding animals is easy so the radio has very little to do with enhancing the guest experience. But try to take away those radios from them and the trade unions and the wrath of the guides will descend upon you! It's because they don't trust their own skills. They're drivers, not guides.

We should acknowledge also the role of the tracker in the operation. In the Sabi Sands, when I was a mere FNG, we had a man sitting high up on the back seat, a spotter-tracker, usually (not always!) very sharp of eye and handy with a spotlight at night. Before I knew all the roads, it was the tracker who directed me about the reserve, speaking in *Fanakolo*, making me look good. In some places, most places, a local tracker sits on the "bait seat", a small seat on the front left hood of the car. In the past this was always a local black man who had grown up in the bush and who knew its rhythms intimately. He knew what animals the guests wanted to see and he watched the road carefully, looking for fresh tracks, signs that would indicate the recent passage of animals. But since he typically spoke very broken English at best, and since his role was to fuel and wash the car, point out wildlife and follow *spoor* on foot if it was viable, it was the ranger that did all the talking to the guests. And, therefore, often took all the credit. Not always, but often. That ego thing again. It's not like that anymore; it is far more of a partnership where guides are careful to give credit to their tracker and his skills. In addition, the tracker, more latterly, has a higher level of English and may even be in training to become a guide, so the new normal is to involve the tracker in the entire game drive process and give him his dues. The guests love interacting with a good tracker. We've come a long way.

Actually, there have been many other changes for the good. While the relationship between the tracker and the guide is better, so it is also between the guide and the clients. There is far less subterfuge than there used to be because the guide gets away with less. If the radio announces, "Stations, there is a relaxed mafazi ingwe in the *Kigelia* tree on the north bank at Paradise Crossing" and there are repeat or knowing guests on board, their response may well be, "Oh, great, we haven't seen a female leopard on this trip; is she in her usual tree?

Paradise is a bit of a drive from here, isn't it?" And it is changing not just because guests are becoming more savvy but because the industry has matured and the guides' approach has grown with it. We were all new young chaps then, but these days, thirty years on, there is so much less emphasis on being the first, on being the smartest, on trying to be clever. I hear that's called maturity.

But, caution, reader! Some of you can be as competitive as the guides. You too want to be the first car to leave camp, to be the first at a sighting, to be the one who spotted it. You too want to hold onto the sighting as long as possible, keeping it secret, before informing other cars. You too love to casually boast afterwards at pre-dinner drinks as the score is totted up that you found it, you tracked it, you saw it do this or that, and to nonchalantly say, "Oh, really, you didn't actually see it make the kill? What a shame, it was so exciting to actually be there." Guests like this, the ones with the biggest cameras and the permanently poised check-list pens, love that radio! They are not put off by the inane yabber. Not for them the gentle perambulation around the reserve, taking in whatever fate has brought before them that day. "What's he saying? *Nkombe*? Rhino? Go! How far? Is it a male? Let's go!" White of knuckle and grim of face, they grip the roll bars and whip the guide on, flexing at the knees at each bump in the road, hanging onto their hats, enquiring every minute, "Is he still there? How many cars are already there? Can we go straight in?" as francolins scatter before the wheels and mere giraffes, already ticked off the list, cease their browsing to consider this unseemly haste. The Land Rover goes swiftly in and it's a great sighting: a white rhino drinking from a pool, oxpeckers fluttering from his back and neck and boring into his trumpet-ears, the rhino reflected in the eddied silver pool. The cameras click and whirr, and then, "Right. Great! Rhino. That's four of the Big Five. Only one to go now. What's that on the radio? *Nyati*? That's buffalo, right? Cool, let's go! How far? Go, go!"

The plague of the Big Five. Mature guides hate it, but the reality is that the Big Five concept has been marketed so strongly to the safari public that without the radio it would be an over-promise. I have had scores of conversations with guests who only half-jokingly have wondered why we don't just radio-collar or microchip all the Big Five animals in an area and go straight to them. Never mind the tracker, or the bush skills of the guide: just follow that massive old lion on your GPS device, straight in and out of the sighting, next please! Use the technology and give us what it says on the tin.

I guided a Spanish family once who fulfilled their national stereotype: late to dinner, late to bed, late to rise, always late, what's the damned rush? I did manage to rouse them for their first game drive, and we had a very productive morning. But Felipe had it all figured out after that activity.

"So you guys talk to each other on the radio and then you go to the sighting, right? So now you know where everything is?" he questioned, yawning enormously as he got off the car.

"Well, sort of, I mean, if the sighting is stable, like a well-fed leopard in a tree or a lion at a fresh kill, then that animal will probably be there later," I agreed.

"Okay, so we don't need to get up early, we just wait until everyone comes back and you ask them where everything is, then we go from sighting to sighting, one, two, three, like that, no driving around wasting time looking at birds and poop and tortoises and those things," he suggested, as if it was the most obvious thing in the world to do. Why on earth does it take a Spaniard to work out the most efficient way to get this done, he was wondering?

"*Ja*, Felipe, we could do that, and we'd probably find most of the animals you want to see. But it would be hot in the middle of the day, and the light would be awful for pictures. Plus, it would feel like a zoo, you know?" I replied.

"Zoo is no problem. Hot is no problem – I'm Spanish! Light is no problem. Tomorrow we sleep and then we go out once only, one, two, three, done!" he declared. The guy had one of those black metal AMEX credit cards, not the kind of person who entertained discussion. Or who wanted to feel any of the rhythm of the African bush. A 'to-do list' kind of guy. I wasn't going to change that in two days.

"Okay, if you like, Felipe, sure." I said.

Everyone goes on safari for a different reason. We all have differing expectations and hopes. I prefer an exploration, though. I don't want my journey to be radio-controlled. No radio-babble, thanks. But sometimes...

"No problem," I said.

Needs must. We'd skip the rising of the great copper sun, then. And I needed the sleep anyway.

6

JUST SAY A NUMBER

Guides say things because they know they're being measured. Here's a favourite: "You should have been here yesterday. I know it's a bit quiet on game drive today, tumbleweed safari and all that, but yesterday it was hectic, man, hectic! Couldn't move for animals, I'm telling you."

He's telling you this because he's feeling inadequate. And he's feeling inadequate because the guests are rolling out a worn out joke, except they're actually only *half* joking.

"Okay, time to bring out the lions. What time do you let the elephants out the cages?" they joke-laugh.

In other words, "How crap are you guide-dude? All you've shown us so far is impalas!" The guide privately rolls his eyes, forces a grin and tries to explain that he's actually really good at his job, it's just that today he's unlucky. So what he says is:

"No, seriously, you should have been here yesterday. Two leopards, plus the pack of twelve dogs made a kill right here in camp, it was bedlam!"

Because he has to say *something*. Sorry won't cut it. So he says a number. Numbers are good. People like numbers.

If he needs to give a small number, then "less than twelve" can be handy. It sounds about right. "About twenty" seems plausible for a larger amount: not too short (or few), not too long (or many). It's got to appear reasonable. Reachable.

But twenty whats?

Safari guests, well, all people really, seek certainty in an uncertain environment, a wild environment, even though they generally know that you as a guide cannot guarantee absolute accuracy. The guide understands this need for information and can handle it in two ways. Either he prevaricates, or he is decisive. If he's overly cautious and afraid of being proved wrong, of being accused by his guests of being inexact, he will use words like "about" and "maybe" and "perhaps", and phrases such as "plus minus." Guides who lack confidence and choose the over-careful option tend to be bland. Vanilla guides. But if a guide is decisive, he'll say a number. A nice clear explicit number. Even if he's guessing a bit. He doesn't mind being wrong because his belief in his ability does not rest upon him being correct every time. And anyway, he gets it right almost all the time. What he says usually gets taken as truth, though, so he has a responsibility not to take advantage of naïveté.

Because first world people love numbers. They run their lives according to them. Train timetables, share prices, electoral results, anniversaries, temperatures, the rate of inflation, their number of Facebook friends, kilometres per litre on their car, budgets, batting averages, Black Friday discounts, and how long before their Uber arrives. It's all about numbers. Information. Right now.

The thing is, few of these metrics are *real* numbers, and they are usually chimeric anyway. They *feel* like real numbers, though, and we depend upon them being so. But, actually, dates and prices and costs and weights and distances and calendars and the level of humidity and even the very time of day are all just systems, measures, that we have invented to create order in our lives. They make the place work. They're necessary. And without the numbers we are lost. Nothing would make sense. We seek patterns, we crave schedules and we desire the substantiation that numbers bring. Naturally, inevitably, we carry our dependancy on numbers with us wherever we go. Even to Africa.

But out there in the uncertainty of the wilderness, life can be a little woolier. Ever heard of an "African kilometre"? It's another old safari joke. The guests have been driven into the bush on a morning activity and they feel out of control because they have no idea where they are or how far they are from camp. All power has been passed to the guide: left or right turns, when to stop, what time they get back, how long they stay at the lion sighting. Many people, and particularly men, innately hate this. They reach for the map of the game reserve and insist that the guide show them "exactly" where they are now, "exactly" where they had morning coffee, "exactly" where the hippo pool is. And they ask the guide to tell them "exactly" how far it is to the camp.

"About ten kilometres," replies the guide. It's a reasonable guess.

He has to say *something*. Silence is not an answer, and if he doesn't give a number, people will suspect that he is lost, or clueless. And being lost is one of our species' greatest fears. But the guide doesn't know exactly how far it is when the question is asked because the tracks twist and turn and who knows what he's going to see and stop for on the way back to brunch. So he drives on, and after a while the emasculated guest says accusingly:

"I thought you said it's ten kilometres. That would normally take, what, thirty or forty minutes at this speed, right? But you told us that at 10.30 and now it's already 11.45."

He's been measuring – he's a Strava hound. The hand-held devices are so sophisticated these days, he might even have the drive plotted on Google Earth. He sounds miffed at the guide's misinformation, as if he thinks he has been deliberately deceived. But there's no chicanery: since that conversation the guide has stopped to look at impalas rutting, crossed carefully through a flooded stream where pied kingfishers hovered and dived, explained the myths and legends of the giant baobab tree and the white-backed vulture's nest in its lofty top, and pointed out a distant herd of zebras. He explains the delay.

"Oh yeah, those *African* kilometres!" says the guest, laughing without showing his teeth.

He's not really amused. Silly man, he's gone and stressed himself out. What does it *matter*? There's nothing else on today: he's on holiday. But the guide laughs along with everyone on the car because never mind African kilometres, there are African hours too, and sometimes they last a long, long way past sixty minutes. The guide *must* say a number because if he equivocates, it's worse. The number needs to be a reasonable guess, of course, but can never be spot on.

"How many elephants in that herd?" a guest will ask.

Jeepers, its hard to tell. They're strung out through the woodland, feeding as they move, and there are plenty of little ones hidden in the shade below their mother's bellies. And why is the number important? Because that's what we do. We measure. We just can't help it.

"Close to twenty," seems a reasonable guess, and a hell of a lot better than "I haven't a clue." And then you drive around the island of vegetation for a better view and you find at least another twenty jumbos out on the floodplain!

"Completely different herd," you say with a delighted clap of your hands and very wide smile. "Another twenty. It's your lucky day!"

The guests can't tell if you're joking, but they're delighted. The number rapidly becomes the truth by the time you get back to camp for brunch.

"Forty elephants," they tell the straight-faced chef who is energetically beating eggs in a bowl at the buffet while the guests wait for their 'omelette with everything.' "Forty! Two big herds, with babies and everything! Brilliant!"

Your fellow guides look at you with raised eyebrows and a smirk. They also saw that herd this morning. One walks over and murmurs:

"I saw that herd, dude. Twenty-five, tops."

And you shrug, because everyone's happy, the number is of no consequence, and the elephants themselves don't care. They just *are*. They don't count things. But people? We need a number.

A guide has to be able to shrug off the pressure of numbers. Many fail. The ones who ply back and forth into the corridor of massive red dunes of Sossusvlei in Namibia, for example, are far too worked up about exactly how high the largest of all the dunes, Big Daddy, is. They argue passionately about it. Some hold out for 280 metres, some for 320, but none of them explain whether they are measuring from sea level or from the floor of Dead Vlei. And since the crest is subject to daily winds, it stirs and shifts anyway. There isn't an actual answer. And why does it matter? The Sossusvlei guides' concern is not actually about accuracy for the sake of science; it is entirely related to their fragile egos. They don't want to be wrong and they most certainly do not want to be found out in front of their colleagues. Fierce recriminations ensue between them as they angrily accuse their fellow guides of making them look stupid by loudly announcing the height of Big Daddy in front of everyone, a number in conflict with the one they told their own guests.

"But Justin," might say a guest, "you told us it's 280 metres high. And this guy reckons its 320. Aah, *African* metres!"

The guide will shrug and affect a smile, but inwardly he's seething. He's a victim of the pressure of numbers, of measuring everything. He wants a black and white answer to a question that has no fixed number. And there are thousands of common ones:

- How long do giraffes live? (Guides always say 29 years. Why not 30?)
- How many eggs does a female guineafowl lay? (Eighteen? But they're not all hers.)
- How old is that wrinkled elephant? (Older than 30. Maybe 40?)
- How much water is there in the Kunene river? (A lot? Especially after the rains.)
- How many stars are there in the heavens? (A lot. But we can only see about 2500 with the naked eye.)
- What day will the rains start? (Any day ending in a "y".)
- Does the sun come up at 05.36 or 05.42? Because according to my app... (Try a different app.)

Sometimes there's no answer, but you have to try. I taught an apprentice guide this truth as we walked with guests along a coarse-gravelled strand on the Mozambican island of Vamizi. Our destination was a sumptuous breakfast, fresh fruit and champagne and seafood, under a pure-white awning in a cove on the northern tip of the island. We'd started off on the hard wave-washed sand closer to the ocean but the tide was inexorable and eventually the rising water forced us up the beach towards the tree line where the going was harder, jagged bits of coral jutting out of the sand and the flotsam zone clogged with a tangle of drifted branches. The sun was beginning to unleash its venom, the going had become tricky and some in the party were beginning to regret their gung-ho decision not to take the Land Rover transfer that had been offered. A stroll along the beach to breakfast had seemed the more idyllic option, the right thing to do. But several of the guests were beginning to wilt.

"How far to breakfast, Matt?" one of them asked wearily.

Matt was brand new at the job, brand new on the island. He pushed his sunglasses up his forehead in a feeble attempt at veracity ('show your eyes') and said: "Uh, it's, like, dunno really, not too far, I think."

The guest looked unhappy, shook her head minutely, and slogged on.

"Dude, you need to be decisive. Just say a number," I advised. "Look at that lady, she feels worse now. Take charge of this. People want leadership from you. Be firm, and say a number."

"Yeah, but, I don't *know* the fucking answer," he said despondently. "I don't want to lie to them."

"Sure, but they need information. You have to take an educated guess, and then if you find you're wrong, just update. People need a number to hang onto, right? That's why they count all the birds they see, and how many hours of sleep they got last night, and how far they paddled in the mangrove swamp yesterday. Ha! But they always forget how many glasses of wine they had at dinner! Well, I do, anyway."

"But I've never been here before," he said plaintively, shrugging off my little attempt at humour.

"Okay, in that case, you either say so right at the start, or you sort of make it up. But you don't really have to fabricate: come on now, think about it. Do you think its one kay to breakfast, or five, or ten?"

"I reckon it's only three but... "

"Exactly! Good enough. Say three the next time someone asks. You have two things going for you. Firstly, people are terrible at guessing distances anyway, and secondly, these folk happen to be

American so they don't have a clue how far three kays is! And don't use the word 'only.'"

Matt took charge. He called a stop and as we rested under the meagre shade of a slim palm tree, he informed the group that there were 'close to three kays to go.' Everyone felt cheerful about that. Three is a plausible number, an attainable number. Anyone can walk three... whatevers. We walked on to breakfast and it was actually closer to four kilometres but no-one knew the difference.

"I can't believe that worked," said Matt, impressed.

"Just say a number, dude!" I said, grinning.

7

AFRICA'S A BIG COUNTRY

A greying ponytail on a middle-aged man with a receding hairline looks rather affected to me. And if he also wears a pretentious little scarf around his neck, it's even more unfortunate – it looks like he's trying too hard. The guiding world seems to attract quite a few of these types.

This one was called Gary. He called everyone "dude." I was going to have to get used to him.

"You know that about half the people in your tour party don't even know they are in South Africa, right?" I said to him.

I was a fresh-faced lodge guide in the Sabi Sands Game Reserve, and had just returned from an afternoon game drive. It had been fun and enlightening; this was the first time I had guided a group for Gary's tour company, an American safari travel outfit that focused their business on retirees living mainly on the golf resorts of Florida. 'Snow Bird Travel', or some such name. Gary had cautioned me to drive very slowly indeed because the guests were elderly, and one of them, Beth, had had a hip replacement fairly recently.

I love guiding older people. I love elderly people in general, actually.

They are so damned *interesting* if you take the time to let them know that you really do want to hear their stories. They tend to feel ignored as they get older but we shouldn't sideline the oldies' wisdom just because they might be crusty and can't hear us properly. And unlike so many of the youngsters, they often have a wonderful sense of the ridiculous. It's far too late in their lives to take themselves seriously. I remember one old veteran requesting with a twinkle in his eye a "quarter of a fluid ounce" of milk in his coffee. I grew up with the metric system: an eminently logical method that counts in tens. So when I looked at him, confused, and asked him how much that was, he chuckled and said, "One finger son. Don't they teach you anything at school these days?"

I had imagined that Gary took himself too seriously. Group guides like Gary, those who travel with their clients for weeks on end, naturally develop a special relationship with them, and when they have to entrust their wards to local guides such as me, they are often sensitive about losing their position as the pre-eminent fount of knowledge. They want to remain the "go-to" person and sometimes don't like it very much if their clients go off on a game drive with the local chap and have too much of a great time. "Gary, Lloyd was *great!* He has the eyes of an eagle! He showed us elephants and lions and zebras and... he's such a *lovely* young man." Venomous look and a cold shoulder from Gary likely to follow. Fragile egos often go hand in hand with ponytails, I think. What do I know? But that's what I've noticed in the safari game.

I was wrong about Gary.

"Oh, it doesn't matter," replied Gary, winking. "Africa's a big country."

Oh, okay, he did have a sense of humour, then. There are at present count 53 countries in Africa, and all of China, India, the USA and most of Europe fit easily into the African continent in terms of land area. The infamous story about George W. Bush calling Africa a country had done the rounds, it seemed. Knowing the press, it may well have been a misquote, but the way they wrote it, 'Dubbya' had displayed laughable and insulting ignorance on this occasion. The fact that he was at the time announcing the most generous USA aid package to Africa ever, including a tranche of funds to train people in the tourist industry, helped shut people like me up.

The fact was that his clients adored Gary. He was kind to them, and they loved the way he fussed over their every need. It was a large group, perhaps thirty – they had arrived in an enormous bus – but Gary knew everyone's name and peculiarities; what they liked to eat, to drink, who they liked to sit with at meals, and most importantly, their various ailments and afflictions. That was a big topic of conversation: which prescription pills they were on, and for which malady. Gary was organised, caring and professional. The oldsters looked upon him as the son-in-law they wished they had had. He was half their age, but he was nearing forty.

To Gary's chagrin, there had been no room for him on any of the Land Rovers that afternoon so he had spent the entire afternoon on a chair at Reception, waiting for the return of the cars, checking every ten minutes with the girl there about what their ETA was. As each one pulled in, he had enthusiastically leaped on to the running board, inquiring as to what they had seen, clapping in delight as they happily relayed information about leopards in trees and great herds of buffalos. He was good at his job, was Gary. Hats off. He was far more genuine than I had thought at first appearance.

"So how come they don't know where they are?' I persisted. "Surely they see the signs at the airport? What about the local currency? Our road signs are in both English and Afrikaans. Don't they notice? What about immigration when you fly in: don't they ask?" I asked, mystified.

"Dude, my job is to take care of them, shepherd them and show them wild animals. African animals. That's really all we prep them about. 'Lions, tigers, elephants,' you know the story."

He raised a cautionary hand as I started to interject.

"Yes, I know, I know, no tigers in Africa, try telling *them* that! I keep all the passports because they can be a bit forgetful, and tend to lose them. I handle all the money, tipping, bar bills, the works, it's all included, so they never handle cash. I fill in the immigration forms,

I do all the documentation for them, all they have to do is sign. Easy peasy, lemon squeezy. Stress free safari for them. They just eat, drink and look at the animals. I even write postcards for some of them; man, I even lick the damned stamps! So yeah, to them, they're in a country called Africa."

I had to swallow my preconceptions. Gary was cool. I asked him to join me on the drive next morning because one of the old folks wanted to sleep late, and I had to admit that he was good fun to have on board. To my surprise, he didn't try to hijack the game drive, but sat behind me and asked really good questions.

Beth was sitting next to me. I drove slowly down the river road, pointing out bushbucks and impalas and hamerkop nests, gently making our way towards where a White rhinoceros had been reported drinking in the Sand river. At this speed it didn't seem likely that we would get there in time, and I quietly mentioned this to Gary.

"Not to worry, dude. They saw some rhinos yesterday on the wildlife video in the bus while we were driving through the Kruger National Park. They're happy," he told me with a straight face.

I stared at him. He didn't appear to be joking. Watching a video inside a national park when there where real live animals, including rhinos, right on the other side of the bus window? Seriously? He laughed, and leaned over my shoulder, whispering.

"We keep the windows closed because of the air-conditioning. And by the way, stop pointing out animals unless they are *right next to the road*, okay. These folk are too polite to tell you, but they can't really see them."

Right. This was a learning experience. He knew his audience, did Gary, and he knew what worked.

We rolled gently on down the river's bank in the shade of the old African ebony trees, just barely keeping pace with the stream on our right as it trickled around thickly reeded islands. I kept an eye on Beth. She seemed thoughtful. After a while she started to fret with her multi-pocketed safari vest, opening and closing zips, patting and unclipping. Eventually she drew a wrinkled rectangular card from some recess and handed it to me.

"It doesn't look anything like this," she announced, looking slightly aggrieved.

Gary frowned, thinking no doubt 'whoops, the old girl is upset, this needs sorting out' and leaned forward to see. It was an ancient black-and-white postcard, the writing faded and illegible. I peered closely at it. Unmistakably the open grasslands of the Serengeti.

"This is from Tanzania, Beth," I said. "Where did you get it?"

"My aunt sent it to me a long time ago, when she was on safari in Africa. She loved the holiday so much, and I kept it because I always knew I would get to Africa before I died. And here I am!" she said. "But," stabbing a crooked finger at the card, "this place looks different."

I glanced at Gary, who shrugged slightly. Good luck dude, he was saying, I've tried to explain all this before.

I stopped next to an open patch of loose sand, and pulling my stick from the car, I got out. Drawing a large outline of the African continent, I added the countries that constituted southern and east Africa, and finally scratched the Equator across the map. Beth and her friends watched with interest.

"Right, everyone, take a look at this," I said, pointing with my stick. "Here we are at the bottom of Africa, in South Africa. In the Republic of South Africa. Africa is one of the seven continents, as I am sure you know. And this country here, is Tanzania. See, it's next to Kenya, just underneath it. This is Mount Kilimanjaro, about here, everyone's heard of that, right? The equator runs though *here*. So you can see that most of Africa is actually in the northern hemisphere, look."

"Where's Egypt? We were in Egypt last year, on the Nile," said one of the old guys.

"Up at the top, on the right, over here," I pointed, and drew in the river.

Beth piped up. "Okay Gary, so, how come we aren't in the Serengeti? I thought we were going to the Serengeti?"

Gary grimaced.

"This is a *southern* Africa safari, Beth, remember we spoke about that? Tanzania is way over there in east Africa," he said patiently.

"Look," I added, scratching at the map again. "Between us and Tanzania you have to cross Zimbabwe, Mozambique, Malawi, maybe Zambia..."

I should have added a scale to that map.

"Well, okay," said Beth firmly, "let's go there tomorrow!"

8

STEVE, AND THE MODERN NOVEL

On the rare days when I had no guests to guide, I used to roam at random from Kirkman's Kamp (as it was spelt), into the vastness of Mala Mala Game Reserve. I'd bow-wave my Landy north through the Sand River at Rocky Crossing, past the chorus of wheezing hippos as oxpecker birds rose chittering from their scarred backs, and hefting my .375 rifle I'd explore on foot the thickly bushed ravines that meandered east of Paradise Valley towards the Kruger National Park fence-line. I went slowly, quietly, cautiously, promising myself that I wouldn't run if something unseen suddenly growled or lumbered to its feet in front of me. The things I came across and the sights I saw! Previously undiscovered hyaena dens, the nests of Paradise flycatchers, sometimes the remains of kills that even the keen-eyed vultures had not yet detected. Once, briefly, tiny leopard cubs, their eyes still blue-grey (where was their mother?), and occasionally lions at their rest, completely unaware of my presence. In the deepening evening I'd be so disorientated by the twists and turns of the eroded *dongas* that I'd have to use the setting sun and a falling western planet to guide myself back to a road I recognised, or onto my own tracks. It was a bit like Winnie the Pooh and Piglet (trying to be brave, as usual) following themselves in circles: look, tracks! More tracks! Oh, they're *our* tracks! It was exhilarating to simply be there, alone and free. It was why I chose to work there. Those were glory days.

Living in Japan was something like that too. It wasn't as edgy but it was every bit as interesting as living in the bush. It, too, was a good place to get lost in. And the people you came across! I would wander the narrow streets of Fujioka, the small village where I worked, and little old ladies in large straw bonnets would round the corner and see me, a big *gaijin* man, apparently menacing, and foreign, and they'd immediately stop dead, their mouths open into a comical 'O', then turn and shuffle away with their funny little short steps, bobbing and nodding and apologising, *sumimasen, sumimasen*. Everything was a surprise there. My first haircut was startling: after a succession of hot towels and soothing balms applied to my face, they then shaved my forehead and ear-lobes with a cut-throat razor and gave me a wonderful neck massage. Only thereafter did the haircut follow. It was all so gloriously strange. The seasons, so distinct one from another, were unfamiliar: bitterly cold and snowing in winter and unbearably humid in summer. Cherry blossoms in spring and the many shades of leaf-gold in autumn. Occasionally, an earth tremor would shake the house, sounding like an advancing wall of wind as it rushed audibly through the building, setting the wine glasses tinkling and the cutlery shaking and dancing in the drawers.

Mala Mala and the bachelor life had run its course for me and here I was in Japan, married to Sue and teaching conversational English. I had needed a completely fresh perspective and I very badly wanted to travel, to see the places that my game reserve guests spoke about. Sue and I felt that we'd rather have a passport full of visa stamps than a house full of stuff. And I was loving it, running in the mountain parks, meeting fascinating people, skiing like a beginner and birding assiduously on my days off in the conifer-clad mountains on the spine of Honshu. My bird "lifer" list was growing fast.

Then I met Steve. My language school arranged a softball game against students from a sister school in nearby Chichibu, and he was one of their teachers. Steve was a tall and gangling Canadian (by way of Scotland) and I liked the way he sized me up. He looked into me as if he was searching for light. It wasn't at all off-putting: I immediately recognised an earnest wish to communicate and the hope that the discourse would be good. That chance gravitation of two foreigners on the edge of a dusty sports field in a remote Japanese hill village was exactly the reason I travelled – I sought out the unexpected – and I knew straightaway that I had found someone who had something to say. His Canadian-Scots accent was intriguing and his eyes laughed from behind his spectacles.

We instantly became good friends and visited each other virtually every weekend after that for the two years I taught English in Japan. We played unskilled yet energetic tennis on an ancient earth-tremor cracked court, visited tiny local sushi bars (where cute dark-eyed local girls who thought all Western men looked like film stars giggled from behind their hands and dared each other to talk to us), drank a hell of a lot of Kirin beer, and sang drunkenly and lustily in karaoke bars until the small hours of a Sunday morning. Sometimes we argued heatedly, and occasionally ended up in a wrestling match from which we both emerged, after the sweating had sobered us up, covered in scratches and pine-needles, laughing and satisfied with life.

Earnest debate was the very basis of our friendship. We spoke about Japan, and its unfathomable strangenesses and fascinations. About ice hockey (he was a Canucks fan) and soccer (Celtic). A lot about politics. About relationships, as men begin to do usually only after alcohol has set free the tongue and enough time has passed to allow confidences.

Mostly, we spoke about literature. Steve was a man for the classics, a graduate from Vancouver in English literature, and claimed (I suspect with at least a little exaggeration) that he had never read a modern piece of poetry, play, novel, in fact anything written since Arthur Conan Doyle at all. Although I had read my fair share of classical literature at university, as well as for pleasure (not necessarily the same thing), I had read a lot of modern stuff too. Steve decried the paucity of great modern writing, and steadfastly rebuffed my point that it was impossible for him actually to know if there was any good latter day writing if he was choosing not to read it.

He had an over-riding (I called it a 'limiting') admiration for the writing of Charles Dickens. He felt that no other writer in English (except Shakespeare) came close to Dickens's greatness, his inventive use of the language, his deliberate irony, his humour, his telling of a tale. I would point out the obvious, that some novelists of today are necessarily the great writers of tomorrow and therefore there *must* be really important stories being written right now. Steve would languidly unfold his long frame from the futon, pour us another Jack Daniels, and announce that in any case everything written today, and always, is based on the classics. He was always annoyingly final about his blanket dismissal of modern novelists. But I persisted, and in a weak moment (not enough ice in his whiskey) he eventually agreed to read one of John Irving's novels. I have had an affection for Irving's writing since 1985 when a university friend told me that Irving is one of the most relevant modern novelists; quirky, controversial and a very fine storyteller. Steve read the book in a single day (or claimed to have done). Slightly triumphant, he shoved the novel at me.

"I have read your man, Irving," he said theatrically. "He's quite good, actually. But this is pure Dickens, my friend. Like so many others, he's a style plagiarist."

I'd been sure that Irving would turn him, so I was put out. Our tennis that day took on a renewed vigour, his serve harder than usual and my net-rushing more abandoned. At the sushi bar that evening I found that I was petulant and inclined to disagree with everything Steve said.

One October day, before the first frosts set in, Sue and I left Japan. It was time to travel again and we found ourselves some weeks later in Kathmandu. The day was going well: I was settled on cushions on a roof-top coffee house in delighted possession of a collection of Irving essays called *Trying to Save Piggy Sneed* that I had discovered that day in a second-hand book store. In perfect isolation from the Tiger Balm vendors and the mad scrambling hubbub of the claustrophobic alleyways below, I opened the book. One of the stories in the collection was called 'The King of the Novel'. Interested, I immediately paged to it, and gasped. It is John Irving's tribute to Charles Dickens. My mango lassi grew warm in the Nepalese sun.

"Almost everything I know about writing stories, I learned from reading Charles Dickens," it begins.

Dammit.

I mailed that book to Steve with a covering note: 'You'll want to read this.' I wonder whether he ever got it. If he did, his eyes would have shone bright from behind his spectacles. He wasn't beyond an 'I told you so.'

"Dickens. Pure Dickens," he would have laughed.

9

FOOL'S GARDEN

The Camp Raider is back, the bugger.

We guides, we who reputedly hold the ebb and flow of nature in deep respect, we who ostensibly are always sensitive to all creatures of the wild, we who honour the earth and give it the space it deserves, we would never hurt a fly. Right?

Wrong.

Especially if it is a mosquito keeping us from sleep in the depths of night. That mosquito will learn about survival of the fittest. Fast. What about the White-browed scrub robin that awakens us with its far too cheerful up-and-down-the-scale whistling at two in the morning, then again at three and once more at four? It has to go. Somehow. Consider the hyaena that on a nightly basis ransacks the kitchen and drags the contents of the rubbish bins across the camp. Something must be done. Or the hippo that tries to get into the lodge swimming pool each night. It's not on.

Anyone who is appalled that we guides would consider getting rid of such nuisances hasn't questioned us closely enough. And most definitely has not run a safari camp. Nature poses challenges.

The Camp Raider is an impressive fellow. We've all got a soft spot for him but he's a bloody nuisance. There is no fence around Kirkman's Kamp, of course, and the animals come and go freely, especially at night. We want it that way. You can't blame the Raider; it's not his fault that there are lemon trees planted in the garden.

Actually, there are all sorts of exotic plants at KK, invader vegetation that should not be there. The place is a riot of purple and crimson when the bougainvillea comes into flower. There are blackjacks too, noxious weeds that leave their "stickies" in your hosiery and render one's clothing unwearable. And paper thorn infests every lawn. But the Raider doesn't care about those: he doesn't wear socks, and he has tough feet. He's only here for the lemons.

Sometimes when I am on game drive, many a mile from the camp, I come across a pile of green and steaming elephant dung deposited with indifference on the two-track road.

"You know that big elephant that was in camp during dinner last night?" I say to my guests. "The one that we tried to chase away? He was here this morning. He left this."

"How do you know it was him? There're plenty of elephants here," they ask.

"Lemons," I say, pointing at the wet pile. The dung balls are studded with pale yellow half-chewed citrus fruits, bleached now by gastric juices, incongruous in this environment. "He loves them."

The problem with the Camp Raider is that he has become over familiar with people. He's not really dangerous, but he's always in the damned way, standing around in the car park, loitering on the pathways, slumbering under the shady wild fig tree and taking long draughts of chlorinated swimming pool water. The old fellow can be a bit grumpy, though, and doesn't like to be bothered. After all, he's been around since before the camp became a tourist lodge; he's probably forty or fifty now. Big guy, too, and nicely tusked. In truth, he isn't really the problem. It's the guests in camp. A highly unpredictable species, the safari tourist, and despite all the safety warnings, we rangers can't tell what they might do. Some of them think the animals that wander through the camp, the dainty bushbucks, the shy waterbucks, the warthogs rootling on their knees, are tame animals. They're not. They are habituated. We call them "relaxed". The difference is that tame animals are dependant on humans for food and attention, but habituated ones are not: they have learned to tolerate us because we don't bother them, that's all, but the moment we change the rules on them, they leave. Or get grumpy. So if a guest does something unexpected, like leaving the designated path to get closer for a picture with the Raider ("I just wanted a selfie with him, I mean, he's tame, isn't he?") or tossing an apple to a watchful baboon ("He looked so hungry and next thing he grabbed the whole bowl of fruit out of my hand!") or feeding the little Bush squirrels ("I couldn't help myself, they're so cute... but now he's got into my bathroom and has eaten my *medication!*"), and the animal behaves badly, well, whose fault is that? The rules changed, and the animals changed with them. They're opportunists.

The Raider is largely immune to us now. He co-exists, parallel to the activity in camp. He wanders through the staff village, exploring their cooking pots, and belly-rumbling his way past Rams, the rangers' accommodation. Just the other day he was standing right outside my window and I reached through and stroked his right-hand tusk. It was billiard-ball smooth, cool to the touch, and finely fissured with a worn notch just short of the tip that he uses along with his trunk as a catch-point to snap soft vegetation off with. I don't know if he even knew I had touched him: he was leaning against the outside wall, day-dreaming. Maybe dreaming about lemons.

But the rules with the Camp Raider do need changing. Elephants are very active at night, often to the detriment of one's sleep and bodily safety. They are noisy eaters and prodigious farters, and yet surprisingly hard to detect in the dark unless they are moving. Therefore, they are prone to scaring the crap out of you because they are grey as the night, and hide in plain sight; you just don't see them sometimes until they are suddenly looming over you, their tusks gleaming dully in the moonlight, their ears held out stiffly like boards. Careful and respectful retreats are always the sane option when that happens. Slow steps backwards, and no running. Elephants chase people who run. I'm sure they think it's funny. Because size *does* count.

So almost always we leave elephants alone. But that's not what Rob, the camp manager is telling us.

"Chase the bloody thing away, boys," is what he's saying. "We're too complacent about the Raider. One day there's going to be an accident. Someone, a guest or a staff member, is going to get hurt when they walk into the Raider at night, and I don't fancy the admin."

Rob's view is widely held amongst people who understand wildlife: this camp area is *our* territory, and we humans mark it, live in it, and defend it. We don't put up a fence, and well-behaved wild animals are always welcome in camp, but only on our terms. Pretty much every animal wanders through camp, mostly at night, including lions (frequently), leopards (every night), hyenas (often) and old buffalo bulls, the *dhaga* boys (too often, the unpredictable and stately old bastards – I love them). But for the arrangement to work, so that the guests and staff are safe, we must assert our dominance in this small patch that we claim.

"So, every time he enters camp, guys, we need to shout and clap and harass him, okay?" Rob is telling us. "He's got the whole of the game reserve to wander about in. Okay, I know he likes the lemons, but we're making it too easy for him. So make him feel unwelcome from now on."

It's not working. The Raider is still blithely ignoring us. His view, apparently, is that it is we who are in *his* territory. Oscar Wilde wrote that there is only one thing worse than having too much attention paid to oneself (the self-satisfied hypocrite!) and that is having none paid at all. The Camp Raider is maddeningly oblivious to our attempts to shoo him away, and it's annoying.

Rob has decided to up the ante. Missiles. He has bought a *cattie*, a hand-held catapult, or slingshot, and a supply of glass marbles. The other morning, when the guests were out on game drive, he fired a few marbles from close range through the open office window at the elephant. The Raider squealed loudly and walked swiftly away with head held high, glaring suspiciously back at Rob, who looked simultaneously guilty and triumphant. But in the late afternoon the Raider was back, casually feeding from the Fever *Acacia* planted next to the reception area. A rapid barrage of marbles aimed at his backside had him trumpeting off once more. The place is going to be full of glass if this goes on. Rob can't always find them after they have thudded into the Raider's corrugated hide, a skin that easily handles on a daily basis the sharp thorns and jagged sticks of the Lowveld bush. The gardener who mows the lawn is going to get a bruised shin one day, I'm telling you.

Mind you, they are having some effect on the thieving apes in camp. The mischievous Vervet monkeys and calculating baboons are feeling Rob's wrath too. I don't think he's managed to hit a single one of them (I don't think he really aims at them, to be fair) because they always spot him when he is sneaking about. At least they run like hell when they see him, usually with an apple or half-eaten croissant in one hand, skipping nimbly away on three legs and smirking back at his feeble efforts to punish them.

However, it is less easy to dislodge a 4000 kg elephant that knows that there is readily available fruit and water. Sticks and stones (and glass marbles) don't break his bones, and no words can hurt him. The eviction programme has now been extended to loud revving of Land Rovers stopped as close to him as we dare, but all that does is create a horrible cacophony and a blue-grey diesel exhaust haze that drifts across the camp. So Rob has tried spraying the Raider with a high-pressure garden hose. The elephant loves it! Spa for elephants. The Raider stands there happily, even turning so that the spray can soak the backs of his great ears. The morning after that mis-thought, we woke to find that the Raider had yanked the hose off the stand-pipe, breaking it off at ground level, drunk his fill at the source of the leak, and walked away while the entire camp's water supply, hard-won by dint of a creaking old pump down at the Sand river, had drained away into the thirsty sand.

Rob looked drained that morning, too.

"Right," he said. "Enough of this bullshit. Now it's personal. It's me, or him. One of us has to go!"

I have a nasty feeling it's going to be Rob.

Because last evening we had dinner in the outside *boma*. The stars twinkled bright and merry through the leaves of the massive *Marula* tree that dominates the tall reed-fenced dining area, and the log fire sparked and flamed. Fetching my guests from their rooms before dinner, I saw the Camp Raider loitering on the fringe of camp, well away from the main area, and minding his own business for a change. In the *boma*, Rob was holding forth to an enthralled audience about fishing again – yes, I know, when there are giraffes and zebras and hippos and interesting toothy things lurking out there to be talked about – but Rob has a thing for fish. I must admit, he knows his stuff. He was just insisting that tiger fish live in the Sand river, "Just little ones, but they put up a hell of a fight" when the *boma* wall fell over. The fragile dry reeds bent and snapped, the thin baling wire and poles that hold the edifice upright gave way, and the tall fence toppled into the open circle.

The Camp Raider had arrived.

The problem is that the lemon trees, ancient gnarly things that have seen better days, planted years ago in cattle ranch times for some fine lady's gin and tonic "with ice and slice", are loosely grouped right next to the *boma*. How the Raider has previously missed any of the fruit astonishes me, but an elephant's eyesight is not that good, especially in the dark, and the Camp Raider usually has a penchant for citrus fruit at night. Seemingly there are still some remaining lemons right on the tops of the trees, and nonchalantly leaning against the *boma* wall, the Raider was searching them out, his great trunk extended, questing for those sour and withered old fruits.

The guests sitting closest to the reed wall yelped, spilling their wine everywhere, distributing their cutlery to the four winds, and scrambled to the safety of the far side of the *boma*. It seemed like the old bugger was barging straight through the fence this time.

Rob's eyes took on a steely look. He gritted his teeth. He stood up. Grabbing his rifle (always carried at night by the duty ranger for real emergencies), and snatching up his flashlight, he looked at all the diners and said calmly but grimly, "Folks, please remain here in the *boma* where you are safe. Rangers, come with me." The guests gasped. Rob looked intimidating; armed and dangerous. If the Raider had seen his expression, he might have scarpered immediately! The rules were about to change.

We rangers gathered in the dark about twenty paces from the elephant, staying close to the safety of the main building, a brick and mortar sanctuary to which we could rapidly retreat if necessary. The Raider had his great baggy backside to us, unheeding as always, intent on his search for lemons. I had a brief and nauseating feeling that Rob was about to shoot the Camp Raider, although I knew that there was no way that could really happen. But Rob was prepared. He handed us each a small hessian sack that he had stashed in the *boma* earlier in the day. Each bag was filled with large clods of mud, some tatty old tennis balls and a selection of heavy glass marbles, *goens*, the big ones.

"Let him have it, chaps," he commanded, holding the beam of light on the elephant. He still had his rifle. Was that the back-up plan? God!

Since the *boma* wall had been buckled towards the dessert end of dinner we had all, except Rob, had plenty of time for several glasses of wine before the disturbance. Now we were being giving licence, even in front of the guests, for a concerted bombardment on the Raider. New rules!

As the first missiles struck, the Camp Raider spun around. Do not think that elephants lumber. They move very smartly indeed when it is required, even elderly fellows like the Raider, and he swung rapidly about at this assault. His ears flared out, and stayed there like flags in a strong wind. His trunk shot up like a periscope. His tail went rigid behind him. And he sent out a long, shrill, piercing shriek that froze us, our arms extended and locked in mid-throw. A babble of frightened voices arose from within the *boma*. God, the Raider was huge at close range. And obviously peeved.

"Round two. Fire!" said Rob, solemnly.

We re-gathered our wits and launched a second volley. The clods bounced off his forehead, exploding in dusty little clouds, and the tennis balls made funny plopping noises as they struck his leathery ears and fell to the earth. The elephant stood his ground. Was he contemplating a counter-attack? I looked behind me: the veranda was close. Good, I might need that. I kept chucking, but our ammunition was running low. The Raider hadn't moved. Suddenly, something else flew through the air and hit him on the forehead with a dry thump. A half-eaten bread roll! The Raider reached down with his trunk, feeling for it in the darkness, picked it up delicately, and thoughtfully popped it into his mouth. I looked in astonishment at the ranger who had thrown it. He shrugged. Out of ammo, obviously. The elephant searched around for more foodstuffs but finding none, turned around and gave his attention to the lemon trees once more. He was still disgruntled, though. His tail was erect, pointing straight back at us, the stiff bristles hanging like a strange dark feather. But as far as he was concerned, the game was over. Victory was his, as usual, and he had better things to do with his time.

"Enough," proclaimed Rob, defeated. "Back into the *boma*."

"Hey, you *okes*, anyone want an elephant hair bangle?" I said quietly. The cabernet was talking. Our curio shop sold bangles made from the tail bristles of elephants, elephants that had presumably been culled in the Kruger, the national park across the fence. Many of us wore them, and they were popular with the guests too, before the noise about elephant culling reached such a crescendo that the practice was halted.

Rob stopped, alarmed. "No, no, Lloyd, hang on," he warned. He knew exactly what I was thinking. We often joked about trying to pull the hair out of a live elephant's tail as a mark of earning our spurs, something akin to a Maasai warrior killing a lion to prove that he has reached manhood. Not quite in the same league, of course, and nothing has to die. Unless it's the ranger.

But the Raider's tail was sticking out at me, I was full of ink, and I do hate the sound of opportunity rushing by. Quick as a flash, I closed the gap on the unsuspecting elephant. The Raider was doing that thing that elephants often do, standing with one rear foot cocked up onto the toes, the sole of his foot exposed to me. I was quick in those days. And impetuous. I leaped onto the upturned heel, grabbed the tail and with a triumphant yell yanked down hard on it. The effect was electrifying.

The elephant screamed! Without hesitation, he plunged forward into the lemon tree, smashing it, leaving me sprawled on my back. The Raider was utterly shocked. He disappeared straight down the earth bank, crashing through the thickets of the *donga* below, trumpeting his bewilderment, uttering a series of small startled parps as he went, dismayed at this radical new approach to seeing off unwelcome animals. We could hear him blundering through the bush for minutes as he effected his escape. New rules, indeed.

I was somewhat alarmed too, sprawled there in the grass. But not as much as Rob was.

"You okay?" he said. Then seeing I was fine, very emphatically: "Jesus! Well, that worked!"

We rangers all gathered again in the *boma*, sniggering. The guests were gathered about the fire in a tight group, looking inquisitive and slightly alarmed.

"Okay folks, well, we sorted that out, nothing to worry about," announced Rob, looking embarrassed. "Um, right, anyone for dessert?"

But today, as if nothing happened at all, the Camp Raider is back.

10

THE ACTRESS AND
THE GIRAFFE

They say that we shouldn't get too close to our heroes in case we find that they are actually human. That they are just like us, only more famous. It is horrible to discover that even Batman bleeds. In the guiding business, we sometimes encounter media celebrities, and sometimes they happen to be our own heroes. Sometimes they really are quite disappointingly self-aware, disconnected, fragile and foibled. But it is a happy revelation to me that they are often much, much nicer than I expect them to be. Human, certainly, but the nicest parts of that condition.

At dinner once in Damaraland Camp in Namibia, I sat by chance opposite a once famous astronaut, an elderly fellow and the loveliest man you could hope to meet. I only figured out that he had been a spacewalker by the time dessert was served. He wanted to know about community conservation and desert-adapted elephants, not whether I had heard of him. I was deeply impressed by his humility. Maybe looking down on Earth has that effect.

At Serra Cafema Camp there was a shy and beautiful woman who wore large sunglasses indoors and a peaked cap and didn't bother much with her hair. It took me three days to recognise her, and even then only by her voice. Hollywood star. She was travelling under a *nom de plume* and I never once let on that I knew who she was. Wonderfully modest, sweet with the staff, very gentle. I'm still a massive fan.

A top ten tennis player pitched up at Mombo Camp once, travelling under his own name but without fanfare. He spoke enthusiastically about the game (but not his own game much) with anyone who asked, and he remembered all our names, which always makes a deep impression. He mingled comfortably with the other guests who soon lost their wonder in his presence, and in no time he was just one of them, asking the same questions about wildlife and enjoying the drives as much as anyone. It all depends on circumstance, though: I was watching the same player live at Queens in London once when a young boy leaned over the barrier and asked him for a discarded sweat band. "Fuck off," said the tennis player to the kid. The player had just dropped serve and lost the set but the horrified look on the boy's face said, "Right, that's it, I hate you now." Too close to his hero.

So you do get the prima donnas too, and they can be exasperating. Often they are self-serving aspirant politicians, not necessarily names you'd recognise, not the prime ministers and presidents and royals (although their over-attentive minions and lackeys can be exhausting to deal with) but the up-and-comers, the self-important ones who claim to be in search of privacy but who just love to be ambushed by the press. We had a good measure of them in the Lowveld at one time. Back then the reserve had the reputation for being the most expensive and opulent, unrivalled for the quality of game viewing. The politicians, sports stars, movers and shakers – often invited for free – poured in, claiming a respite from the world and its complications. The reserve benefitted from the association with the glitterati.

One morning our manager called us guides together.

"Lots of heat coming down from HQ," he said. "Triple VIP. Big actress and her entourage. Don't mess it up."

The actress flounced in, dressed in what she imagined was safari chic, her toy-boy following closely behind, the poor devil, picking up discarded handkerchiefs and leopard-print shawls and bossing waiters around to bring drinks that never touched her lips and plates of canapés she never once glanced at. I don't know where the Reserve management team gathered them from but a group of small black children were bussed in for her to play with, and she instructed her sycophantic pressmen to make sure that they got photos of her holding hands with the confused little tykes and kissing them on the cheek. I was faintly disgusted. Afterwards, she quickly disappeared back to her room, presumably to wash her hands, while the children drank glasses of warm orange juice and ate Marie biscuits.

We didn't go out on game drive that afternoon because all she wanted to see was a leopard – the reserve traded on its amazing leopard sightings – but she didn't want to drive on bumpy roads for more than thirty minutes. It usually takes more than half an hour to find a leopard, unless one just happens to be lolling about in a *Marula* tree nearby, so the actress stayed at the pool drinking tall pink concoctions while her boyfriend fanned her with a small towel. She had been married three times then, and has managed another two since, but I'm not sure he was ever one of them. I didn't keep up with that stuff. I must say she had worked assiduously at retaining her famed beauty. The poor woman was trapped by her film-star looks: she was so conscious of being looked at, and acutely aware of the ravages of age. There were, of course, plenty of rumours about botox and plastic surgery. Who knows? There was a hell of a lot of make-up on display and plenty of self-awareness, as well as an awful amount of fawning, which she seemed to like. And yet she seemed somehow quite vulnerable and requiring of approval. I couldn't put my finger on the reason but I sort of liked her, to my surprise.

I also liked it on a game reserve when something really big died. Like a giraffe. 900 kg of meat and bone, a banquet for a succession of scavengers: lions, sometimes leopards, always hyaenas, jackals, various kinds of vultures, marabou storks, maybe crows. It's nice because the guides have it all on tap for at least three days. Straight to the carcass, park upwind and hope for a stiff breeze to carry the smell of putrefaction away, settle back and watch the fun and games as the predators box and squabble for days for possession of the rotting meat. It is at times like this that people suddenly realise how real it all is out there in the bush: that this is not a zoo where the lions with their combed manes are chucked half a donkey and some vitamin pellets twice a week, that this is the *actual* Circle of Life and that death comes easily to the old and the weak in the wild.

Not everyone has the stomach to watch a kill, either while it is actually happening or even after the fact. Every guest clamours to see one: the next question after, "Are there snakes here?" is, "Will we see a kill?" They have seen the sanitised version of sudden death on Nat Geo Wild, and they fancy a bit of live action themselves. But when it happens (and very few safari guests actually witness a kill happening live, primarily because carnivores mostly hunt at night), most people find it too bloody, too violent, too visceral, too real. And I'm not talking about sensitive souls either. I've seen grown men cry. Grown men who will happily eat a nicely presented cellophane-wrapped supermarket steak, and who now realise with sickening impact that meat actually comes from something that had to bleed and die. Removed as we are these days from the origins of our food, it can be disturbing to see death, to watch carnivores doing what comes naturally, to see them doing what they must. Oftentimes, guests will beg me to leave a sighting. Africa is not 'The Lion King' and it's not for sissies.

Early in the morning before the waterbucks had ventured up from the riverine thicket to drink from the camp swimming pool (apparently, like elephants, they prefer their water chemically treated!), as I sat on the camp veranda clutching a mug of coffee and wondering whether the actress would even emerge that day, three hyaenas sprinted across the lawn, taking a focused and direct route. I knew what that meant: action! They had heard something, almost certainly a fight between other hyaenas, or something dying, and the game was afoot. I drained my coffee, sprang onto the Land Rover, and followed. I'd pick up the actress later, once she had adjusted her face and made herself presentable for the day. And sure enough, not ten minutes from camp, something big was dead. A giraffe, killed by lions overnight. A pride of lions, a dozen Spotted hyaenas, squabbling and jockeying for position, and already some low-gliding vultures struggling in the thick cold air onto the exposed dead branches of an old *Acacia* tree to wait their turn. Game viewing was about to become an easy task for us guides as long as we were first there and grabbed the up-wind parking spots. The smell of flesh and guts was already overwhelming. I drove back to camp for sweeter air and more coffee.

The actress emerged at noon, looking glamorous. The toy-boy emerged, looking sulky. I explained the excitement of the day, expecting a bored, "Oh whatever, dear, just make me a Bloody Mary, will you?" but to my utter astonishment, she clapped in delight.

"How wonderful!" she exclaimed.

Well, we would see. We set off from camp, and soon began to encounter the first signs of the struggle: lions low-growling at the hyaenas that skulked at close quarters with upraised tufted tails, giggling in fear and excitement. Her boyfriend cowered down in the seat but the actress was enraptured. She laughed out loud and started taking pictures with a silly little camera that she removed from her purse.

It was fantastic: all hell was breaking loose. Another pride of lions arrived to contest the meat, and wary Spotted hyaenas lurked on the fringes, overcome with hunger and trying to grab a haunch but terrified at the same time of being surprised by their mortal competitors. Blackbacked jackals darted in from time to time to snatch a morsel, and the thorn trees were now festooned with vultures, Hooded and Whitebacked, patiently awaiting their opportunity. A dynamic sighting, with male lions rushing past the cars as they tried to harass the hyaenas, then spinning back to the hulking dead giraffe, now blackening in the sun, to defend it against interlopers. The giraffe's eyes were gone, pecked out soon after death by opportunistic crows, and the guts of the beast lay disembowelled and heaping to one side, ignored by the carnivores. The maggots and the birds would have those later. A sweet and heavy aroma pervaded the entire scene, and after a short while two cars, their pale-faced occupants holding handkerchiefs to their noses, drove quickly away from the sighting, their guides looking resentful and cheated at being forced to miss all the fun.

I watched the actress. She was a role-player all right, a vision in cowboy boots and flared, camouflaged pants, a brilliant white safari shirt, big hair and a wide-brimmed hat, always ready for the photo opp when the eager yellow press might surprise her again. Yet there she sat, quite composed, perfectly at ease amongst the earthy reality of mortality, with all this chaos and noise going on around her, once again adjusting her make-up. Her toy-boy, looking wan and trying to be brave, glancing anxiously about him as animals dashed past the car, was holding a mirror for her.

"Oh, do hold it still, darling, for goodness sake, or I shall send you home," she said archly. "Honestly, stop being such a ninny, I don't know what you are fussing about. These people – waving a hand at me – know what they're doing. This isn't Sloane Square, you know!"

I was instantly starstruck. I've watched everything she's ever been in. Now, I *do* keep up. If she was in Strictly Come Dancing (Dancing with the Stars, in the USA) – and she should be – I would vote to keep her in every week.

11

I CAN NEVER SPEAK
OF THIS

Twice that day, I rescued him from the waves of North Beach in Durban as he floundered in the shallows while attempting to fill a plastic two-litre Coke bottle with sea water to take home as potent medicine to the people of his village north of Francistown. No-one learns to swim in a village north of Francistown.

Twice also, the same day, I took him to the Durban Aquarium, where he watched the dolphin and sea-lion show, and looked at sea-turtles through the smeared thick glass and stared in amazement as divers fed the slow-circling Raggedtooth sharks with great chunks of pink meat.

After the sea-lions had finished batting beachballs about, and the dolphins were done with their somersaults, he sat there silent and contemplative as the excited crowd thinned and then, when the children's chatter had abated, he said:

"What are these things? Are they real, these creatures? I mean, are they real animals?"

I laughed, and walked down to talk to the trainer at the pool's edge. I explained that Patrick was from Botswana. Land-locked Botswana. And that this was the first time that he had ever seen, not only the sea, but some of its denizens. The trainer could not have been nicer. She invited Patrick into the display area, whistled up a dolphin, and invited Patrick to kneel down and touch it.

"*Yo, yo, yo...*" said Patrick in wonder, "I can hear it breathing! It is *warm!* This fish is real." And then he added sadly, "But I can never speak of this in Botswana."

"Patrick," I said, annoyed, "The whole idea of bringing you to KZN is to show you things you have never seen before. Like those White rhinos at Weenen Game Reserve yesterday. The Indian Ocean. And these dolphins. You *must* tell people about all this. You're learning new things. That's the point! Why *wouldn't* you talk about all this?"

He shook his head. "With the guests, the *lekgoa*, and maybe some of the Batswana guides, I can speak about this. But not in my village. They will tell me that I am lying. They will say that you have put some bad magic in my head here in KZN, and made me crazy," he explained.

I had briefly met Patrick's mother. On our journey south with Patrick from Selinda Game Reserve in northern Botswana, we had popped in at his family compound, a small rustic settlement somewhere in the *Mopane* belt near the Zimbabwe border. It was a traditional place, with simple wattle-and-daub huts under corrugated iron roofs, and a mixture of cattle, chickens and a donkey or two wandering freely about. His mother had been sitting quietly in the sun, and she shook Sue's and my hands gently, and spoke to us in *Setswana*.

"She says that she never sees white people here," explained Patrick. "But she is glad to meet the people that work with her son. The ones who help him."

We'd not stayed long. Patrick was picking up some clothing for his journey – his Zionist Christian Church uniform, mainly – because after the Durban sojourn he would be making his way to the church city of Moria in northern South Africa to attend the ZCC Easter celebrations. It was an isolated little village, the place where Patrick grew up, at the end of a series of winding two-tracks through the never-ending *Mopane* scrub, and I'd never be able to find it again. It wasn't the kind of environment where your father taught you to drive in the family car and your mother sat and did homework with you. It was a very different world to the city of Durban, and its sea and strand and sea-lions.

I understood Patrick's predicament, though. I too grew up in a small town. So when I went back to where I came from and talked of the things I had seen – the marine iguanas of the Galapagos, the trading floor of Wall Street, hidden *onsen* in the mountains of Japan, Giant otters in the Amazon, and climbing the frozen Cotopaxi volcano of Equador, well, how did all that translate? How relevant was it, really, except to me? We only know what we know. Even so, it was disappointing to think that this experience might simply end with Patrick stroking a dolphin.

He was quite a fellow, was Patrick. When Sue and I arrived at Zibalianja camp on the Selinda Reserve, he was a waiter, but no mere waiter. He was tall, handsome, hard-working and although he was a little shy, he was excellent with the guests. The thing that struck me most, though, was his quiet determination: he wanted to be a guide. That was a very big step up from whence he came. Just to speak English the way he did was an achievement. Patrick was one of those rare people who was busy transcending his roots, and when you find a character like that, they need to be supported. Plus, I was exhausted: the strain of guiding twice a day for nine months on end, almost no days off, and delivering a first-class safari experience was wearing me out. Sue was running the camp, managing the staff, handling the logistics, doing all the cooking: she too was wondering whether it was worth it. It was tough on both of us, and tough on our marriage: the safari trail is littered with broken couples. It's possible to become jaded in paradise.

We needed a second guide. Fat chance on *our* budget: I knew that idea would gain absolutely no traction with the boss in Kasane. Zib was a tiny six-bed camp, with seven employees including Sue and me, and although we were chock-a block for nine months of the year, a lodge that size made very little money. But Patrick might at least ease our burden. If he could do some of the guiding, then I could be at camp more to help Sue... but there was a problem.

A professional guide requires two licences: one for driving, and one for guiding. Patrick had neither. But he had infectious energy, drive and a certain cunning. He wasn't one to allow opportunity to slip by.

"Right, Patrick, here's the plan. I'll teach you to drive. And you ride shotgun with me on game drives and learn as much as you can, as fast as you can. I'll give you the wildlife reference books you need to study, I'll do mock exams with you and get you ready for the guides' test in Maun. *You're* in a hurry, *I'm* in a hurry. But you still have to fulfil all your waitering duties too, so it won't be easy. How badly do you want this?"

"Lloyd, I want it," he said simply.

"Good. Now, if you get both those licences, *this* year, Sue and I will do something for you. When we go on leave, finally, at the end of the season, we'll take you with us. To Durban. I want to show you the sea."

Patrick's eyes shone bright. "I'll do it," he promised.

And I just knew he would. Even so, he surprised me.

The very next day, he announced that he had severe toothache, and needed to go the dentist in Kasane, the frontier town on the border with Zimbabwe. He looked fine to me but Patrick was no shirker, so Sue arranged a seat on a departing Cessna, and off he flew. Within four days he reappeared at Zib, having hitchhiked his way back to camp via the elephant-bedevilled sandy roads along the northern Chobe/Linyanti cutline.

He smiled sheepishly at me, ferreted around in a pocket, withdrew a credit-card sized plastic licence, gave it to me and said: "Okay, I have a driving licence. Now, please teach me to drive."

"But..?"

"I bought it in Victoria Falls," he announced. "I am half-way to Durban!"

"And your tooth?" I asked, hands on hips, pretending to be indignant.

"The tooth? Oh, it is fine now. Everything is fine," said Patrick, innocently.

"Well, okay then!" I said, impressed. "Now, 'trainee guide Patrick', get to your books! Or is the Botswana guides' licence also for sale these days?"

"No, that one, *yo*, that one will be difficult."

But he did it. Of *course* he did it. Patrick paid attention on game drives, studied, asked questions, and most importantly, polished his English. He learned to relax with the safari guests and not to fear their foreign ways, and he passed that exam the very first time he sat it, an unusual achievement. Zib would soon be too small for Patrick, I knew, but for now, he made all the difference to our little camp; he and I took turns guiding, and he was as good as I expected. And I was able to spend time fixing leaks, keeping the gas oven working and unblocking the bogs, the chief occupations of every camp manager. It was a weirdly welcome change!

And in November when the rains came and the impalas lambed, and the grass stood tall and green, when the Linyanti area breathed at last after the dry white season, Sue, Patrick and I turned the white Hilux south towards Francistown, and eventually, Durban.

To go and make some good out of bad magic.

12

MALARIA DREAMS

"This is going to go one of three ways," the doctor stated. "You'll get better, you'll stay the same, or you'll die."

I stared at him for a moment. I assumed he was joking but... then the doctor grinned.

"No, you'll be fine," he said.

"Hell of a bedside manner you have, Doc," I said.

"You'll be fine for three reasons," he continued, smiling. "The drugs are very effective, you came to see me in time, and you're healthy; your immune system is strong."

Malaria. It was called "bad air" by the Romans, and some historians claim that it was a major factor in the fall of their thousand-year empire. It's by far the biggest topic of conversation in safari camps among the guests. Malaria scares them. These days it is chiefly restricted to tropical and sub-tropical areas of the planet, across about 90 countries, but most people have forgotten, or never knew, that it was only eradicated from Western Europe in the 1930's and that the USA was only declared malaria-free in 1951. It is still to be found in most of the places in

Africa where wildlife lives. Hell, mosquitoes *are* wildlife. And because it is endemic in some places, first world governmental health and travel advisories will always err deeply on the side of caution and recommend that tourists take the anti-malarial prophylactics. In almost all cases, these preventative drugs have no side-effects at all. In just a few cases though, the effect is dramatic. Nausea, fevers and general malaise but – most interestingly – lurid dreams. Night time imaginings in all the colours of the rainbow. Often, sexual fantasies and, sometimes, murderous thoughts. Bizarre visions quite uncharacteristic of the sufferer. Stuff from the dark recesses of their subconscious brain that they really don't want to reveal at breakfast after a restless and deeply unsettling night. But side-effects hardly ever happen.

We guides seldom take the prophylactics. While it's perfectly sensible to use the stuff on a temporary basis, it's a powerful drug and those of us who live in or visit malaria areas frequently can't afford to be taking it every day. Instead, we choose to use the bug spray, sleep under mosquito nets, cover up the arms and ankles and neck in the evening, and cross our fingers. The thing is, it's an easily curable malady nowadays.

The chance of a safari guest contracting malaria is tiny. Miniscule. You have to really *concentrate* to get malaria. You have to *want* it. Firstly, you need the transmission vector – the mosquito. Not just any mosquito, either. There are more than three thousand species of mosquito in the world, almost all of which are completely harmless to people. No, no, you need the *Anopheles* mosquito. And even then it has to be a female of the species (the males don't carry the parasite because they feed on plant sap, not blood, as the females do), and it has to be dusk or nighttime; that's when the *Anopheles* feeds. Secondly, that female *Anopheles* mosquito needs to be infected: she needs to have very recently bitten a person who already has the mature plasmodium parasite in their red blood cells, and then, of everyone present, she needs to have chosen *you*. The unlucky one. And in the safari camps there are very few people, relatively speaking. Just a few dozen, typically. So it is unlikely that there are carriers there. And that's the third thing. To get malaria successfully, you need people. People are critical to the life cycle of the parasite. You need a lot of them, too, some of whom are infected already, otherwise your chance of getting sick is very low. So if you fancy a little bout of malaria, you need to hang around in a busy tropical town for a while, where people are in passage, bringing the parasite with them from malaria areas. And, of course, do not use DEET or cover up exposed skin in the evenings. A safari camp is a very poor choice of places if you want malaria.

But the village of Kasane in north-eastern Botswana is perfect! That's where I got it... the first time. Lots and lots of people moving through town on the great Dar es Salaam to Johannesburg road route, by boat down the Zambezi river and out of Namibia's Caprivi Strip. It's a swampy, highly populated place. I spent a fortnight working in Kasane, playing touch rugby in the steamy evenings on a rough field near the Chobe river and walking around without a shirt afterwards, sweating heavily, batting away mozzies and thinking, "Oh, it'll never happen to me, I've been here years and I've never got malaria." After two weeks of this hubristic behaviour, I suddenly one day came over all dizzy and sick and fainted while waiting in one of those interminable bank queues that Botswana is famous for: the ones where you stand in a slowly moving line, the teller never once looking up to acknowledge you and then, as you finally reach the counter, she suddenly draws down the blind, gets up and walks away because she's "on lunch." (Health warning: If you bank in Kasane, you'll contract malaria by default, you'll be in the queue for so long.)

Some kind soul took me to the local hospital and I joined another slowly shuffling people-stripe, waiting my turn to consult with the doctor, sliding my bum incrementally down a long wooden bench towards the medical room, flanked by dejected old crones actively coughing their lives away and fly-infested children with snot running down their faces. Eventually, a stethoscoped doctor in a hurry curtly beckoned me in, took one look at me swaying there, and said:

"Malaria."

"I reckon," I replied.

"Blood test," he said, indicating another butt-polished wooden bench along a different wall, crowded with more distressed humanity.

I didn't fancy it at all.

"Can't you just prescribe the drugs, Doc?" I asked. "We know what I've got."

"No. Unprofessional. Unethical. Blood test. Next!" he called, showing me out of the consulting room with a flick of his chin.

It took ages. Hours. Bugger, I really should have covered up after rugby. What happened to bullet-proof? Eventually, mercifully, I ended up with the same doctor again, who brandished a blood report at me.

"Malaria," he confirmed. "You ought to know better."

Not much small talk with this man. He looked drained, and exasperated. Almost condemnatory, as if he thought I was deliberately wasting his time.

"First time," I said, shrugging apologetically.

A nurse rapped on the open door, urgently summoning the doctor.

'Wait," he commanded me, and left.

I sat there and tried to memorise the human bones from the plastic life-size skeleton standing in the corner of the office. (It's a big call, there are 206 different bones, but this was Africa; I had the time.) After a short hiatus, though, he reappeared but almost immediately was called out again.

"Wait."

I studied the bones. I'd barely got past humerus and ulna before he was back. He began to write up a prescription for me. Coartem, the new wonder drug: three days and you'll be right as rain, just take it easy. The harried nurse popped her head through the door once more. Yeah, yeah, I know. Wait. Off the doctor hurried. Okay, the spine then: C1, C2, C3...

When he got back, I asked: "Where do you keep going to, Doc?"

"The wards. Signing death certificates," he replied resignedly.

"Three times in half an hour? What are they dying of?" I asked.

"Malaria," he said. Vindictive blighter.

"Oh, great. Excellent news, Doc! What happened about this wonder drug? Coartem?"

"I'm giving it to *you*, too," he said, suddenly relaxing. "By the way, you're going to have some wild dreams."

The ice was broken at last, and we had a proper conversation. The doctor was massively frustrated.

"Look, it's like this," he explained. "You'll be okay... But those people that have just died today *in my hospital, under my care,* what do you think they died of?"

"Um, malaria? Oh, I see," I replied, with dawning understanding.

"Exactly. The death certificate says malaria, right? But I can fix malaria. I'm going to fix *your* malaria. No, they're dying in my hospital from malaria, and TB, and pneumonia and common bloody influenza, all curable, but they die because their immune systems are compromised. I'm not allowed to write it on the certificate but it should read *died of HIV-AIDS!*"

I really felt for him. His reputation was at stake among his peers, as with the local community, people who trusted him to make them well, and the numbers didn't look good at all.

"It pisses me off!" he proclaimed vehemently. "They get sick and they go to their tribal healers, and sometimes the traditional medicines, the potions and lotions and powders and infusions, do seem to work, but if they don't they eventually come to me as a last resort and they're already half dead out there on that hospital bench before I can even get to them. I admit them to hospital, we take the best care of them we can, but sometimes they literally only have days left to live. It doesn't matter what I give them at that stage, it's too late, I might as well give them Smarties. Coartem won't work on any HIV positive person who isn't already on anti-retrovirals. Bill Gates spends all this money on malaria prevention – new drugs, mosquito nets – but there also needs to be a stronger message about sexual behaviour and societal taboos."

He's jabbing a cheap plastic ballpoint that says "Extra Strength Disprin" in the air and bitterly, rapidly, clicking the button at the top of the pen.

"But you'll be fine."

And I was. It wasn't a pretty three days – what with the diarrhoea, the feverish day shivers, the night sweats that left the sheets a soggy mess, the total loss of appetite, the crazy hallucinations and the blinding headaches – but the Coartem fixed me.

No death certificate. And he was right, the dreams... just great. Disquieting, but great!

13

MARY 28

Someone unexpectedly drove him in from the narrow gravel airstrip to Zibalianja Camp, the camp my wife, Sue, and I were managing in the Linyanti region of northern Botswana, and I went to the reception area to see who had arrived. He had a ready smile spoiled by a startling assortment of crooked teeth, and a firm handshake, but his workman's clothes were dishevelled and his glasses were starred in one lens. The bridge of the spectacles was held together by a lumpy combination of grey putty and sellotape.

"My name is Stephanus Ignatius van Zyl," he announced formally. "*Ag*, but you can just call me Fanie."

I had no idea how Fanie had ended up at Zib or who had sent him ("Bloody Kasane HQ, they never tell you a thing!"); he just pitched up, saying that he had a job with us. He was very welcome: we needed help with the annual maintenance now that we were about to close our little tented camp to tourists over the rainy season, and he assured me that he was handy with a spanner.

"I can fix almost anything with just a roll of number eight wire, a *waterpomp plier* and some cable-ties. Sometimes they even stay fixed," he said, grinning.

He was from the Ghanzi farming community south-west of Maun: the proud descendant of a bunch of tough Boer migrant trekkers who had left the old Transvaal Republic in the 1890's to escape impending British rule and who had settled amongst the Bushmen, or Basarwa, in the dry, featureless Kalahari grasslands. The *trekboers* were cattle people, hardy survivors, who knew how to make a plan.

I set Fanie to work and, keen to impress, he fell with utmost vigour upon the malodorous task of rebuilding the collapsed roof of the latrine soak-away, while I took the last guests of the season, a lovely French couple, on a game drive.

In the dying of the light, we returned to camp and I immediately went to inspect Fanie's work. I was astonished. Working alone, Stephanus Ignatius van Zyl had completely remodelled the cesspit roof, lined it with plastic to hold in the smell, covered it over with earth, and was now sitting with a satisfied look behind the kitchen holding a can of St Louis lager (I know, weird, hey? Who comes up with *that* name for a beer in land-locked Botswana?) in a grubby paw. I invited him to join us for dinner.

"Not like that, Fanie," I warned as he leapt up hungrily and started towards the dining tent. "You need to clean up first! Plus, there are going to be vegetables," I added, winking.

He made a face. Fanie seemed to think that washing was a vanity and vegetables something best left to cattle and effete urbanites to devour, but he acquiesced readily enough, and soon reappeared at the bar, his incongruous spectacles askew, looking slightly presentable. I eyed his grimy fingernails with suspicion, but decided not to send him back for further smartening up lest the soup grow cold. He was wearing the same blue Johnson's work trousers and heavy boots as before, but at least he had a fresh plaid shirt on, no doubt a uniform much favoured amongst the fashionistas of Ghanzi. I poured him a double Captain Morgan and Coke without needing to ask and introduced him to the guests, Phillipe and Irene.

"Fanie," he said shyly, sticking out a hand, obviously not used to speaking to foreigners. They gallantly shook it but I noticed Phillipe surreptitiously wiping his own hand on his jeans in the half-darkness. Irene was charming, though, and chattered away to Fanie in her cool French accent while I talked about the game sightings of the day with her husband. Somewhere between our discussion about the pride of three male lions on a hippo kill and the recent sudden birthing of the impalas, I overheard Irene ask: "Fanie, did you study history at school? What do you know about France?"

"*Ja, ja*, we did," he said. "We studied the French Revolution. I can't really remember much about it, but." After a thoughtful pause, "I think there was a queen who had her head chopped off."

"Marie Antoinette," said Irene encouragingly.

"Exactly!" said Fanie excitedly. "Mary 28! That's her!"

Don't underestimate a Ghanzi education.

Irene clapped her hands in delight and shrieked with laughter. Fanie looked pleased with himself. Dinner was wonderful fun that night, as Fanie tucked into his kudu steak ("You get two kinds of kudus, you know. The mountain kudu with seven stripes and the *platteland* kudu, much bigger, with ten stripes. Completely different.") I rolled my eyes but Fanie had already launched into a retelling in graphic detail of a recent murder in Maun where two Ghanzi cousins had had a disagreement while drinking at The Bull and Bush and one had taken a hunting rifle from the trunk of his car in broad daylight and shot the other dead. ("They're calling that pub the Bullet and Ambush now," he told us, chuckling, waving a forkful of meat and potatoes at us.) No green stuff skewered on that piece of cutlery, I noticed.

Irene and Phillipe left camp the next morning with many tales to tell, mostly about Fanie, but he hadn't finished entertaining me and Sue yet. He approached me with a look of misgiving.

"Um, Lloyd, can my girlfriend come and visit me?" he asked hesitantly. "I don't know what the rules are, and... "

"Sure Fanie, of course she can. It's pretty quiet now. You'll have to pay for the seat on the Cessna from Maun, though."

A week later the little fixed-wing wobbled over the camp and touched down in a cloud of fine dust. When the haze cleared, I saw there were two people disembarking, one of them with a cascade of blonde locks and the other a short, old-looking, yellow man. Odd. I looked at Fanie, seated next to me in the driving seat of the Land Rover.

"Who's that?" I asked, jerking a chin at the pair.

"Hestie," he replied with a little frown. "My girlfriend."

"No, man, Fanie, the other person, the small one."

"Hey? Oh, him, that's Kleinjan, her bushman."

"What do you mean, ... 'her' bushman?" I stuttered.

"*Ag*, we all have a bushman while we're growing up. They're our friends. They take care of us. Hestie's only nineteen, she's still got hers."

"Where's yours, now that you're... older. How old are you? How old is *Hestie's* bushman?"

"I'm 25. Mine's on the farm, I don't need him anymore. He herds the cattle and fixes fences and stuff these days. But Kleinjan still takes care of Hestie. He goes everywhere with her. He doesn't know his age. They don't keep count like we do."

There was no time for further questions because the Land Rover was already bumping towards the plane, and in a few seconds we were all greeting each other. Kleinjan loaded Hestie's small bag on the back of the vehicle, and climbed nimbly onto the rear seat without a word. I looked at him but he politely averted his eyes and I sensed that it would make him uncomfortable if I spoke to him. We drove back to camp, Fanie and Hestie speaking rapidly in Afrikaans, catching up on Ghanzi gossip. As far as I could tell, everyone in Ghanzi seemed to have the same name. Or were they talking about just one person?

Sue came out to welcome us as we reached Zib. Fanie was keen to show off his girl.

"Hi Sue, this is Hestie," he said proudly, helping her off the vehicle.

"And this is Kleinjan," I said, waving towards the back of the car. But the bushman was gone, and so was Hestie's bag. I stepped around the car, and there he was, quietly standing hidden from us, presumably awaiting Hestie's bidding, her suitcase in his hand.

"*Ag*, don't worry about Kleinjan, man, he doesn't speak English. He takes care of himself," said Fanie, looking at the bushman fondly.

Sue raised an eyebrow at me. I shrugged. In the harsh world of the Kalahari sandveld, a different order pertained, it seemed, and we really had no clue how it worked. Early the next morning that little yellow man was working shoulder to shoulder with Fanie, both of them chattering and clicking in the San language, sweating and cackling together at a shared joke in the warming November sun, dividing the labour and the lunchtime plates of food which Sue brought them. Food, and sweet tea.

Tea. I too have drunk tea with Fanie.

The Selinda Game Reserve in those days was a 'multi-use' conservation area. You can't hunt in Botswana any more, thank the gods – although that policy is subject to change – but back then it was still possible to buy a licence to shoot big game, including elephants. The east of the Reserve, where I worked, was set aside for photographic safaris, and the far west for so-called 'sport' hunting. The middle piece was a buffer zone. The theory was that relaxed big game animals from the east – lions, elephants, buffalos, leopards, the ones that had learned to trust us, but also the ones the trophy collectors most wanted to kill – were territorial there, and would not venture down into the far-away hunting area where they might be shot. To a large extent this was true, except that lions and elephants are wide-ranging creatures, and there is no doubt that some trusting animals ended up hanging as trophies on a den wall in Texas. There actually wasn't very much hunting at Selinda, but it brought in some tidy income to a reserve that only had two small safari camps, which is a marginal business.

So although the hunting went on occasionally, we simply did not mention it to our guests at Zibalianja because it created so much friction and dinner table heat. Occasionally we would have cross-over guests, people who mixed hunting with photographic safaris, and we hated that: people were very quick to take sides on the argument, and it could become unpleasant. On one occasion, I was driving a mixed group that included a pair of hunters who had recently been on a bird shoot in northern KwaZulu-Natal in South Africa, where they had had poor sport of it. Selinda, on the other hand, was thick with guineafowls and francolins, coveys darting from the grass and feeding in great numbers from the bird table I had set up.

"Why are there so *many* birds here?" wondered one of the frustrated hunters.

"Because they *don't* shoot them," one of the non-hunters replied, her voice heavy with reproach.

But make no mistake, Fanie was a hunter. The Ghanzi farmers have never debated the merits of killing wild animals for food or sport – it is part of their DNA to shoot for the pot. Indeed, had they not done so on their long trek away from the hated British invaders, they would have starved. And any predator that threatened their livestock, then and now – jackal, cheetah, lion, leopard, caracal – would certainly be shot on sight, or cruelly poisoned, or trapped, without remorse.

So, when the news came that a hunter had shot an elephant down in the western sector, and that fresh meat for the making of *biltong* was available – thousands of kilograms of it – Fanie lost all concentration on his camp maintenance schedule. Please, please, please, his eyes beseeched, let's go! I had no interest in seeing the carcass – I had seen dozens of dead elephants in my time as a guide – but the reserve manager wanted some meat for the *biltong*, and we were despatched to collect it.

It didn't take long to find the scene of the slaughter. The elephant had been shot that morning and the hunter was long gone, back in camp, no doubt already sipping a whisky in celebration of his manhood and admiring the bloodied tusks set up for his edification, but the vultures had already gathered. Birds – and human ones too. A sensible part of the deal with hunting was that the local communities living just outside the reserve were allowed to take the meat when a large animal was killed, and word had spread fast. Whitebacked vultures by the score festooned the *Mopane* trees around the dead elephant, patiently awaiting their turn as the frenzied villagers took their axes and *pangas* to the great mound of flesh, depositing huge gobbets of muscle into plastic buckets which overflowed with blood and gore. The guts, unwanted by the people, lay in a horrible purple heap, and Blackbacked jackals sniped in and out, daring to snatch at titbits even from between the smeared legs of the voracious villagers. Hyaenas, too, were in the vicinity, keeping a careful distance, lying in the shade and biding their time. There would be plenty for everyone in the grand scheme of things.

Fanie got stuck in without hesitation. Very soon he had collected some choice ropes of meat and was enthusiastically detailing his personal recipe for the making of the *biltong*: Worcestershire Sauce, Mrs Balls's Fruit Chutney, salt by the handful, pepper, coriander, vinegar... brown sugar. I eat *biltong*, but I couldn't stand the indignity of the slaughter any longer, and went for a walk. One of the things that makes kills in the wild interesting, albeit gaggingly odiferous after a few hours, is the number of birds that gather at the scene. Apart from the Whitebacks, there were a few massive-beaked Lappetfaced vultures, plenty of the smaller Hooded ones, a pair of Whiteheaded vultures, a plethora of swifts skimming over the mayhem collecting the flies that were swarming about, and the inevitable Pied crows – those great cohabiters with humans – ever alert to the opportunity for food. But there were hyaenas, too, reluctant to give way as I approached, and I wondered whether lions from the buffer zone, unaccustomed to humans, might, despite their fear of humans, venture closer through the woodland to investigate the bedlam. I returned to the butcher's shop.

And there was Fanie, nicely settled around a small fire, the burning *Mopane* twigs cracking, and a giant yellow enamel mug full of bubbling water on a little metal stand above the flames. A creeping lake of blue-red blood, thickly congealing, was oozing slowly past him as he sat happily on a raised mound not ten metres from the frenzied scene.

"Hey, Lloyd," he cried out, beckoning me over. "I'm making tea. Have some."

I didn't want tea in that revolting place. I hesitated. But Fanie's child-like enthusiasm and genuine kindness made me think twice. I didn't want to be over-delicate about this, so I navigated my way across the blood-soaked leaves to where he sat. He offered me the huge mug. I put it to my lips. As the first taste struck my tongue, I drew away, appalled. It was pure sugar water with only a hint of tea in it. God, how much of the sweet stuff had he put in there? You could virtually stick the spoon upright in it, it was so thick with sugar. Fanie's face fell: he could tell I didn't like it.

"*Ag*, sorry man!" he said, looking chastened and pushing his wonky glasses higher up his nose. "I knew it! I wasn't sure how much you wanted. Hang on."

And taking the mug back from me, he scooped yet another heaped tablespoon of refined white sugar into the mug and energetically stirred it into the liquid.

14

SHE NEVER SAW THAT COMING

I heard later that it didn't last six months, that marriage. There was an opportunity to forge the relationship in fire; but it melted instead. Bloody hippos, they don't go quietly into that good night, do they?

The honeymooners arrived in our little safari camp for lunch and to meet their guide, David, who was going to lead them out on a walking and camping safari for three nights. Middle-twenties, fresh-looking, despite the overnight journey south from Europe and then the light aircraft hop from Johannesburg into nowhere. Fresh, but perhaps not so eager. The bride, Emma, confided to me as David loaded their heavy duffels onto the Land Cruiser that this was in fact a *surprise* honeymoon booked by her husband, Rupert; she had been rather hoping for a tanning holiday at an Indian Ocean island resort, not an overland tramp sleeping in simple tents in landlocked Botswana. What was she going to do with all her beach wear, a different bikini for each new day of the holiday? She didn't even have the right shoes for bush walking, she complained. I agreed, looking doubtfully at her sequinned pavement trainers; well, they would have to suffice.

I've never got the knack of beach resorts myself, not in the conventional sense anyway, all that lying about in the sun on uncomfortable plastic recliners reading Jack Reacher novels, feeling like human sandpaper as the grit accumulates on your sunscreen. I actually went to one once. It was okay, to be fair, because I spent the entire time sailing, playing touch rugby on the beach and diving amongst the bleached Comoros coral. The shore birding was good, I have to admit, and the beer was fine. Come to think of it, I've never met a beer I didn't like (except for Swan lager in Perth, but I think I'm finally getting over the shock). I'd rather have been hiking in the mountains, though, or skiing. Especially on honeymoon.

So here were Emma and Rupert in camp, embarking on their married life – their very first time in Africa, indeed, their very first day – preparing for a walk amongst large, hairy, tusked and toothy animals and nary a beach umbrella or azure lapping ocean in sight. Rupert had already had an earful by the look of it, probably from the moment he had handed Emma her boarding pass at Heathrow – "Surprise!" – and he departed on the Land Cruiser looking chastened. Not a good start, pal.

David drove them to the first camp site, which was beautifully appointed on a short hippo-cropped grass sward nestled between a giant baobab and a pleasant lagoon decorated with lilies and dabchicks and snow white egrets spearing fingerlings amongst the vlei-ink lilies. A small domed guest tent was set up in the shade, a hand-wash basin on a tripod with creamy clean towels to one side, two proper old safari-style director's chairs under the fly-sheet, paraffin lanterns on a small table, and a double bed made up in cotton linen and plump pillows. David and his team had made an assiduous effort: the walking safaris were a new concept and he was determined to do them well. Emma relaxed visibly: this might be all right, actually, she was thinking, as a flight of Whistling ducks vee-ed overhead and a waiter brought her a tall gin and tonic with plenty of ice. A white-smocked chef hovered over an open fire, and a second communal hearth, the gathering point for the dinner that evening, burst brightly with sparks. On the floodplain fringe a herd of Red lechwes splashed out of the shallow water, making their way to higher ground for the night. Yes, this might just be okay, she thought. Hippopotami grunted beyond the reeds.

"Hippos," said David as he poured the wine. "We'll see them tomorrow."

Tomorrow, eh?

Lions eat hippos, if they know how to catch them. And in that part of northern Botswana there was a small and dominant lioness that had taught her brood how to do just that. Hippos graze at night, sometimes many kilometres from their lagoon sanctuary, and we'd wake in the night sometimes to hear the horrible lingering death scream of one that had been ambushed far from safety. A hippopotamus is a thick-skinned beast and a lion can't strangle it in the normal way by clamping its jaws onto the windpipe, so instead the pride swarms all over the hippo and bears it to ground, then bites and tugs and tears at it until eventually a major artery is severed and the hippo bleeds to death. In the meantime, some of the lions start to feed, ripping in via the softest part of the body – the belly and the anus – and beginning the evisceration process. The hippo lives through all this agony for many hours, thrashing and screaming, until its life's-blood finally gushes out. The death sound carries for many kilometres in that quiet bushveld air and it brings in other opportunists: Spotted hyaenas.

It's hard to watch a hippo die. It's not beach sports in Mauritius.

The honeymooners had a final glass of Merlot and went early to bed. David drank no alcohol: tomorrow the walk would begin, and he wanted to be fresh and alert. His tent was discreetly placed about thirty metres from their's, within hollering distance for safety's sake. He had a heavy Maglite torch and his rifle with him, and the Cruiser was parked over at the kitchen area, some distance away. The support staff had long since retired to their own tents, tucked away behind the baobab. As the lanterns were doused the night reclaimed the little camp, and a sliver of moon rose, true and eternal. Africa, at peace. Emma snuggled into her duvet.

The loud and surprised grunt of a hippo, very nearby, punctured the quietness. David sat up immediately, listening hard. Nothing unusual. He lay back. But now the crashing of reeds followed, and the hippo bellowed in real alarm. David loaded his rifle and flashed his torch out from his tent. No further noise. His wrist-watch told him it was midnight.

"David?" called a nervous voice from the honeymooners' tent.

"It's okay, Emma, just a hippo that got a fright. They don't see very well at night," he reassured them. "Nothing to worry about."

Another scream, more crushing of reeds, and a massive hippo lumbered straight into camp. Under the broad beam of his torch, David could make out the pride lioness hanging tightly from the jaws of the hippo, trying to hold the mouth closed, trying to cut off its air supply and its tell-tale roars: the fewer guests at this dinner party the better, no hyaenas need consider themselves invited. More lions clung to the hippo's back and flanks, tearing at the heavy grey skin, scoring the sides with sharp claws, kicking their back legs like manic giant house cats, trying to stay on board and keep a grip. The hippo tottered into the centre of camp between the honeymooners' tent and David's, stumbled over a pile of firewood, and fell. The rest of the pride were upon it in an instant, like *Mopane* bees to a sweaty brow, and the hippo knew it would never get up again. It windmilled its stubby legs in the air, and the metal dining table went flying, pots and a kettle clanking into the night, lanterns smashing and chairs crushed to sticks and canvas strips in the bedlam.

"DAVID!!!!!" A high scream of sheer and unadulterated terror.

"STAY INSIDE YOUR TENT! DO NOT LEAVE YOUR TENT!" roared David.

He shone the Maglite towards his vehicle. Too far away to chance a run. In this madness, a blood-crazed lion could easily chase him down. A literal shot in the dark with his .375 might have a temporary effect but there was no way the lions were going to leave their prey. The hunt-lust was upon them. And with this cacophony, there were definitely hyaenas coming, in numbers, coursing even now towards the campsite, bold as brass at night, and ever eager to snatch at anything that moved. This was going to go on for hours. The car had a two-way radio to contact camp with... but the car was over there. They were trapped. The chef and the waiter were yelling to him now too.

"BE COOL, PEOPLE! STAY STILL. WE'RE OKAY," he shouted.

The lions tore at the hippo and slashed at each other, squabbling for access to the meat, and the hippo shrieked its life away. The Spotted hyaenas came, giggling and whooping, teasing the lions, darting in and out, tripping over the guy ropes of the tents, nosing amongst the kitchen paraphernalia, and above all of it, David could hear Emma's terrified sobbing: a woman mired in her worst nightmare, wondering if it would ever end, wondering if she was going to die on honeymoon. Just one night in Africa. One night only.

There was a brief lull in the noisiness of death.

"David! What do we do? What are you going to do? Are you going to shoot them?" came Rupert's voice.

"No. The lions don't want to eat us!" yelled David, "They won't come into our tents. When I can, I'm going to get to the car and drive to you and fetch you... if it's safe. But I can't go now, not yet, there are lions all over the place."

"But we need to pee, David!" shouted Rupert desperately.

"Use a plastic bag then," instructed David, "but keep it inside with you. Do not open the tent!"

The sound of duffels being ransacked, then after a while, the dry rustle of a supermarket bag. A pause.

"Oh shit, its got a hole in it!"

Then, a long and exhausted, resigned silence from the honeymooners' tent. Chaos continued without.

A bulge appeared on one side of the tent, pressing in towards David, sniffing enquiringly. David punched it as hard as he could. A lion rocked back, gruff-barking in astonishment.

"One to me," said David. There were no other enquiries.

The hippo bled and died, the lions grumbled, the hyaenas tittered, the darkness persisted and then slowly, slowly, the dawn came. David cautiously unzipped his tent and peered out. Plenty of predators lying about, replete and gore-smeared, but things had settled down a bit. He reckoned he could make it to the car with a bold approach. He levered a round into the rifle's breach, zipped the tent door all the way open, gathered himself, then bolted for the car. Pandemonium! Startled lions coughed in fright and leapt to their feet, heads lowered, yellow eyes wide. Hyaenas on the outskirts yipped and bolted. Audacity prevailed, and David, legs pounding and with a horrible tight pain in his gut, scrambled aboard the flat bed of the *bakkie* and spun around, ready to repel invaders. Safe! Not a lion had followed. David clambered through the side window and gunned the car, picked up the staff, then drove to the honeymooners' tent. Lions lay fat and satiated just metres away and David drove the car directly at them, shifting them by main force, hitting the hooter, blaring and revving and outmuscling the predators. It was his turn! He parked right at the tent entrance, and spoke in what he hoped was a soothing voice.

"Listen folks, slowly open the tent, I'm right outside. Leave all your luggage, ALL of it. We'll get it later. When I say go, just barrel out of there straight onto the truck. Emma, jump into the cab, left hand side, I'll have the door open, okay? Rupert, jump onto the back with the guys, okay? The tailgate is down."

"Where are the lions? Where's your gun?" asked Emma doubtfully.

"I've chased them off. They're here somewhere, though. You'll be fine. Just be quick. Ready? GO!"

Some younger lions had approached again, intrigued by this new development. It had been a grand night already for them, what with murdering a hippo, repelling hyaenas and getting in a good feed, and now here was a new game!

The honeymooners came rocketing out of that little dome tent without much regard for each other in a flurry of knees and elbows and thrusting legs and dishevelled hair and big wide terrified eyes. Emma piled into the cab in a tangle and the chef hauled Rupert onto the back. David floored the accelerator and the Cruiser took off with a leap. Too fast, much too fast. Rupert had a grip on the roll bar but his feet slipped as the truck crashed over a low termite mound and with a scream he plummeted right off the back of the vehicle, right into the path of the curious lions following.

The chef screamed. "David, stop, STOP, STOP!"

There is nothing that concentrates the mind so rapidly as impending death, apparently. David had barely even touched the brakes before Rupert was back on the truck. I have seen safari walkers climb straight over one another on the way to the very top of a thorn tree when charged by a rhino and later they have no recollection of this prodigious athletic feat. So it was with Rupert.

David drove straight to our camp, explaining the drama to me on the radio as he came. I stoked the fire up and made coffee. It was still just getting light when they pulled into camp.

"Get me out of here, *today*," said Emma to me as she alighted from the cab.

"Look," said David beseechingly, looking at Rupert, "we will move camp. I know a really lovely little place... "

"*Today*."

"There's no way that that sort of thing will happen again. Actually, you're quite lucky... " David faltered, realising that this dog wasn't going to hunt. "Okay, well, why don't you just stay in this camp instead and... "

"David. TODAY!"

He radioed to HQ and arranged it. Rupert and Emma boarded the little Cessna and David and I watched it bank south towards Maun into a gathering storm.

15

INVESTIGATED

A wooden bread-board wielded as a weapon can hurt. Not as much as a dent to a man's ego, but still, it's sore. She just kept hitting the poor guy with it, thrashing at his shoulder in a torrent of uncontrolled frustration until it became too embarrassing for me to watch and I said: "Hey, hang on now, in actual fact your husband has done amazingly well to get this far, there's no way I could have done it. You folk are very brave just being out here at all!"

The German guy looked grateful for my intervention. How was he supposed to know about this wilderness stuff anyway, he was from bloody Hamburg! His wife dropped the board, wiped her tears away using a gritty sand-soaked sleeve and abruptly sat down on the road's edge.

"Okay. But can we follow you now? Please can we follow you?" she begged.

"Of course!" I promised. "I'm not going to abandon you. I'll take you as far as the Ghoha gate. You'll be fine from there on."

And she promptly burst into tears again. Relief will do that to the most hardy of souls. Especially after an unscheduled night all alone in the African bush.

It is a long, long, arduous drive from the town of Kasane to Selinda Game Reserve, all along the far north-eastern edge of Botswana, and the road just gets progressively worse. It is lonely country and you have to be well prepared: a full tank of diesel, two spare tyres, food, plenty of drinking water, and a taste for adventure. There are no road signs except to a few rustic villages and there is no obvious route. Once you've passed between the two baobabs of Kachekau village, the road deteriorates into a series of deeply-incised sandy two-tracks that rise and fall over the longitudinal dunes of the Kalahari basin, splitting, re-joining, wandering in a confusing fashion through the Silver clusterleaf sand forest, now looping this way, then twisting that.

"Just keep heading south-west after Kachekau until you hit the Linyanti double cutline," Brian, our Director, had told us the first time Sue and I had ventured into that untamed vastness. "Then go north-west until you hit the Linyanti river. Then sort of west again until the Savute Channel. You can't miss it. Oh, and watch out for the elephants up there, especially the tusk-less females, I don't know what their story is, but they're *hectic!*"

And then as an afterthought: "*Ja*, and if you have any issues, engine problems or something, don't worry, just sit tight, a TFC (tsetse fly control) *bakkie* or a BDF (Botswana Defence Force) truck will usually pitch up after a few days. It's *lekker* out there, though; enjoy the drive. Did I mention the elephants?"

That very first time, Sue and I drove out to Selinda with a knot in our guts. It was a sort of initiation, an unspoken rite of passage. We had already secured the job as camp managers of Zibalianja Camp… but we still had to find the damned place! And it was hot. Really hot. 40 degrees celsius in the shade. And we were not in the shade. A clusterleaf sand forest is a limitless, monotonous stretch of stunted shrub-trees that goes on for ever and ever, punctuated too seldom by massive baobabs that stand like sentinels amongst dwarves, each giant tree so prominent and noteworthy that it actually has its own name: the Triple Baobab, the Island Baobab, the Kachekau Baobabs, the Split

Baobab, the Broken Baobab. Later, at Mombo, I came to know a baobab called Bob. That was the baobab where Tish and Terry... no, no, that's another story.

These ancient tree monoliths are comforting markers on a long journey. They feel like old friends, showing the way. And on that first journey out to Selinda, we counted them down. Brian had said: "After the third one on the right of the track, the one with the bee's hive hanging under the horizontal branch that looks like a skeleton arm, look for a track that turns north-west. There's a burnt out Nissan *bakkie* at the junction, been there for years, don't know what happened to the driver, maybe he's still there. Head along that. If you haven't come to a big pan surrounded by *Mopane* trees next to the track within twenty minutes, go back. Or don't. I think it probably joins up with the Linyanti eventually, I can't remember, I got lost there once. But you can't miss it."

Oh, really?

"Three more things," advised Brian. "Drive with the air-conditioner off. It saps the power of the car, and you'll be needing plenty of oomph in the soft sand, especially as the day heats up. Secondly, load up the *bakkie*. If you haven't got a lot of kit, put sand bags in the back of the truck directly over the back axle. Your Toyota Hilux has a stiff leaf-spring suspension, and you'll be going like the clappers in high-range four-by-four, so if you don't dampen the springs with weight, you're going to be flung all over the place in the driving cab. Or wear a helmet, ha ha! Oh *ja*, and lastly, don't stop. Never ever lose momentum. Of course, if an elephant walks onto the road in front of you and blocks your way, you're stuffed. And there're a lot of elephants out there. So take a shovel."

All right, then.

But fortune favours the bold, and we made it. We anxiously watched the fuel gauge, we drove with the windows down and the A/C off, we made several wrong turns, we banged our heads on the cab roof a few times, we counted baobabs and swerved around some annoyed female elephants that had neither tusks nor a sense of humour, and late in the afternoon we drove carefully over a narrow, weathered

Mopane-log bridge that forded the delicious cooling waters of the Savute channel, and found our little camp. We felt pleased with ourselves, and hugely relieved.

We'd made the same journey several times since, and the anxiety of the unknown had abated significantly. We didn't need to count baobabs any more to find our way, and the elephants turned out to be reasonably friendly provided we slowed down as we approached them. But on this particular occasion, there was trouble brewing. Because on this day, there was a *bakkie* blocking our way. As we came over a rise that offered a view of the next kilometre or so of the track, there on the far side of the valley, halfway up the next distant vegetated dune, and smack in the middle of the road, with no chance of getting past it, was a white pick-up truck. It was stuck fast. On a harder patch of sand, an area that would allow me to halt then easily drive away again, I braked the Toyota to a stand-still and reached for my binoculars. The distant white *bakkie* swam into focus. A rental. I could make out the sticker on the door. "Britz 4x4 Rentals", with a GP registration. Johannesburg. Gosh, this car was a long way from home. The contents of the vehicle were strewn about in the grass: camping chairs, water containers, sleeping bags, a hi-lift jack, suitcases of clothes. Clearly, this *bakkie* had been stuck here for some time. A young woman sat disconsolately in the paltry shade of a straggly tree. Her companion, a man, beaten down by the heat, lay on his stomach next to a back wheel, still slowly scraping up a pile of sand from beneath the car.

"To the rescue, Sue," I said with mock exasperation, and grabbed the sand shovel from the back of our Hilux. "Bloody tourists, eh?"

"Man's work, babe," replied Sue, and settled down in the shade of the car with a book and a flask of iced-water from the twelve-volt fridge. This wasn't the first time we'd had to save lost travellers from the clutch of the Kalahari. I could not drive closer for fear of losing momentum in the unforgiving sand. That slope needed to be taken at a run and there was no way I would be able to leave the deep track to get around that stuck car. I trudged down the road towards the bogged-down *bakkie*. This was about to become extremely sweaty.

The listless woman looked up wearily, and suddenly saw me.

She bolted to her feet, electrified, and began to yell, "Hey! Hey! Help!" Her companion, too, rose and began to wave a coloured cloth, a sarong or a scarf, above his head. I plodded towards them at a judicious pace: no point in wasting energy in the desert. Even though they could see me getting closer, they kept screaming at me as if they thought I might just disappear suddenly into the sand forest. I waved, and called out encouragingly, but I was still several hundred metres away, and my words were lost in the heat-shimmer. The woman started to run towards me, then sensibly stopped, and went back to the car to wait. The man draped the cloth over his head and stood quietly, but as I came up he stretched out a hand and, in an unexpectedly formal manner, introduced himself.

"Hello. I am Hans-Peter, and this is my wife, Gisele. We have been here since yesterday afternoon. No cars came. Only elephants! Many elephants were investigating us. Please help us."

In a small and wretched voice Gisele added, "There were other things too, at night. Other animals. Making noises... We slept in the car," she added. And then, miserably, "We are on honeymoon!"

Something next to the car caught my eye. It was the digging tool Hans-Peter had been using. A bread-board, for goodness sake. Mine was the only shovel in sight.

"Don't worry," I told them. "I'll get you out of here. Do you have drinking water?"

"Some water, yes. But no food."

"Okay, I have food in my car back there," I said, pointing at my distant vehicle. "Sit in the shade with your wife, Hans-Peter. Drink water. I'll sort this out," I reassured him. "But what on earth are you doing out here? Where are you going? This road is only used by safari operators, and government people, not self-drive tourists."

"We are going to Maun, via Third Bridge in Moremi. But this road is very bad. Why is it so bad? It is a brown road," he said.

"Eh?" I asked. "How do you mean, a brown road?"

"Look, on the map," he said, taking it from the dashboard. "You can see, it is a brown road. And the main roads are black. So this is a secondary road. In Germany, a brown road is a good road.

So we thought we could drive on this road. But this road..." He shook his head.

I wanted to giggle at his naïveté, but it wouldn't have been fair.

"*Ja*," I said. "Here in Botswana, we only have two kinds of roads. Black ones, which are bad. And brown ones, which are terrible. And they both have lots of elephants on them."

Plying the shovel, I began clearing the differential from the high middle hump of the road and creating smooth, grooved tracks for the wheels, scraping a clear path so that I could reverse the vehicle back down the slope to a firmer stretch of sand. Partially deflating the tyres so that they would be able spread out on the sand and gain better purchase would also help. But something was nagging at me. This particular section of dune didn't look all that tricky to drive up, actually. And then I realised: only the back tyres had dug in. Not the front ones. That meant that the front wheels had not been spinning. What? So that meant..."

I climbed into the driver's seat. Yup, as I thought. I engaged the low-range gear shift. It went "clung" as it engaged the hubs. I started up the car.

"Gangway aft!" I bellowed, and very gently, without spinning the wheels and with a minimum of fuss, I eased the vehicle back down the track and onto some reasonably compacted sand.

The Germans watched this miracle in astonishment, and the woman began to clap her hands.

"The car was in two-wheel drive, Hans-Peter," I said. "No wonder you got stuck. Only the back wheels were pushing the car."

"No, no," he said vehemently, "It is a four-wheel-drive car. Look," he gestured, pointing at the sticker on the car door, "It says 'Britz 4x4' here!"

"*Ja*, but you still have to actually engage it in four-by-four. You have to use this lever to put it into '4x4'. You have been driving it in two-wheel drive," I pointed out.

Gisele has approached to watch the explanation. To my amazement she suddenly reached down, grabbed the bread-board and started to beat her husband with it. Hans-Peter yelped, but he let her do it, taking his punishment manfully, as if he felt he deserved it. He didn't.

"Hang on," I said, "Your husband has done amazingly well. There's no way I could have got this car all the way out here in two-wheel-drive. This guy is better than Michael Schumacher! Come on, let's get all your stuff packed. Then I'll get you some food, and afterwards you can follow me all the way to the park boundary. From there the road is easy, and there are many cars. You'll be fine. You were never really in danger here, anyway."

But as I started the tramp back up the hill to my Hilux, I noticed them for the first time. Elephant tracks, of course, dozens of them. But others, too. Large pug marks. Lions. All around their car.

They'd been investigated all right.

16

PICTURE MAN

You'd think safari guides would have a tattoo (or three). Wouldn't you? Before I became a guide, that's what I thought. I'm not sure why, really, it's not like we play professional darts or soccer, but it just seemed to go with the territory. But in fact I can only remember a single colleague who did have one: Peter had a sort of a cheetah thingy inked across his ribs. He didn't seem to like it much.

I've got one, though.

I love it. It's funny how things play out...

The London adventure is over, and I'm back in Botswana. It's damned awkward clambering into a Cessna 210 airplane, these functional little puddle-jumpers we move people and freight around the Okavango Delta with. They might be cramped, but they're also wonderfully reliable. And they're the only way to get in and out of the Swamps. They're bumpy though. And hot. I'm wearing khaki trousers, which I seldom do, even in winter, even on bitterly cold early morning game drives. As I manipulate my legs under the yoke, trying to not to nudge any of the knobs and levers, especially the very important looking red ones, my right trouser leg rides up my calf.

"Hey, what's that, chap?" asks Ritchie, the Australian pilot, pointing gleefully at my inside right ankle.

"It's a tattoo, china. What's it look like?" I reply testily.

I'm strangely annoyed at his discovery. I'm still getting used to it myself. Hence the trousers. I think it's because I have always associated tattoos with rough people. (Like guides?) People with class don't have them. Right? Or didn't use to, anyway. My grandfather was in the Royal Navy and even he didn't have one. Which, actually, was always a bit of a disappointment.

Anyway, there it is. Ritchie is a blabber-mouth. The secret is out now.

"It looks like a bloody umbrella, mate, that's what it looks like. Why'dya have a bloody umbrella taddoo done?"

Taddoo. Australians speak funny.

"I had a moment," I reply. "And for your information, *mate*, it's a scorpion, okay?"

It's supposed to be very cool scorpion. I hope it's a very cool scorpion but I still have my doubts.

"Scorpion? Why a scorpion?"

"It's personal," I tell him with a tone of finality. "Shut up, Ritchie."

I don't want to talk about it. Not with bloody Ritchie. He's a pain.

He waggles the wing-flaps, raises a thumb to the perspiring guests crowded into the little cabin behind us, and guns the engine. We rattle down the runway, ignoring the Crowned lapwings which shriek and scold as we rush by, and wobble into the still, blue sky, Mombo-bound out of Maun. Actually, I quite like Ritchie but he can be annoying. He goes on a bit. Now he's saying something like, "Wait till the boys at the Sports Bar hear this one," but fortunately the drone of the engine blocks out most of his chirping, and I moodily contemplate the streams and islands below us, waiting for the buffalo fence which indicates the start of the unadulterated wilderness area that we call 'The Swamps.' Three months ago I was taking off like this, too, but in the reverse direction, out of Mombo Lodge heading for Maun, then Johannesburg and eventually London. Wearing shorts and sandals – and no tattoo.

London. Bright lights, big city. It's a marvellous place. No-one knows you. You can be anyone you like. You meet strange and eccentric people who everyone else seems to regard as normal. It's all going on and you end up doing unexpected stuff.

Like getting a tattoo.

I blame the Australians, really. They have much to answer for in my life. I'm happy to say that they have often led me astray. If it weren't for the Aussies, my life would have been very much more mundane.

I had been on a sabbatical from the bush after years of intensive guiding. I needed a break, somewhere foreign, somewhere entirely unfamiliar, somewhere alien. My intention was to explore every nook and cranny of the old city, and the new, taking it as it came. I immediately moved into a dodgy communal house in Stoke Newington, north London, inhabited by a motley assortment of other travellers. Guides might lead bankers on safari but they are not paid like bankers (no automatic bonus even when they mess up), so pretty much straight away I found a job as a carpenter on a building site, helping to lay insulation flooring in the refurbishment of the Smithfield Meat Market. I am not a carpenter. I was paired with an Australian chippy called Deano. Most Australian names (and plenty of other words in their lexicon) end in a vowel. It's in their constitution. As I say, they can't help speaking funny. On the first morning Deano watched me butchering a piece of timber with a handsaw and shook his head.

"Lloydo, you're not a chippy's arse, mate," he said, laughing.

"No, but I need the money, china," I said, grinning back.

"Okay, Springbok, we'll make this work, no need to make a noise about it. You fetch and sweep and bring me nails, and I'll do the clever work. Hey, I like that guy of yours, Francois Pienaar, that boy can play rugby!"

And so our friendship began, based upon the usual metrics of young men from the ex-colonies: a shared appreciation of cricket and rugby, beer, large milky cups of sweet tea on lengthy work breaks and every expat workman's desire to thumb a nose at his English supervisor.

I spent a fair bit of time with Deano, and it all got a bit hectic on weekends. One Friday night while Deano and I were out drinking (cold Foster's lager for him – "fizzy piss", he called it in that blunt Aussie way – room temperature Director's Bitter for me), he came up with his Weekly Bright Idea. Deano, a self-confessed authority on the fairer sex and always keen to test his theories, wanted a "Tweedy Bird" tattooed on his backside.

"You'll have to shave your own arse first," I told him. "Why would you want a yellow cartoon canary inked permanently on your bum, anyway?"

"Chicks dig cartoon taddoos. It makes guys seem vulnerable. Seriously."

"Whatever, china. You're going to have to shave your arse. The Picture Man isn't going to do it for you. And by the way, Tweety is *not* cool. In the unlikely event that you get lucky, the unfortunate lady will be off at the same time as your pants."

He smiled a superior and knowing smile.

"I'll keep you updated, Springbok," he said. Then inclining his head, he said brightly: "You should get one, mate."

I had to admit that the idea intrigued me. I put it to my housemates when I got back to the hostel that night. They weren't really the right people to ask, now that I think about it. Gazza, the ex-policeman from Melbourne; Monica, his girlfriend (who was always finding him jobs which he never pitched up for – the relationship didn't last); Peta, the Irish purple-haired supply teacher; and a mysterious South African we named Feckless Dezzy, who did absolutely nothing at all except drink cheap French wine (with screw tops) and smoke dope in the lounge.

"Totally cool idea," they instantly agreed.

It was a few days before my thirty-first birthday, and I wanted to mark the occasion by doing something memorable. Get the tattoo, and an earring, I thought. It seemed I was about the only worker down at the Smithfield Meat Market building site who wasn't so adorned, and the heavily inked local English lads, egged on by Deano, went on at me to do it, teasing me over our 10 o'clock white-bread baps while they contemplated the bare-breasted beauty on page three of *The Sun*. I was primed to do something novel, though; life was a little edgy, living and working without proper papers in London, an officially vilified white South African in the apartheid era, earning minimum wage at three pounds and a penny an hour, and enjoying living a slightly subversive life sheltered amongst many thousands of Pakistanis, West Indians and other hopeful illegal immigrants who had dodged the British immigration laws. It was other-worldly, rather intoxicating. It felt like a tattoo was in order.

I looked at Deano over my mug of builder's tea.

"See you at Portobello in the morning, china," I said. "We're on."

The famous Portobello Road Market was packed that Saturday morning, as always. 'Sandy's Tattoo Parlour' had the reputation amongst the colonial beer swillers down at our local, 'The Coach and Horses', for being nice and quick and clean. Despite the milling throng that heaved and jostled amongst the vegetable barrows, the mime artists, the purveyors of cheap Indian clothing (guaranteed to fall apart in the first wash) and the stinking street drunks, 'Sandy's' was dead easy to find; there was a queue out of the door and down the pavement. Mostly, they were white guys and girls like us (more Debbos and Daveos.) Suddenly, having a tattoo seemed much less appealing to me. Commonplace doesn't equal cool. Deano (backside freshly shaved) and I joined the line anyway.

The train of people moved rapidly. This was disconcerting to us. Either this Picture Man dude was a really fast artist, or there were a hell of a lot of people chickening out. And if they were, that was a bit scary. And if he was fast, I foresaw a problem: I mean, this was for life, this picture! The guy needed to do it right. Deano and I tried to look relaxed. We soon saw how to tell whether the emerging person had been tattooed: a pink Elastoplast over the work, a triumphant (or relieved) grin, sometimes a worried expression which said, "I hope my new girlfriend likes it. 'Charmaine' does start with 'C'? Right?" Whereas the fainthearted rolled their sleeves down or smoothed their skirts as if they had just had a tattoo done under there, and their faces said, "Man, that was close. That would have been tricky to explain to my girlfriend. Especially if the guy had spelled her name wrong."

We shuffled closer to the door. Then we were in.

The place was dimly lit, and the blanched yellow curtains made the place look tacky. We sat gingerly on plastic-covered benches (is that so they can wipe the blood off more easily?) along the walls and steadily slid along them towards an interior room from whence came an electric buzzing noise. A sudden shriek startled the waiting clients. They'd said down at the pub it can really hurt. And that they use the same needle over and over again, and that it gives you AIDS. A tough-looking blond Scandinavian type immediately got up and left, muttering something in his native tongue. So much for the modern viking, I thought. Deano and I kept sliding. Towards a picture. For life.

"No Tweety Bird," I noted. The tattooer's 'flash' – his displayed designs – were stuck up on laminated sheets, life-size, across the walls, with numbers below each one.

"He'll know it," said Deano. "He's famous, Tweety." It suddenly struck him that he had never asked what tattoo I wanted. "Hey! What're you going to get, Springbok?"

"Scorpion," I said. "My star sign."

There had been no debate in my mind, once I decided to do it. "On my ankle, so I can hide it later if I hate it." Forward planning. Going for a job interview with a naked woman painted on your forearm could count against you. Or not. Depends on the job.

"Scorpion? Geez mate, that's a bit obvious. Everyone has scorpions."

"No, everyone has dolphins. Behind the shoulder. Or butterflies."

"Yeah, chicks do."

He was looking a bit uncertain, though. We butt-shuffled towards the sound of the buzzing. A very pretty girl in sandals and a sarong came out, holding a plaster to the back of her shoulder, and went over to a desk to pay. She pointed out her choice on the 'flash' to the attendant: a two-toned leaping dolphin.

"See?" said Deano, and I simultaneously.

The pictures on the wall looked good. Professional. You could choose from several colours, mostly blues and shades of red for the in-fill, black for the outline. Colours cost more. There were several scorpions to pick from. I decided on number thirty-two. Smallish, mostly dark blue, with red pincers. Discreet, I thought. Quite classy.

We were next. Deano dithered (second thoughts?) so I pushed in front of him, and went straight in. Picture Man did not disappoint: his arms were absolutely covered with indistinct faded blue marks (some of his earlier work, I hoped), and a swirling Maori motif swarmed across his right cheek. He was sitting, frowning, with his electric pencil poised (wearing surgical gloves, I noted with some relief), and he looked... well... busy. Bothered, even. His red and gold T-shirt read 'The Gunners'.

"Yeah?" he said curtly. Business was obviously good, the guy was definitely in a hurry.

"Thirty-two, please," I asked. "And an ear stud, left ear."

"Eh?"

"Thirty-two."

"Whatchoo mean fir'y two?"

"Number thirty-two. On the wall. Picture number thirty-two. The scorpion," I offered.

He leaned forward, interpreting my meaning and deciphering my accent.

"Fir'y two is the price, innit mate!" he explained. Then helpfully: "Quid. Stud's an extra ten."

Jesus, forty-two pounds! That's, uh, forty-two times, how much is it these days, ten, so that's, shit, 420 Rands! I swallowed. Forty-odd Brit bucks was the equivalent of about two weeks work. I had exactly twenty pounds in my wallet.

"Do you take credit cards?" I asked nervously. I was again doubting my decision. Surely you can't pay for a tattoo with a credit card? Here was my out.

Picture Man narrowed his eyes, and I thought he was about to say no. The guy was just an honest skin-artist making a living, but still, he gave me the jitters. Sweat stood out from his brow, and his breath reeked of something... Asian.

"Yeah, course, watchoo fink? You been drinking, mate?"

"It's Saturday morning!" I protested.

"Yeah, mate, I know." Exaggerated forbearance. " 'ave you been drinking? Don't do no tattoos if a bloke's been drinking. Bleeds too much. An' 'e don't know wot e's about, does 'e?"

"No. Sure. No, I haven't."

He fitted a fresh needle (aah, good, good) to his machine and went to work. It barely hurt, even against the bone, and there was very little blood. Within minutes a very satisfactory scorpion had appeared on my ankle; it was exactly what I wanted. There was no idle chit-chat with Picture Man; any attempt to start a conversation was met with a non-committal grunt. He left the tattoo for a minute, having completed the outline of the scorpion, and picked up a stainless steel gun which I realised he would use to puncture my ear lobe. He grabbed the ear, a bit roughly, and placed the gun.

CRACK!

I jumped.

He looked down at me briefly with an expression that made his Maori design dance and went back to work on the tattoo, filling in the colours. Very soon it was done: painted and plastered.

"Pay at the desk, mate," he said, pulling off the gloves and tossing the used needles into a bin. "Keep it covered for a week, yeah? Use moisturiser. Baby lotion's good. Don't pick the scab, you'll bloody ruin my work. An' wash the stud 'ole with alcohol every day."

Hesitantly: "Uh, okay. So when do you put the stud in?"

He looked at me pityingly, and sighed. Bloody foreigners; you could see him thinking it.

"It's in mate. Goes in with the gun, innit."

I fingered my left ear lobe. Oh! There it was! It felt strange. Strange but... cool!

Deano got his little yellow Tweety Bird all right. I suppose Picture Man had placed tattoos in stranger places than men's backsides in his time. You hear stories about vaginal and penile tattooing. Crazy. My ankle scorpion was as brave, as out there, as I was prepared to be.

We scored a few free pints of Foster's and Director's Bitter down at the 'Coach and Horses' that night, Deano and I. None of the locals had thought we would really go through with it so we were temporary celebrities until the Manchester United/Arsenal game came on.

I loved my tattoo and ear-ring. I felt so different to the person

I was used to in the bush. I wasn't, but it felt that way. It was fun and exhilarating.

A week later in the same pub, I saw Deano chatting up an expat, a new Aussie arrival, fresh off the plane and straight from Heathrow down the Piccadilly Line into Earl's Court, London's Kangaroo Valley. He was leaning in on her, sort of whispering, and it seemed to be going really well until she suddenly pushed back from the bar and laughed loudly.

"Seriously? Like in "Bad ol' Puddy Tat'? No way!"

In the ensuing silence, I walked over to Deano. He looked crestfallen, and I tried to control the smirk that threatened to creep across my face.

"Toldja! Should have had a scorpion, china," I said.

17

NO LAUGHING MATTER

"The bullet bounced off him, that's why," said the official from the Department of Wildlife, his beer-breath permeating the short space between us.

"No, you completely missed him," I said tightly. "You're drunk." And then sarcastically, as my temper boiled over: "I suppose you believe that witches ride upon their backs in the midnight hours?"

A look of sullen indignation: "Of course."

"*How* do you know this?"

"Everyone knows. It is known."

"I *don't* know this," I said in a hard voice. "Have you actually seen it happen?"

"No. But my grandmother saw it," in a tone of finality, as if that settled the matter.

Grandmas just know, in every culture. Mine did. She had some fondly held and unswerving beliefs, such as the fact that we should all be driving American-made cars "because the Yanks helped us in the war," but she never filled my young head with stories about witches.

She would have called it superstitious nonsense.

"But you have a college diploma in Wildlife Conservation, right?" I asked the guy. "A science-based course. Evidence-based. Yet you still believe in witches. Do you really believe the bullet simply bounced off that animal?" I questioned.

"Yes. It is a hyaena. I studied for three years in Tanzania. But that is western education. We inherited that from the British. It was good. But witchcraft, they don't teach that there. That thing we just know. We all know."

I was extremely angry and deeply frustrated. Worse, I felt guilty. I had initiated this whole horrible mess and the Department had sent this inebriated idiot to deal with the problem. It wasn't the magic and sorcery that was vexing me. It was the fact that the guy was armed, and drunk, and *enjoying* it.

Poor Jimmy. We were trying to kill him. And it wasn't Jimmy's fault. We had created the problem.

Jimmy was a Spotted hyaena. He had become a damned nuisance in camp, but I liked him. We all knew him: he had an obvious scar across his nose and a mangled left ear, and an attitude which said that this was his place, not ours. You couldn't help but admire him. "Take your shot," he seemed to be saying. "You can't touch me."

Magic. I read recently that the Sri Lankan Minister of Sport had employed an oracle to divine the likely fortunes of the national cricket team for a grudge match against Pakistan, presumably to create good luck for them. Maybe in order to place a more accurate bet, too. And that one of their recent Presidents consulted a soothsayer who encouraged him to hold a snap general election. An election that he promptly lost. Come on now, who believes in this stuff anymore? Well, let's start with, "Most of the world, actually."

Looking back, it was a bizarre life, growing up in South Africa at the time that I did. As a white boy, I became accustomed to living alongside the largely unknown parallel world of black people. I hardly thought about them. The uncivilised folk, we were taught to think of them as, who could only progress through the dual benefits of a western education and the moral influence of the church. My own education was nominally Christian and emphatically Eurocentric, and of course we were exposed to the unquestioned myths of that culture, at school and at home, just as the black kids were to theirs.

I think most South Africans of all races went to some version of a Christian church back then. There are plenty of scarcely credible mysteries associated with all religions, certain articles of faith, but what I never grew up with, unlike many of the black children, was a dual system of belief in the One God as well as in the power of the ancestors. We dismissed witchcraft and a belief in omens as so much rubbish, but a walk down any township road in South Africa, then and now, would reveal a robust trade in snake venom, bones, skins, medicinal powders, healing lotions and magic potions. We laughed at the notion of raising one's bed on bricks so that the short *tokoloshe* – a mischievous and evil dwarf-sprite – would not be able to climb onto it at night. We did not paint our outside doors blue, or scatter ashes on the hearth, to ward off evil spirits in the belief that someone had *thakathi*-ed (invoked an evil spell upon) us. But Anna, our Zulu housekeeper, who lived with us for 42 years, and who was an avid church go-er, certainly did. She ultimately succumbed to the belief that a wizard had invoked an evil spell upon her and she simply lay down to die. She was gone in three days despite all that western medicine could do. I thought I was growing up in a civilised world guided by reason and logic and science and yet I was surrounded by a great majority of people who had a very real belief in the power of the spirits. African mysticism was and is a deeply ingrained, inherited part of their social fabric.

So, who is to say that witches do not ride upon hyaenas at night?

My grandfather told the story of a man who came up from the Maehle mission station, a Methodist (Wesleyan) church-owned area in the Mzimkulu valley, to buy an Easter goat for slaughter.

"It must be a strong goat," the Methodist said. "It must scream as it dies, when I thrust my spear down its throat and then catch the blood in the basin. I don't want a sheep, they die too quietly."

"I thought it was for the Passover feast," my grandfather asked teasingly. He had grown up with black children in this place, and spoke isiZulu fluently. "Why does it need to scream?"

"So that the ancestors will hear it," the man replied.

"But you wear a cross around your neck. You are a Christian," my grandfather pointed out. "Why are you making sacrifice to your ancestors?"

"This," said the man pointing at the cross, "is the religion of the Whites. And it is my religion also. But I still worship the ancestors, and make sacrifice to them. They are the important ones. They are the ones you have to be respectful of."

He saw no hypocrisy in the duality of his belief systems.

And who amongst us that considers themselves civilised chooses to sit in the thirteenth row of an aeroplane? Who tosses salt over their shoulder when it spills? Would you accept a new wallet as a gift if the giver has failed to put a dollar note inside it first? Who gives knives as a wedding present? Who thinks it bad luck to put a shoe on the table? We, too, are superstitious, inherently afraid of teasing fate, or the mysterious spirits that control it. We are forever knocking on wood.

So when the man from the Department of Wildlife said that Jimmy wasn't dead because the bullet had bounced off him, I was incensed at his lack of professionalism, but not remotely surprised. So now Jimmy had magic on his side? Boy, Jimmy was a survivor.

The problem was the rubbish pit. For an eco-tourism company, we had made some elementary mistakes in the early days, and one of them was chucking all the biodegradable waste, mostly vegetable peelings and uneaten food, into a vast open hole at the back of camp. It was supposed to break down and re-enter the earth but the volume of waste was too high, and it was impossible to persuade the kitchen and maintenance staff to stop throwing other rubbish like glass bottles, tin cans, old tyres, used oil and building material into the hole. We burned what we could but it created a horrible drifting haze and a lingering miasma that permeated the camp and surrounding area, and was always the indicator to experienced guests that we were approaching camp. It was pretty embarrassing.

The wildlife loved it, though! Porcupines nosed voraciously by night amongst the bruised pumpkins and rotting butternut squashes, African badgers made the pit their home, warthogs snuffled about

gorging themselves on unidentifiable mulch, Marabou storks and
Hooded vultures roosted habitually in the old dead knobthorn trees
next to the pit, and Glossy starlings rose in raucous shining flocks at
our approach. Baboons and Vervet monkeys dragged old food away
and ate it at their leisure. And the hyaenas. The hyaenas ate everything.
They're cunning, hyaenas. They figure things out. When we fenced the
place off, they simply dug their way in. When we covered the refuse
in ash, they ate the ash too. When we re-fenced the pit and added an
iron gate, they wrenched it clean off its hinges. When we posted a day
guard armed with a bag of calcrete rocks, they blithely ignored him and
squirmed through the wire regardless. The food piled up, the animals
came and went at will, and the problem grew worse. By far the best
game viewing in the reserve (not that we took our guests there!) was
at the rubbish pit at the back of camp amongst the rusting old trailers
and discarded coils of black 20 mm plastic piping. It was a disaster.

Not for Jimmy. He moved in on a permanent basis.

Who wouldn't, if you are a hyaena? Free grub. Lovely and warm
among the rotting foodstuffs. It reeked, but anyone who has witnessed
a foraging hyaena eagerly entering the body cavity of an elephant dead
a week will know that a bit of a pong never stopped *Crocuta crocuta*.

Familiarity breeds contempt, and Jimmy lost all fear of us. We were
perfectly used to driving right up to wild animals in broad daylight
while on game drive, animals that had learned to trust us not to
interfere in any way in their lives, content to allow us to watch them do
what they do. But had we just once got out of the car, everything would
have changed in an instant, provoking a "fight or flight" response from
the startled animal. Once you have made the rules, you can't change
them. The animals don't like inconsistency. The problem with Jimmy
and the other animals in camp, though, was that we *had* changed the
rules: we were actually feeding them! Jimmy liked these new rules. Plus,
he learned that we humans actually just weren't that scary. Jimmy had
figured out that once we were on foot we were both slow and scared,
and we couldn't even see in the dark. Who knew? Jimmy was habitually
in camp now, not only lurking about by night, but in broad daylight,
watching us at work, noting how warily we eyed him and how useless

we were at chasing him away. Jimmy knew. Now.

The cheeky devil took advantage of this new revelation. He actually started to follow us in the dark. It was bloody unnerving. As duty manager at night, one's final task was to extinguish the paraffin lanterns that adorned the dining area and lined the pathways. There were no elevated wooden walkways to the tents in those days. Boots on the ground, folks, and it led to some exciting moments, with all sorts of large animals. One night my heavy Maglite torch batteries had died during dinner so I carried a lantern with me as I walked the length of camp, shaking the pathway lamps to put them out. Hearing a soft sound behind me, I spun about with my inadequate yellow light and saw Jimmy walking right at my heels, his terrible yellow teeth exposed in that classic hyaena grin. I jumped back and yelled at him, brandishing the lamp, standing my ground. He retreated a few metres, and sat down like a house dog, still smirking. Each time I walked on, Jimmy followed. I abandoned the rest of the lamps and walked swiftly back to my tent, but sideways, like a crab, keeping an eye on Jimmy. He followed me all the way to my door. Bastard.

A week later, I tried to get my own back. I was sitting with a few guests around the fire after dinner when a sudden clatter erupted from behind the bar. It was late, around midnight, and I had sent the bartender home so I knew it couldn't be him. Sneaking up, I peered over the bar counter. Jimmy! His nose was deep in the bin, snuffling amongst wine corks and damp serviettes, lapping at spilled alcohol and stale cigarette butts. Hyaenas, eh! Just no class at all. I bellowed at him, and for once I briefly got the better of him. He took off, bounding from the bar past the startled guests with me chasing close behind, howling at him and throwing empty beer cans. He headed for the flight of steps that led from the polished teak deck to the car park. It was slippery, providing no purchase for the blunted claws of a frantic escaping hyaena. Jimmy slowed a tad as he approached the top of the stairs, and I struck, more in hope than expectation, aiming a mighty right-footed kick to Jimmy's backside as it tilted up at the top of the stairs. To my surprise, I got him arse and centre and Jimmy turned a very gratifying somersault and catapulted down the stairs. He fetched up against a railing at the base, rose quickly, unharmed but with a rather non-plussed look on his face, and walked rapidly away into the darkness. The laugh was on me however; I was wearing only a pair of light deck shoes, and it turned out that a hyaena's backside is bony and *hard*. I limped back to my seat at the fire, my foot swelling already. The joke was on me and the guests loved it. Jimmy had won again.

We had long since totally re-built the rubbish area, digging deep holes for vegetable matter and placing heavy metal grids across the openings. Now only the primates could get into the enclosure, and even they couldn't open the lids. But the damage was already done; the badgers, the monkeys, the scavenging storks still hung around camp expectantly. As did Jimmy.

Jimmy started to raid the kitchen even while the chef was actually cooking in there. Brazen as you like, he would stroll in and take an entire haunch of meat from the preparation table. All the screaming and fluttering of tea towels from the haunted kitchen staff could do nothing to stop him. The incensed chef laced a chunk of beef with the hottest chilli concoction he could create, a real devil's brew, and allowed Jimmy to take it. Jimmy devoured it in a few greedy gulps, and licked his lips. He wanted more. Then one morning we woke to find that Jimmy had climbed onto a Land Rover and bitten great chunks out of the seats and steering wheel. Over the next week, he helped himself to mouthfuls of the expensive leather couch, a large basket of decorative ostrich eggs and the beautiful tooled-leather visitors book. We could shrug our shoulders about that, but then it got ugly. Strange. Something would have to be done.

Because one early dawn a guest arrived in a state of near-hysteria at pre-drive coffee.

"That fucking hyaena has gone too far," she said, and she looked terrified. "I couldn't sleep last night. You know how he followed us to the tent after dinner? He never left. I could hear him the whole night, walking about in the fallen leaves. I could hear him *breathing*. He kept pushing his nose against the zip of the tent, trying to get in. But eventually he started biting the tent wall right next to where my head was! Go and look! There are huge *holes* there!" She began to sob.

This had happened once before. Jimmy had several times terrorised a lady manager in camp; she felt that he had targeted her specifically, as a woman, but only at her time of the month, which I had found hard to believe then, but perhaps it was so. We erected an electric fence around her tent. Jimmy munched right through it and chewed at her tent all night. Now Jimmy was at it again. No; Jimmy had to go.

I reluctantly radioed the company HQ who after much debate contacted the Department of Wildlife who eventually sent a uniformed official with a rifle and silencer. The moment that guy stepped off the plane, I regretted it. He seemed to be relishing the idea of executing wildlife, far too excited about the job. And he went straight to the bar. The safari companies danced to the Government's tune: they had a far-sighted approach to wildlife conservation but even so we still had to mind our P's and Q's with petty bureaucrats in a business environment where work permits depended on good behaviour and a carefully judged measure of respect. When I politely reminded the man from Wildlife that he would be using a weapon that evening, and that maybe getting drunk beforehand wasn't professional or safe, he dismissed me with a wave of his hand and demanded another beer.

So, later, when he fired at Jimmy, at close range from the back of a vehicle with Jimmy standing in the full glare of a spotlight, he missed entirely. I couldn't believe it. Garbage scattered wetly, Jimmy leaped in the air, and bolted for his life. Hyaenas are wily, and they learn very fast. We weren't likely to get another shot at Jimmy.

"The bullet bounced off him," shrugged the Wildlife guy. "It's magic."

I was incandescent with rage. I radioed HQ again the next morning, requesting that they have this clown removed, only to be reminded that now that we had asked this unusual favour of the Wildlife Department – think about it, permission to have an animal shot inside a National Park! – we could not send the guy back until the job was done. A hyaena had to die. I felt sick.

Jimmy stayed away for a day. I hoped it would be forever. The man from Wildlife spent most of his time eating, and drinking at the bar, his rifle beside him. I could barely bring myself to speak to him, but in the late afternoon when all the guests were out on game drive, a hyaena appeared, skulking about in the carpark right in front of the main area. I grabbed my binoculars but before I could focus on the animal's face, a muffled thump rang out and the hyaena went down, spinning in the dust with a horrible yelp.

"Wait, wait, dammit!" I shouted. The hyaena struggled upright and started to limp off on three legs, struck in the hip. For god's sake! The Wildlife guy was chuckling. A second shot. The hyaena fell again, shuddered, blood ran from its mouth, and then it died.

"Put away your fucking gun," I screamed harshly. "No more! Goddammit!"

I dashed down the stairs to where the animal lay. A scarred nose and a tattered ear. It was Jimmy all right.

I was ashamed. I took off my hat, crushing it in my hands. Suddenly, I wanted Jimmy back.

"So sorry, Jimmy," I said, and I wept.

18

COOKIE CUTTER

"Guys, what's a 'cookie cutter' guide," asks Dieter, breaking our contented silence.

"Mmh?" we ask. It's late and it's cold and we guides are huddled around the lodge campfire. All our guests have gone to bed in anticipation of another compelling day in the bush tomorrow but we are still here, indulging in our evening ritual of a whisky before we blow out the paraffin lanterns and drag ourselves off to our spartan tents. The moon is reflecting silver on the wetlands and we usually don't talk much at this time. It's a period of reflection after a long day, an exhalation of breath. It is our meditation to the sounds of reed frogs piping amongst the floating vegetation of the Okavango creep-flood and the distant furious shriek of a startled elephant. So the question surprises us. Dieter has obviously been brooding on this as he considered the low flames.

"You know how I sometimes go off and guide for that American safari travel company?" He doesn't wait for an answer. "I got a phone call today from their guide co-ordinator. She fired me."

This is stark and unexpected news. We all sit up with sudden interest. Dieter is a well-known and much-liked guide and has worked off and on for the US company for several years, so this is an intriguing revelation. He leans forward, his face lit up by the dying embers and tugs at his collar the way he always does when he's anxious. Although I know Dieter pretty well, I have never seen this particular look before: he's bemused, slightly incredulous, and a little embarrassed.

"*Ja*, I was hellava surprised, hey. It started out as a nice friendly catch-up chat like always, I mean, she's a nice lady, you know, but she sounded a bit funny, sort of, uh, syrupy and trying too hard, and I was trying to figure out what's up. I thought we were going to talk about my upcoming trip for them in Uganda but instead she kept asking me about my *last* safari for them, you know the one I told you guys about where I had that lady who refused to walk to the gorillas? *Ja*, I don't know, something's happened, man. I'm not sure what's changed. She was being nice, all 'yes, yes, I'm listening' and I was trying to figure out the real reason for her call. Anyway, finally she got there."

Dieter takes his job seriously. There are some guides who just wing it, greatly dependent upon their charm and gung-ho youthfulness, and they mostly do a great job, but Dieter isn't one of those: there is nothing *laissez faire* about his approach to his work. He is serious and solid, and he is taking this news to heart. I have never heard him talk so much in one go. There are lions calling now behind camp and normally we would take a guess as to where they are and in which direction they are moving – our guests will want to see them when we sally out in the dawn. But tonight no-one even mentions them.

"So what did she actually say, Dieter?" I ask.

"Man, I don't really remember all of it. I've never been fired before." It's a small attempt at humour. "I was a bit shocked, I love doing that east Africa trip for them. Something about how they've loved having me on their guiding team, and for years I've been their go-to guy, you know how they talk, but now they're looking for a change in personnel, something fresh. And then she said what they need is 'cookie cutters.' What the hell is a *cookie-cutter?*"

We look at each other across the half-shadow as the last *Acacia* logs pop and smoke to their end. Someone tosses another thin branch onto the fire, and it quickly flares up bright and lively: this disclosure from Dieter is worthy of a few more minutes at the hearth. Actually, I don't really know what 'cookie cutter' means either, although I've heard Americans use it. One of the guys says it has something to do with everything being uniform, all exactly the same and predictable. What a horrible idea. I really feel for Dieter: he loves guiding, and he is damned competent at it too. Furthermore, I know this American company well. I like their ethics, their *modus operandi* and I like the people that work for them – I've met several of them on the ground in Africa, including the owner, and have been impressed. He's no cookie cutter. He's well known for a vibrant approach to the outdoors and a focus on fun and adventure. They have always wanted quirky and charismatic guides who know their stuff, who interact easily with people and who create an atmosphere of laughter and conviviality: they want characters, who also get a professional job done.

What's going on? We are surprised, and disappointed. Why on earth would he want to fire a guy like Dieter?

There are fruit bats chiming in the mangosteen trees, and the roosting baboons are muttering to themselves in their restless sleep. Dreaming of the dreaded leopard, the night phantom, it sounds like. No wonder they're always so drowsy in the mornings, flopping half-asleep in the welcome sun with their pale eyelids drooping.

'Cookie cutter.' We mull on it for a few seconds. It sounds odd in the context of what we do as guides, which is to lead our clients into the wild places of Africa where every activity is unique and where the unexpected happens all the time, where the unexpected is *welcomed*.

Dieter continues.

"*Ja*, she said that they want to have a guiding standard across the board and they need all their guides to be 'singing from the same hymn sheet.' She actually said that. So they're rationalising their staff, and trying to get consistency. Stuff like that."

It's all rehearsed corporate gobbledygook, of course. False mutterings and prevarications. We believe that each safari experience we offer our clients is idiosyncratic and distinct so this nod to the formulaic Lego approach to guiding in the wilderness – a pre-packaged and boxed holiday – is exactly what we hate. Furthermore, Dieter is one of our own. We naturally close ranks. More whisky is splashed into our tumblers, and someone fetches some ice.

"But Dieter," someone asks, "I thought you were getting *great* reviews from the clients on these trips. What are these people thinking?"

"*Ja*, I thought so. I asked her that. I said, 'How come I suddenly don't match your guiding standards? Because you said the previous client reports were pretty good. Outstanding, even. You've always seemed really happy with my efforts. What's happened?'"

He pauses, looking resigned. Then he brightens a little, smiling, but with tight lips, and polishes his glasses carefully, each lens in turn, with a perfectly folded white handkerchief. So Dieter! Actually, ironically, so cookie cutter!

"*Ag*, but guys, never mind the cookie cutter thing. Let me tell you what happened on my last trip to Uganda." He shifts in the old camp chair and the worn canvas squeaks in the darkness. "That lady who just didn't want to be there. Weird, hey! I think her daughter and husband persuaded her to come to Africa, and she hated it. I tried really hard to talk to her, to encourage her, to include her in the group, but you know how it goes sometimes, she was just sullen and quiet, sort of, I don't know, *sulking* all the time, looking miffed at everything. *Jussus bru*, she was tough to handle. Then, when it came to walking to the Mountain gorillas, she managed a kilometre of flat road and then she just stopped! It was still easy walking! She just wouldn't go on, man!"

Dieter is one of those folk who divides his world into clear and easily managed compartments: yes and no, black and white. So it isn't easy for him to understand how someone could travel so far and be on the brink of what many guides consider to be the most evocative wildlife experience on earth... and turn it down. Some of us at the fire have never had the privilege of seeing Mountain gorillas in their natural habitat so we are in full sympathy with Dieter. We consider this for a long moment and a Barn owl screeches unexpectedly, sounding forlorn.

"So what did you do with her, dude?" someone asks. The fire is burning down again to a mere glow but the cold is forgotten.

His reply comes out in a rush.

"I don't know if she was afraid, maybe, of the gorillas, or the humidity and mud, or the forest, maybe the bugs; I don't think so. It just wasn't her kind of holiday. I've been to Uganda eleven times, and guided more than 100 clients, and I have never before failed to get a person to the gorillas, and lots of those clients were worried about their physical ability, but they all made it. And you know, on that morning, I even persuaded the park rangers to give us access to the closest family of gorillas so that this lady had the best chance of seeing them. The shortest walk, like two hours. So when she stopped, I really talked to her. Her daughter talked to her. But she was adamant that she couldn't make it, and she went back to the lodge. Man, she looked so pissed off! I don't know if it was with the whole situation or just with me. It was a hell of a shame."

Guiding is a people business. Sure, you have to know plenty about the environment, the wildlife, about the safari business, about the world at large. But, most of all, you have to know about people. And they come in all shapes and guises, and carry with them all manner of fears, eccentricities, prejudices and pre-loaded views of the world. Just like we guides do. It can be awkward at times dealing with some guests but I know that a guy like Dieter has the greatest patience and is more accommodating than most when dealing with his clients.

"But did this just come out of the blue, Dieter?" I ask.

"Not really. She was a bit snippy before, like I said. She didn't like one of the lodge managers but everyone else found him really charming and hospitable. Then she had a major problem with people who smoked, even when it was done discreetly. And on one walk she chewed me out for talking too loudly while I was explaining something to some of the other clients. It was like she was *determined* not to enjoy herself. It started on the very first day at Entebbe airport when she got off the plane. They had a delayed flight. *Jussus*, she had a face like thunder, man. "

We all nod; we know how it goes. You meet a group of people at the airport, they meet you, and none of you know how it's going to go. But you can usually tell within minutes whether you're going to get on with each other, and what allowances will need to be made. As a guide, you can almost always do something about unhappy guests, especially once the jet lag has worn off and folk have got to know each other. But it can be difficult. On rare occasions there can be very little bonhomie, small cliques form in the common areas at meals and drinks, and there is not much laughter or repartee. An unusual combination of strangers, tossed together for twelve days, some of them sharing a room with people they have never met before, all with different expectations of what will unfold, can lead to tensions. But almost always there is enough obvious delight in experiencing all the wonders of Uganda to ease the strain, and the problem dissolves. The trip begins to flow with excitement, and anticipation, and the clients generate a lot of the energy in the group even without your input. Many of them become friends for life, with each other and with the guide, and everyone delights in each other's company. But, once in a blue moon, it just doesn't gel with a client and all you can do is be as professional and pleasant as possible, and hope that the client warms to the experience, to the rest of the group, and to you.

"So, anyway," Dieter continues, bringing us back to the present, "Today this lady on the phone says to me, once she's finished with the cookie cutter bullshit, 'On your last safari for us, there was a bit of a complaint.' That's when I knew what the real problem was. Never mind cookie cutters. It's this lady, the one who wouldn't walk; she's bloody torpedoed me! A hundred happy guests but they only listen to her!"

He's working through his disappointment, talking it out, ruefully shaking his head, his glasses reflecting the lamplight, and I see that he is actually grinning a little. We've all dealt with the rare complaint before, and we always take it personally. It is very difficult for us guides to understand that just the very fact that a client is in one of the greatest wildlife areas on earth is not already enough... but, of course, that is only our perspective.

"Did you read the client feedback on-line once you got back from Uganda, Dieter? I mean, before the phone call today?" I enquire.

"No, I haven't read the feedback. It's hard to get on-line out here in the bush, and we've been busy. But, anyway, I almost never do."

Most guides tend to share this approach. Feedback can be useful sometimes but it is too often simply a case of a rushed post-trip "rate your experience/the accommodations/the food/your guide" on a scale from one to ten. If you fill in the online report, you can 'win a free holiday' sort of thing. Our attitude is that if we do the best we can on the trip, and make sure that we all have a lot of fun together, that will always work. Many of us also ignore the pre-trip speculation from safari agents about their clients: we prefer to take our fellow travellers as we find them instead of being influenced by the opinions of trip-reservation staff who only have an online or telephone relationship with the clients. Guests described by the operator as "difficult" are frequently anything but, and turn out in person to be lovely to deal with.

Heavy splashing in the shallows of the swamp. Probably a hippo on its nocturnal ramblings. Their paths run through the camp so we'll have to be wary on the way back to our tents. We all stare briefly into the gloom, and then Dieter carries on.

"*Ja*, she said that one lady said that I ignored her and spent much more time with the other clients. She felt neglected. I asked her what the other guests said, and apparently they were very happy but the overall feedback wasn't up to my usual standard. And what they're looking for is consistency. Cookie cutter guides."

There is much tut-tutting around the fire. That's what our friend Dieter was told but we don't buy it. Poor Dieter. This isn't about cookie cutters at all. And can it be just because of one complaint? Surely not? No, something else has happened, and the lady on the phone isn't telling him. She's feeding him a line.

He is rising to his disillusionment, however. He pushes his glasses back up the bridge of his nose and picks up his tumbler. The ice has long ago melted and the whisky twists in honeyed swirls as he raises a toast.

"Listen boys, it's a pity. But Uganda was an amazing opportunity. The gorillas are awesome. So you know what I told that woman on the phone? I said, 'Okay, hang on, I don't know what's going on and I don't know what the hell cookie cutter guides are, okay? But I don't like the sound of them at all. So if you want some of those, go and look in the bloody cookie jar. But don't look for me; I don't live in there!'"

19

I NEVER WENT FOR THE SCHOOL

There was an exceedingly anxious week at the Old Mombo camp in the Okavango Delta during which we did a lot of short, unscheduled and completely illegal walking safaris. The lodge was located in the Moremi Game Reserve, an area where we were not, according to the Department of Wildlife and National Parks regulations, actually allowed to be on foot outside of the camp perimeter. Game drives only. It was all my fault.

Sloppy management, you see. Hell, I only ever really wanted to be a guide and rove about in paradise looking at wildlife but the actual manager went on leave and the silly buggers from Maun HQ put me in charge of the camp for three months. Now that I think back on it, that makes it *their* fault. Poor judgement on their part, you see.

Lodge management requires a lot of forward planning. The big six-wheel drive, high-clearance, can-go-anywhere delivery truck only arrives once a month, and everything you need for the forthcoming weeks had better be on it. Toilet paper, cases of well travelled sun-baked wine, screws and planks of wood, furniture, canned goods, bags of mail, solar panels, spare parts for the vehicles, tools, thatching materials (and the thatchers), errant staff members returning late from leave, their pockets empty and their eyes still bloodshot and – most importantly – diesel. Multiple 44-gallon drums of diesel, their contents audibly sloshing about within and sometimes seeping from the lids when the truck suddenly brakes as a herd of elephants crosses the road, causing the fuel to leak and creep down the length of the truck, soaking into the dry goods and sometimes also the passengers.

Diesel was everything. In the days before the lodges went green and eco-friendly, before the modern-day solar farms stretched out behind the camps in vast arrays of bright panels and blinking warning lamps, before the USP was about environmental footprints and sustainability, everything ran on diesel. And it is filthy stuff. The generators that powered the fridges and the radio batteries, that gave life to power tools and kitchen blenders, all consumed diesel in alarming quantities. The old Lister thundered away in the back of house, spouting engine oil and spilling fuel into the absorbent sands of the Kalahari basin. And our game drive vehicles ran on diesel too. No diesel, no game drives. No game drives, well, game over.

Naturally, we had a system. On a weekly basis we needed to dip a special stick issued by Shell into the overhead fuel tanks. This required propping a decrepit ladder against the tank, slithering along the slippery, rounded rump of the container and dropping the stick into the fuel via the refilling cap. It was a horrible greasy job and I certainly didn't fancy it. We were only issued one pair of uniform shirts, and the camp laundry staff was already doing a fine job of destroying those with their heavy-handed ironing. No, no. So Precise, our cheerful camp assistant, was tasked to do it. The stick was calibrated for that particular size tank only, and the wet mark on it after dipping pretty accurately reflected how much fuel remained in the tank. What could possibly go wrong? After all, I also had a fail-safe back-up plan: the fuel tanks were on the way from the office to our quarters at back of house and I habitually rapped a knuckle on each of them several times a day as I passed by. A dull sound was good: fuel within. A hollow echo was bad: empty! Which was fine as long as only one tank made that echo.

Precise did his job. He would arrive each morning at the office in his grimy overalls, the dip stick held aloft, the wet mark obvious and reassuring. Plenty of diesel, he would say, and the stick proved it. Good, two more weeks and the big truck from Maun, the Deutz Magirus, would be here, the only vehicle that could ford the waterways and river crossings of the rising waters of the Okavango. We were okay. The Lister hammered on, the fridges hummed, the lights worked and the Land Rovers went out each day loaded with excited guests.

Until one morning I knocked with expectant satisfaction on the two tanks. The first one was empty. Fine. It was halfway through the month, after all. I knocked on the second as I walked past. A resounding reverberation. I stopped. I went back. I knocked again. The dull empty resonance of a hollow drum.

"Precise!" I yelled. No answer. "PRECISE!" I could hear the contained alarm in my voice.

I fetched the ladder and struggled up the tank stand. I peered in. A very disappointingly low smear of fuel met my eye. And yet yesterday Precise had shown me a dip stick that indicated enough fuel to last for the remainder of the month. I rushed to the cars. Full. Thank god. I sped over to the generator. Full. Thank all the gods. But even so, at our usual rate of consumption, we only had enough fuel for a few days. The fuel truck, if available, and at a considerable premium, could reach us at best in a week, provided the driver could negotiate the tricky, sticky water crossings between the islands. There was going to be a proper fuss about this in Maun, and it was going to be me answering the questions.

Three things needed to happen immediately. First, a rapid emergency meeting with the managers and guides.

"Right, listen up," I tell them. "Don't tell the guests anything. Minimum use of the generator, just enough to pump the water tanks to capacity and to run the fridges. Short game drives with long coffee and sundowner stops. Drive in circles near the camp; the guests never know where they are anyway. Drive slowly. Stay at sightings as long as you possibly can. Stop often. Talk about the small stuff. Butterflies. Obscure little brown birds. Dung. Chat, tell stories, draw it all out.

No all-day drives, no picnics out there, no exploring to distant parts. And walk. Lead the guests on short, safe walks in the vicinity of the car. If guests want a morning sleep-in, do not discourage them. Remind them that they need to catch up on their travel journals. Pile as many guests as there are seats onto one car. Airstrip runs will include the guests' luggage; no separate vehicle for bags. Do all these things but don't tell the guests!"

Second, I needed to get on the radio to HQ and order more fuel. That was going to be a difficult conversation. The boss was going to raise his anxiety level from permanently peeved to temporarily apoplectic. "You want what? More fuel? Why didn't you order enough last month? You know this is busy season! I want to see you in my office in Maun. Get on the next plane!"

Third, where's Precise? "Show me that fuel stick, chap. Show me what you do every day. Yesterday you filled the cars and the genny and the stick showed half a tank still remaining. Plenty to last us the month. Get up there and show me what you do."

Precise had re-appeared now that it was obvious that I was not going to go postal on him and he looked annoyingly cheerful. He knew he had done his job just as I had shown him. Up he went, stick in hand, screwed open the lid, dropped the stick in to its full extent, withdrew it and handed it down to me for my inspection.

Upside down. He handed me the dipstick upside down.

"See, nearly full," he said in deluded triumph despite the blindingly obvious. I could barely believe the illogicality of it.

"Get down, Precise," I said slowly, closing my eyes. "I need to explain something to you. I have made a mistake. I want to show you again how to use this stick."

"Thank you," he said. "But you must show me better than before. There are many numbers on the stick and I never went for the school."

You might think that this was a lesson that I had learned, absorbed and internalised before. Who needs the stress? You'd think. Apparently not.

Because north-east of Mombo, in the Linyanti, along the verges of the Kwando river, lay Zibalianja camp, a small tented haven on a remote palm island, now and then surrounded by the shallow waters of the encroaching Zib lagoon.

It was a tiny island, barely large enough to house the guests and staff, so fuel-stuffs needed to be stored away from camp for fear of accidental fire. It had never happened at any camp I had worked in, but it was, nevertheless, a sensible precaution. On a nearby island that I dubbed Shell Ultra City (after the many roadside refuelling services along highways in South Africa), we built a rudimentary stand of gum poles with a ramp and we would roll each 44-gallon drum up as we needed it, horizontally laid with the cap bottom-most so that we could gravity-tap the diesel from a height of about five feet straight into the fuel inlet pipe of a Land Cruiser parked next to the stand. It was simple and effective and required no pump. Easy as you like. The problem was that the fuel depot wasn't actually in camp. In other words, it wasn't directly under my daily supervision. And I was busy.

Roadblock was the Zibalianja maintenance man. He was an able and ingenious fixer, a wizard with a few basic tools, a man who called himself 'Roadblock' because he played in the last line of defence in our occasional inter-camp soccer games and who claimed that nothing got past him. (That didn't explain why the Zib team always lost, but I think he secretly blamed me, with considerable justification.) Amongst his daily tasks was the regular refilling of the generator and the Cruiser, and for months it had all gone along very well. He would let me know whenever the diesel supply over on Shell Ultra City was running low, and I would make sure that I ordered sufficient for delivery by the monthly truck. He steadfastly topped up the car whenever the fuel gauge indicated half. He and I used to joke that if the needle of the gauge indicated F, that meant 'Finished' but that if it dropped to E, that meant 'Enough'.

One week I noticed that the needle was showing that only half a tank remained. The camp was full so I was doing two long drives every day as well as shorter trips to and from the airstrip to pick up and drop off guests. A lot of diesel was being used but I knew I had just enough in the car for the next day. All was well. But the next lunch time, with the tank now less than a quarter full, I called for Roadblock.

"Please fill the car," I said, surprised that I needed to remind him.

"I cannot," he said flatly, looking evasive.

It suddenly occurred to me that the steady throb of the generator was absent.

"Eh? Why not?"

"There is no diesel," he replied, looking at his feet.

"None? Is Shell Ultra City dry? Is there no diesel in *any* of the drums?"

"No. It is finished."

I immediately felt sick, and angry. It was high season and I hadn't personally been to the fuel island for two weeks. Roadblock had been away on leave, returning only the day before. No-one had been checking. My fault, again. A clever plan to purchase fuel from a distant neighbouring concession was going to have to be made, a plan that meant a long drive through the night with no sleep before dawn game drive and some embarrassing explanations to the Reserve manager when he received the over-inflated bill. I tried to speak calmly and evenly.

"Roadblock," I said, "you got back to camp yesterday. Why didn't you tell me yesterday there was no diesel."

He shot me a pitying look.

"Because yesterday there *was* some diesel," he said. "E for enough."

A torn hat.

We take a walk and you smile with the sky.
Photo: Norbert Grafe

Contemplating the nature of all things.
Photo: Norbert Grafe

Courtenays.

Hush Puppies.

Nice office.

Step away from the jack.
Photo: Anthony Paglino

Paying attention.
Photo: Norbert Grafe

Sorry, Jimmy.

Not for eating.

Sweated up vaquero.

Not lost.
Photo Credit: Gerhard Thirion

Guide training at Mushara, Namibia.

Tools of the trade.

Motsamai: one of the new breed.

An elephant passes.

Malaria dreams.
Photo: Norbert Grafe

The red sun leavens the outer edge of the earth.

Investigated.

In a baobab called The Maw.

First world problems.

All whom you love: Lloyd and Sue.

Watching the evening light fall.

20

HI, I'M FROM HQ,
I'M HERE TO HELP

"They're bloody useless those *okes* from HQ, they expect us to drop everything to go and fetch them from the airstrip and then they arrive hours late, they pull in to camp wearing all the latest branded uniforms when we can't even get hold of the old stuff, they park off at the bar drinking wine but they tell us *we* can only have two beers a night, and then they want to have meetings about performance standards and quarterly goals and make us do personal SWOT analyses and they say, yes, yes, we're listening, we hear you, we know you work long hours in harsh environmental conditions and your roof leaks and there's no hot water in the staff showers but what are you doing about the complaint from that really major agent? The bloody Parachute Brigade: they drop in, fire a few shots, and then bugger off to a cocktail party in town."

It's an old refrain, and you'll hear it at every camp in Africa. You'll hear it in every company, actually, *anywhere*. "The HQ guys are here, and they haven't got a clue about what it's like on the ground. C'mon, just leave us alone to get on with the job. We know what to do. Just send us the stuff we need to keep calm and carry on."

And then what happens? The Peter Principle kicks in, that's what happens. People get promoted beyond their level of competence. An excellent guide or manager secures a promotion to HQ, quickly acquires a T-shirt that says, 'The beatings will continue until morale improves', and plans a lightning visit to the very camp he has just left, a tour of inspection ostensibly to lift the spirits of the people on the ground. Sometimes they indulge in some hypocritical sabre-rattling, telling the lodge staff how much better they are than the competition simply by dint of the uniform they wear. They bemoan the ethics of their safari rivals, how they steal their ideas, their staff, their designs, quite forgetting in their ardour that not only will many of the incumbent staff inevitably move with bewildering speed through all the safari companies but that they themselves will in all likelihood do the same the moment they are offered a hundred bucks a month more. What tune will they be singing then? The staff ignores this nonsense anyway. They have mates across the boundary fence, family quite often, and all the muscle-flexing by the HQ folk runs off their backs like so much water. "Don't come here and tell me who I should like! Your company bullshit is not reflective of how the people at ground level feel."

Those HQ folk! But okay, different skills, different priorities, and *someone* has to run the show. The camps would be empty if the marketing guys didn't send in the travel agents and the private guides to check out the lodges and activities; there would be no jobs at all if the town accountants didn't keep the books in order and hold the lodge managers to budget; and it is not given to all to be able to represent the company proactively at an overseas trade show where directors shindig together, work out preferential rates, and get to grips with market trends. It is always a real shame and a disappointment though when the HQ guys show no actual interest in the *environment*. You don't have to know a thousand birds to be a good accountant (I asked one of them once about birds and she said, "As far as I'm concerned there are only three kinds of birds. The small ones are sparrows, the medium ones are pigeons and the really big ones are ostriches") but it would be lovely to see the HQ folk in camp really revelling in the delight of a herd of springbok meandering down to the waterhole or getting excited to go on a game drive. Far too often, though, they're in the camp office trying to log on and wishing they were back in town where the download speed is faster and the air-conditioning works. They're busy people, you see, running the show.

So what usually happens is that the guys with the specialised skills, the numbers and legal skills, become the bosses. Too right! If they had me in charge, I'd spend all the cash on rebuilding the staff quarters, on wildlife monitoring programmes, on guide training, on hiring excellent mechanics to keep the Land Rovers in tip-top condition, on road maintenance, and the company would probably be bankrupt in a year. That's why the ideas guys, the progenitors of these ecotourism concepts, the people with the passion and the drive and the energy, never last in the top echelons of their own companies. They eventually get ousted by the company bean-counters on the Board because their ideas are too grandiose, too futuristic, too expensive, and the reality is that the company needs to pay for itself. That's how it should be, too: the imaginative ideas guys need to move on, take their passion elsewhere, start up new projects that are good for the environment and the surrounding communities.

I have been one of those HQ guys too. When I was Area Manager for a reserve in the Namib desert region of Namibia, and very new at it, it quickly became obvious that the camp managers would judge my performance simply by whether I provided what they believed they needed to run the place properly. I was in essence nothing more than a shopper for supplies: building materials, food and drink, personal toiletries for the staff, light bulbs, coils of wire, Land Rover tyres and spares, fuel, bottle openers, the nuts and bolts of making a far-flung camp work in a remote place where the supply truck arrived only once a month, and everything they needed had better be on it.

"How's it all going?" I asked one Namibian manager who was determined at all times to point out that, just because I had managed a lodge in the Okavango Delta, it didn't mean I knew anything about the desert camp business.

"I'll tell you when I see what comes off the truck," he sniffed.

Fair enough. But very often, as a camp manager, when it doesn't go as hoped, you simply have to make a plan. I'd learned to get by in Botswana, often. But there were limits.

One day at Mombo Camp in Botswana I reached that limit. HQ had sent out a beautiful brand new Holland and Holland tractor to help with the rebuild of the new camp. I expected the boss to recall it once the work was done but, to my surprise, we retained it, and it was brilliant. The roads were dragged, the supplies were fetched in a single run from the river crossing, water tanks and other heavy materials were moved about in camp, we shifted storage containers and built vehicle ramps and gum-pole bridges, and the maintenance manager was in heaven with his new toy. I swear he surreptitiously polished that thing under cover of darkness. But shortly after he went on leave at the start of the rainy season, a supply truck became bogged down 30 km from camp. I sent the Holland with chains to haul it out, normally the work of a day only, and the driver radio-ed in the evening to say that now the bloody tractor was mud-jammed too. I went out to have a look. Hi, I'm from camp, I'm here to help.

I'm no mechanic, I just drive the things, and that tractor was not only stuck, its big back lugged tyres churning helplessly in black cotton soil, but now it would not start either. I radio-ed HQ in the morning. Given time, I can extract the tractor, I said, but only of it starts, so please send the town mechanic, the guy who can fix anything, the guy who knows. Send The Guy.

"He doesn't fly," I was told.

What? That's how people get about in the Delta! What do you mean, he doesn't *fly?* Send him, dammit! We're in trouble here!

"He refuses to fly. He's scared of flying. We'll ask him what you need to do to get the tractor started. Meanwhile, start by building a coffer dam around both the tractor and the truck. Pump the dam dry, let the mud dry and drive the things out. Make a plan! That's what managers do."

Oh, for... give me some credit! I'd already done that! The dam was ready... and then it began to rain again. Hard. Every day the swamp rose until it spilled into the dam. We pumped. We pumped

and shovelled for five straight days. That little Yamaha EP-50 petrol
pump did sterling work. The rains fell, we worked in the mud, and the
dam filled with water. I tried what The Guy had said about starting the
tractor. He said I had "wound it up", whatever that meant. I couldn't
get it unwound. I loaded Land Rovers with the dry goods from the
truck and ferried it all to camp. The rain slackened, we began to gain
on the flood, and I radio-ed HQ again.

"What? Are you *still* cocking about out there? We need that truck
back in town," said HQ.

Through gritted teeth I said: "Send The Guy. Just send the mechanic
that knows. With tools. In an aeroplane. Send him now. You asked me
to make a plan. I made a plan. The dam is almost empty. Now send
the bloody mechanic. It's time YOU made a plan!"

"Okay, okay, I'll send The Guy," said the boss. "And you get yourself
onto the first plane into Maun," he added icily. "We need to talk."

The Guy arrived, carrying tools and some used air-sick bags. He
tinkered about in the guts of the tractor, tut-tutting, for about fifteen
minutes, shouted a few swear words in some European dialect, no
doubt at me for breaking the thing, started the tractor up and drove
it straight out. I felt elated. Then he attached long chains and hauled
the truck out too. I felt deflated...

I flew to Maun. The boss took me to the pizza place and we drank
beer. He didn't take kindly to open criticism on the two-way radio,
he said. A public thrash at him was not the way to get things done,
he said. Can't be having that, he said. How would you feel if one of
your guides had a good old harangue at you over the radio, he asked.
No, I said, you're right, I apologise... but the bloody tractor is out now
and The Guy seems to have overcome his reluctance to fly, hasn't he?
He'll be out at Mombo all the time now, I expect, on bloody tours of
inspection. "Hi, I'm from HQ, I'm here to help." The boss grinned
and bought me another beer.

"Bloody HQ, hey," he said. "Now, let's talk about rugby. Province
are looking good this season."

It didn't go quite as chummily when the Fly Boss came calling
though. It was a hectic time at Mombo, run off our feet, guests in and

out every day, at full capacity and the game viewing as good as ever. I was supposedly the manager of the camp but I was guiding almost full time and, as usual, the camp was actually being run by Sue and the ladies. And then it started to rain, far too early in the season. Every day it came, the whole flipping season's bounty in a week, the skies purple and angry with wind and wet. The laundry staff couldn't get the sheets dry, recently washed guest clothing hung festooned from every rafter in the back-of-house, staff clothing remained unwashed and the game drive ponchos were still saturated when we put them on and ventured out again into the water and the wilds. The animals took shelter as all sensible mammals ought to do, hunched against a driving rain, and the birds stopped singing. The guests were very understanding about our challenges but some finally dropped the facade of having a good time and became openly sullen. I spent the days rescuing stranded guests and embarrassed guides from sunken Land Rovers, caught in water crossings that a week before had been perfectly negotiable. How long could this go on for?

So in the midst of this when the Fly Boss radio-ed camp to say that he was coming in to inspect the new "no shut-down propellor pad" that I was supposed to have built for the Cessna Grand Caravan and to give me training on the safety procedures, his timing was way off.

"Meet me at the air strip in fifteen minutes," he instructed. "I'm in the air, I'm on the way."

"No can do, I'm afraid," I said with considerable irritation. "Too much going on here right now. I'll send a guide to fetch you."

"No, no, I don't have time. Meet me at the strip. The strip!" he shouted above the engine noise.

I sent a guide. When the Fly Boss arrived in camp he was exactly as incandescent as I hoped he would be. We sat at the long dining table and without preamble he launched straight into how the new procedures for the Caravan would be more time efficient, safer and provide a better guest experience all round.

"Oh," I said innocently. "I thought it was to save money. All that shutting down, starting up, wear and tear and stuff?"

Fly Boss looked narrowly at me.

"Yes," he replied heavily, "yes, there is that too. But anyway, back to the pad... "

I listened with growing impatience. I'd heard it all before. The air charter company HQ had sent a file detailing the reasons and safety procedures and I was perfectly happy to comply. These new Caravans were great machines, so much roomier than the old claustrophobic 210's and 206's, and the guests loved them, but how could I even build the damned pad if the cement hadn't been sent, I pointed out. And where was the wheeled safety barrier? And the steps?

Fly Boss went crazy. Why weren't they here? Dunno. Weren't they on last month's truck? No. Well, where were they? Dunno. Someone needs to take charge of this! You're right, I thought, *you* do!

Guides and other staff kept interrupting us to check the flight schedule of arrivals and departures that kept changing, looking meaningfully at the man from HQ as they did so, and it was obvious that they were not best pleased to hear him having a go at us. He simmered down a little and sipped at his coffee, and I couldn't help myself.

"Um, I just wanted to check on something. Since you're here and we are talking about flying safety and policy. These pilots of yours... "

This really got his attention. In those days the pilots were mostly characterful bush boys, young men fresh out of flight school, getting enough hours to move up the ladder towards bigger flying jobs, working on a thousand take-offs, a thousand landings and a thousand hours, never shy of a drink and of wooing the girls in the lodges. Perhaps the latter two were also measured in thousands. One of them, a New Zealander, memorably asked me what I was doing as I peered down at the Mombo countryside from the air just post take-off in an Islander one day. I was always trying to figure out how to get to exciting places on game drives, and you couldn't always work it out from the ground.

"I'm looking for a route," I said.

"Ah, mate, story of my life," he replied. (A "root" to a Kiwi means casual sex).

They gave Fly Boss a hard time, the pilots. They loved a prank and were naturally youthfully disdainful of authority. They were damned fine pilots but they were kids, and they liked to play. And what are aeroplanes if nothing but big toys? They loved to beat up an airstrip after take-off for example. They'd never do it with guests on board; with clients it was always steady and level with nice, slow turns, nothing stomach-churning, a long safety briefing before every take-off, "stick-it-in-one" touch downs and a gentle run towards the terminal. But sometimes when alone or with consenting staff members, they'd climb hard and high after take-off, tip a wing over, race down the arc and come screaming at low level back down the strip towards us on the ground, their passengers white-knuckling and whooping all the way, and us ducking beneath the racing shadow and screaming roar of an aircraft doing what it was built to do. It was strictly illegal, of course, but Fly Boss had undoubtedly done exactly the same when he was a young pilot. But not anymore. Now he was from HQ. He was supposed to be here to help. But he went onto the offensive instead.

"What *about* the pilots? They tell me that you lodge people keep forgetting to give them lunch packs. They can't fly all day on an empty stomach, you know! And your guides are always late at the air strip!"

This was mostly true. I simply could not get the guides to remember to take the lunch packs out to the air strip. I sometimes forgot myself. And getting the guests out of camp and to the airstrip was difficult. Why would they *want* to leave? One more cup of coffee for the road...

"Okay, you're right," I said. "We do need to sort that out. No, I'm talking about the barrel rolling. The barrel rolling in front of camp. Just asking."

People really do turn purple when they're apoplectic, you know. I saw it happen that day. There was a strict rule about the pilots not overflying the lodge at any time because it disturbed the tranquillity of the place and woke slumbering guests. And the pilots very seldom broke the rule. As for barrel rolling, it just didn't happen. The pilots may have got up to high jinks when alone up there, but they didn't have a death wish, and flinging a small plane upside-down wasn't on their list of tricks. But Fly Boss wasn't in a good mood and he completely lost it. He rose from his seat and leaned over the table at me. At first he couldn't speak but eventually he spluttered:

"I want *names*, I want plane *registrations*, I want *times and dates*. I want... "

He sat down abruptly, struck dumb again, staring crazily at me. He couldn't think of what else he wanted. But pilots were going to pay. Or I was going to pay. *Someone* was going to pay! And then he saw me grinning.

"Fuck you! Fuck you, man. Aah fuck, you had me going. Oh, shit, no, I can't believe I fell for that."

And to his immense credit, he started to laugh. I started to laugh too. It was becoming a long hard wet season and we all needed a bloody good laugh. Even the guys from HQ needed a laugh. *Especially* the guys from HQ.

Eventually the rain stopped. I built him his propellor pad, I ordered the safety equipment and the Caravans came in. It all worked just like the book from HQ said it should. I think the guides may even have got the guests to the airstrip before the planes arrived. A few times, anyway. I believe it no exaggeration when I state that some pilots may even have received their lunch packs.

I liked the Fly Boss after that. He could take a joke. He was a good man. A stressed man, but a good one. Even if he was from bloody HQ!

21

DON'T MENTION THE MONKEY

You never want to be unkind to animals and it would be especially infra dig in a game reserve but these particular animals just keep coming at you. They're relentless. We tried everything we could to keep them away, but it was like facing the Zulus through the blood-sun afternoon at Isandhlwana: there was no end to them, and they easily won the day. The Afrikaners call them '*blou ape*' (blue monkeys) and the vivid colouring of the male's balls would make you think that's why. We called them by many names, often profane, but the lodge checklist had them down as Vervet monkeys.

In the end they did get their come-uppance, though. It wasn't pleasant for anyone.

They're quick and they're clever, Vervets. They're natural foragers and raiders in the wild – the nests of birds, fruiting trees, swarming insects, whatever is available at that time of the season – and as soon as they figure out that they are faster than us humans, as soon as they figure out that they in reality have very little to fear from us, the moment they realise that they can rob and steal and plunder at will, without retribution, they become a safari camp manager's nightmare.

There is a strong school of thought in the lodge management world that wild animals in the camp ought to know their place, and the only way for them to know it is to teach it to them using the same rules that the animals themselves use to organise their own societies: fear and intimidation. The thinking goes that when we humans move into a wilderness area to build a lodge, we become the dominant species there. By day, anyway. After dark we retreat to our fires and our beds to wait until dawn, and when we can see again, we reassert ourselves. Through the night the animals take the camp back, which is why part of the wonderful drama of the safari experience is finding lion tracks outside your tent in the morning, or being kept awake by the sloshing of hippos and the nocturnal feeding of elephants just metres away. But by day we need to demonstrate our dominance by a show of force. Few animals have developed much ability to reason but overt power is a language they do understand.

At one of the lodges I helped manage in Botswana, the Concession Manager, our direct boss, encouraged us to carry a pocket full of palm nuts – a hard-skinned fruit – to hurl at monkeys and baboons every time we encountered them in camp. It was impossible to actually hit them – they read our intention before we had even got a palm nut into our hand – but the message was nevertheless clear: this little patch of wilderness belongs to us humans, and you monkeys (and elephants, and buffalos, and the rest) can have it at night only. When we go out to see you on game drive this afternoon, we will behave with decorum and respect and will seek not to interfere in any way with your lives... but here in camp, please keep your distance and be nice.

The problem is that this strategy requires the cooperation of the whole staff, as well as the guests. Three things happen that ruin the plan almost immediately. Firstly, the rubbish pit is often mismanaged, and food waste overflows the bins, or is not buried properly, or burned as it should be. Where's the best place in camp to see porcupines, Spotted hyaenas, African badgers, Marabou storks, Pied crows (that often suddenly appear in swirling cacophonous clouds when camps are built, having seldom been seen there formerly) and Hooded vultures? Go straight to the pit. Secondly, the guests (and staff) do what all people do: they feed the animals and the birds. Who can resist dropping a crust or crumb or bacon rind for the cute little Familiar chat that flicks its wings and looks up at you with a cocked head and shiny, inquiring eyes? One lodge in the Caprivi Strip (Zambezi Region) of Namibia used to invite their guests to toss breakfast muffins – yes, muffins – to a crocodile that waited in the shallows below the dining deck. After a time, that croc started to haul itself out of the Kwando river and laze about on the manicured lawn, as close as it dared come to the muffin supply. And, since humans have been on the crocodile's menu ever since we made our appearance in Africa, we all know where that situation is heading to... Lastly, the staff members in their village at the back, the bit that is hidden from the guests' view behind a tall reed fence, are seldom much concerned about the environmental policies of the lodge. It is often a disappointing mess back there, empty cans of food and old bones littering the place, plastic bottles blowing about and cooking grates uncleaned. It's a picnic for scavengers, both birds and mammals.

So if you are a scavenger, be it bird or beast, insect or reptile, why wouldn't you take the easy option? It is always easier to get take-away food than to do one's own cooking. And they do.

I have guided in lodges where the managers in desperation have posted staff armed with BB guns to shoot at monkeys (they never hit them, and it seems to work... somewhat, but it feels weird having people shooting at monkeys while you're having breakfast) and in others where elephants, buffalos, lions and baboons that venture into camp by day are shot at with paintball guns. The great fear about wild animals in camp is that the guests might be injured. Obviously they are pre-warned not to approach animals at any time but even so they do some really stupid things, like selfie-stick poses with an elephant only metres behind them, or walking right up to a passing old buffalo bull as if it is a tame pasture cow. So a stinging pink paintball splotch to the flank of an animal can become the only solution.

But monkeys are a class apart. They are overt brazen thieves, and cunning to boot. They can plan and scheme and work things out. It's one thing to dash in while guests are dining and snatch a breakfast croissant from their very plate, or escape with an apple snatched from the afternoon tea buffet (and then sit not far away in a tree nonchalantly eating it and awaiting further opportunity), but at Old Mombo camp, the troop of Vervets there learned to undo the door zips of the tents. They only needed a small gap through which to squirm. Tugging on the zip toggles, they effected a small entrance and could, while the guests were out on activities, raid at leisure: plundering make-up bags, toiletry kits (they loved to eat the toothpaste), camera equipment, whatever lay about. They were perfectly *au fait* with luggage zips too, and had learned to pull them open. What treasures lay within! If rumbled by a housekeeper doing her rounds, and trapped in the tent, they would set up a fearful screeching, dashing wildly from one side of the tent to the other, swinging from the overhead fan, upsetting carafes of water, tearing at the curtains, and worst of all, shitting themselves in fear, leaving the linen besmirched. The housekeepers, afraid of the little pirates with their long canines and scratching claws, would call the managers. All we could do was to open the tent door zippers fully while the trapped monkeys wailed in terror, retreat as fast as possible, and watch them make their escape, but not without their booty: running on three limbs, a handful of camera memory sticks, specialised medications, contraceptive pills and various articles of clothing clutched to their chests. Then they would scamper up a shady jackalberry tree and examine their haul, biting on every piece to test its palatability, and discarding anything that could not provide sustenance. Many a time we retrieved watches, jewellery, passports (pulpy and bitten through) and bits of underwear from the prickly love grass that grew rank and horrible below the tree.

For a short while it was quite funny – "clever little fellows, so quick-witted, so *human*" – but soon they became a real trial, and they exasperated everyone in camp, staff and guests alike.

We tried putting realistic, life-sized rubber snakes in the tents. They scared the guests – my goodness, didn't they just scare the guests! – and the housekeepers more than they did the monkeys, which quickly realised that the snake never actually moved, and soon the monkeys were stealing the snakes, too.

We tried posting guards armed with sticks but, as soon as their patrol took them to one end of camp, the *bandar-log* flitted through the tree canopy to the other end and commenced raiding there instead.

We tested the monkey's intellect by fixing the zip toggles together with coils of wire, and we were triumphant for a while, but, within weeks, the Vervets had figured out how to unwind the 'monkey puzzle' and then they stole those, too.

They were driving us mental and taking up far too much of our time. Worse, they were now so deeply habituated and insouciant that they were becoming aggressive towards people, particularly women, and especially if we threatened them. They fought back! A Vervet monkey can be extremely intimidating at close range when it bares its yellow fangs at you and growls like a yard dog. It is a mistake to try to hang onto your bread roll with a Vervet attached to the other end of it. An accident was bound to happen.

We reluctantly turned to the final, fatal option. We would have to kill them. The solution had to be swift and as humane as possible. They'd have to be shot.

The conservation rationale was that, if we removed the entire troop (there were about 30 of them), we would have a respite, a monkey vacuum, and we could start again. We would have an opportunity to re-educate our staff and our guests, fix the rubbish pit, allow the monkeys to slowly re-populate but without the benefit of understanding that we were a source of easy food. There would be no monkeys to teach the others bad habits, no learned behaviour. A new beginning. Not good news for the current Vervets, of course, but we looked forward to welcoming a new band of well-behaved apes into Old Mombo.

We needed permission from the Department of Wildlife, and we needed a .22, a small calibre rifle that, well-aimed, could despatch a monkey mercifully and with little noise.

Rather to our surprise, we got both. We were probably not the first lodge to apply for this extreme measure. As the camp manager, Gary took charge of the shooting. With heavy heart, he set to. Timing was crucial: it had to be done quietly, when all the guests were out on game drive, and without a word of it getting out. We knew that some guests would understand the process (especially the ones who had recently had their passports stolen and mangled) but the majority would certainly not. It went against the grain, culling the wildlife inside a game reserve, especially when the issue was human-created. The whole operation needed to be conducted in secret. We debated shooting the troop at night, since they all gathered to roost in a few select trees come evening, but the rifle was not silenced (no shot must be heard by the guests) and it wouldn't do to simply wound them. No, it had to be done in broad daylight to be sure of our aim. It was an onerous task that needed to be done efficiently.

Vervet monkeys are the most successful and widespread apes in Africa because they're fast learners. Gary easily shot the very first one clean off the railing of the main deck as it sat casually gnawing on a stolen peach. The troop scattered in alarm, chattering madly, staring down at their fallen comrade in consternation and hiding behind the major branches of the jackalberry trees. A few that could not contain their curiosity and emerged to look more closely were easily despatched too. But after that they saw Gary coming every time. This new and deadly game made them cautious but even so they continued to raid the kitchen, the bar, the bins and the tents, only less boldly. It was important to kill each one outright and immediately. A wounded monkey would be intolerable, unprofessional and embarrassing, so Gary took no half chances, no fifty-fifty shots. But the Vervets simply could not stay away from the buffet so, each day, he would get one or two more. It was nasty, unpalatable work and it was taking far too long. Eventually, however, eventually, the troop was down to one.

The captain of the sinking ship – the big bull monkey with resplendent blue testicles and a gruff rattle-bark. The canny one. If Gary emerged from the lodge office with the rifle, he would disappear in a trice, but this was, after all, his territory, and he wasn't leaving. He had no place else to go. We deliberated about simply leaving him alone, we *wanted* to leave him alone, but we knew that monkeys, like humans, teach each other through demonstration, and this guy knew all the tricks. He wasn't strutting confidently along the railings in full view as he once did, glaring at us as we clapped our hands at him and not giving an inch, but he was still there. For several days he evaded us, but then his greed overcame him as brunch was being set up one late morning before the guests had returned from game drive. He hesitated over the fruit basket. It was his final mistake. And ours, the only one we made in the executions. Gary's shot took him in the chest; but it wasn't a kill shot. Instead of instantly dropping dead to the polished teak deck, he emitted a dreadful shriek and sprang up the tree that shaded the brunch table, right to the very top, where he perched in the apex, swaying slightly, gripping tight and in full view. Awaiting the final bullet.

Quickly, Gary moved to put him out of his misery but just as he raised the rifle, the first game drive car came rumbling into the lodge car park, full of guests chatting excitedly about lions, elephants, hippos and the glories of the African wilderness. The rifle was rapidly stashed in the office, and the happy tourists descended upon their brunch. The table had been set up on the teak deck... almost directly below the wounded monkey.

"Don't mention the monkey," we said in hushed tones to the waiter staff. "Don't even *look* at it."

A bright drop of blood splashed onto the deck. Without looking up, a waiter casually mopped it away. Another drop. More swabbing. The guests devoured breakfast, probably engrossed in animated conversation about how we took care of the land, how everything here just existed as it always has. There may have been talk around environmental ethics, or the natural balance of nature. Mention may even have been made about how pleasant it was that the damned monkeys were no longer bothering them in the tents during afternoon siesta, trampolining on the outer shade netting and keeping them from sleep. More scarlet drops of blood, faster now, and another surreptitious wipe by the waiter. The monkey swayed with closed eyes, its pale eyelids showing clear even at a distance. We managers grimaced and tried not to watch the Vervet. It was obvious that the guests were in no hurry to leave. Several of them ordered Bloody Marys and moved to the deck seating to compare their game drive photographs. The monkey above them clung on, silent and dying. More blood.

And then ever so slowly as the life ebbed from him, his head sank onto his chest, he loosened his grip, and he toppled gently from his perch. Straight down. Straight down onto the teak deck, landing with a nauseating wet thump, his crumpled and bloody corpse sliding to a stop directly in front of several guests enjoying a post-breakfast coffee.

A lady screamed and leaped to her feet, spilling cappuccino and staring in incredulity. A Bloody Mary found its way down the front of someone's shirt. There were startled yelps from a large man from whom you wouldn't have expected them, and an eager young fellow collected himself and reached for his camera. He was denied. With the greatest *sangfroid* the waiter, quite unaffected by the fuss, shouldered his rosy-tainted mop, grabbed the old bull monkey by the tail and dragged it across the deck leaving a bright bloody smear behind it, descended the staircase into the car park, the monkey's head banging and bobbling down each step, and without a word hauled the lifeless ape, its limbs spreadeagled behind it, around the corner and out of sight.

We gaped at the scene. The monkey was dead. *All* the monkeys were dead.

"What the *hell?*" gasped the big man. Cappuccino lady was vigorously fanning herself with a napkin, looking stunned.

"Yes, um, uh, monkeys, you see... " said Gary, trying to gain time, "they sometimes, uh, die, uh, when... when... " and then in a flash of inspiration, "when they get a fright. From snakes and things. Eagles. Probably a Martial eagle flew over and he saw it and he thought... " but his vapid explanation stumbled to a close, and he stood there looking perplexed, sweaty and embarrassed. And then in a rush "... but anyway, sorry about that, folks, everything's fine."

Not for the monkey it wasn't.

22

BAD CHEMISTRY

That guy, Stan, he got me good!

"Well played, sir!" I shouted to the aircraft – and I laughed. I know he was having a smirk to himself too. I still don't really understand the message he was sending, but I knew for certain the joke was on me.

The departing Cessna 210 that he was a passenger in had just skimmed over the Fan palms at the end of the Mombo airstrip, and with a high turbine scream had climbed into the light, thin air, leaving me coated in fine calcrete dust from the propeller wash.

When guides get tipped, they don't want it to be of the "Never run with scissors" and "Don't go swimming for an hour after lunch" and "It's a bad idea to look into the sun with binoculars" variety. Those kind of tips they get from Grandma. But a small wad of green United States dollars or some of those lovely pink Great British 50 pound notes... now we're talking! Guides are usually in the bush because it's their calling, but it's never a well-paid job. Usually, a lodge guide gets all board and accommodation thrown into the deal, and the uniform is typically free too – although the booze isn't; that'd be a mistake! – but even so, after the tax man has got involved, there's generally not much left over. And, therefore, tips are very welcome indeed.

It can be damned awkward, this tipping thing. Some nationalities are relaxed about it, most obviously the Americans, who seem content to tip even for poor service (see *Vanilla Guiding*). We guides love the Yanqui (as we affectionately call them). They're up front: "Hey buddy, great job, best time of our lives, here's some cash for you, ya gotta come and see us in Minnesota". The Brits are often embarrassed about it, and will sometimes leave the cash in an envelope with the camp manager or hide the money in the palm of their hand and present it to you in a clumsy handshake, mumbling "thank you" in a low, flustered voice. Israelis tend to be mean and hard-arsed about it, Australians mostly candid and generous, and Germans and Swiss are also usually open and munificent. With South Africans, you just never know: they either give you plenty or zero (primarily because they often think of themselves as bush people, even if they grew up in urban places like Benoni, Ballito or Boksburg. There's not a thing they don't know about the wilderness, or so they think. How do you know there's a South African on the Land Rover? He'll tell you! So why would Saffers pay the 'driver' to tell them things they already 'know'? Not always easy to have on a safari vehicle, especially if there are other nationalities on board that they can show off to. Bless them.)

Tipping. What is appropriate? How much is enough? How do you avoid giving offence by either tipping too little, or, nearly as bad, too much? And if you've been in the company of a guide who you discover is a bit of a Renaissance Man and knows much, much more about life than just the life cycle of an impala, a raconteur who has travelled to your own country and visited more of it's iconic places than you have yourself, who can talk sports and politics and music and movies and wine and books... well, in a few short days, you've become friends now, haven't you? And you don't tip your friends, do you? You sort of want to, you feel you should, but you don't quite know how to address the issue... and so it sometimes never happens. Which leaves the guide wondering if it all went okay, and if not, what was the problem? It can get a little weird.

But that's not quite what happened with Stan. We were never friends.

Stan was travelling alone through Botswana, visiting several camps. He was a pretty decent bloke, fairly reserved, very keen on photography, armed with a Canon EF 200-400 bazooka lens and a Manfrotto monopod. As a solo traveller who had not booked a private vehicle, he was grouped with two couples for his time at Mombo, and they all seemed to get on quite well. We were seeing fantastic animal sightings – lazy leopards languishing in leadwood trees, spiral-horned kudus posing high on termitaria, flights of egrets against a setting sun – and Stan was quietly but avidly capturing it all.

But for some reason Stan and I were just not amenable. He'd said nothing untoward to me, there were no apparent problems, certainly no frank exchange of views, all very civil, he was in good health... but the usual banter wasn't there, that indefinable feel-good factor that I wish we could capture in a bottle for re-use. Sometimes on safari, people don't gel. It happens. Rarely; but it happens.

At first I thought he was just shy, but I quickly realised that Stan was his own man, seemingly quite at ease, and perfectly respectful and polite. He was pleasant with the other guests and the staff, nothing more, but quietly assured. And he treated me with courtesy. But that feeling of congeniality just wasn't there. And I was not used to that. There are very few folk I can't get on with, with whom I cannot find some common ground, very few that I can't make smile and engage with at some level. So it was both confusing and troubling.

Chemistry. I never understood it at high school, and I did not understand it now.

The happy vibes were missing.

"What's up with you and Stan?" asked one of the tourists as we disembarked from the Land Cruiser one evening after a wonderful game drive.

I played dumb. "Why?" I asked.

"He doesn't seem to like you. What's that about?" the guest replied.

"Dunno," I said, shrugging.

Gosh, so it showed! Disappointing. Was it my style, my little jokes and stories? My accent? Did he feel that I was paying undue attention to the other folk on board? I was being very conscious of *not* doing that.

"Has he said anything to you?" I asked.

"Not at all. I mean, he's a bit of a strange fish, but he's nice. He just doesn't seem very relaxed with you."

Bad chemistry. That's all I could put it down to. You know how it is: sometimes, to your surprise, you just don't like someone. They're strangers, you are thrown together, it's hard to figure out why, but you just don't want to talk to them or be with them. Perhaps they're bland, or self-absorbed, or needy, or just plain annoying. They don't mean to be, and they'd be mortified if you told them how you feel about them.

So I accepted that I just needed to be as professional as possible. But I knew that Stan wouldn't be tipping me. Obviously, guides shouldn't be working for tips; they are never a true or consistent reflection of one's ability, and a very poor measure of one's worth. But they're nice, a random and pleasant bonus, a welcome addition to the Swarovski EL 50 fund, that gradual progression towards acquiring the best binoculars in the world.

So imagine my surprise at the Mombo airstrip on Stan's last day when he publicly and with a straight face handed me an envelope, a rather startlingly *fat* envelope, right in front of all the other guests, saying, "I got some great pictures," and squeezed into the Cessna. Just that. Not even a handshake.

But that was far more than I had been expecting. I felt exonerated, relieved, and happy.

We guides had a superstition at Mombo. That envelope burned a hole in your pocket, and you wondered how much was in there. How close were you to those Swarovskis? (Sometimes it was a thank-you note, or a sketch, or an invitation to visit, which could mean more by far than cash). But you had to discipline yourself not to open it until that little six-seater had taken off safely and dipped a wing towards its next destination. Then, only then, could you take a look. And sometimes it was a very nice surprise.

The Cessna dipped. I dusted myself down and polished my sunglasses. I extracted the bulky envelope from my shorts-pocket, and carefully tore it open along the top edge. It was thick with dollars. Packed. Pregnant with cash. I was gobsmacked. Well, I thought, it just goes to show, you think you know someone, eh?

I drew the wad of cash out. Thirty notes. Thirty of them! What? Wow! I counted them.

Singles. All singles. Thirty one-dollar United States bucks.

I grinned, and waved at the aircraft as it grew small over the Delta. I knew he couldn't but I really wished Stan could see me. An elegant riposte.

"Well played, sir," I shouted to the wind, laughing.

23

FIRST WORLD PROBLEMS

"I'm sending charcoal tablets on the next plane," said our safari company nurse to me over the two-way radio. "Tell her to take two immediately, keep drinking as much water as she can stomach, and stay close to the toilet." A pause, and then the radio crackled again. "And the boss says you have to say sorry to her."

Okay. That was the pre-emptive shot across the bows and very sound professional advice it was, too. But to my mind, nothing had really happened, there was no actual issue there. At the time, we all thought it was a bit of a laugh. We *did* laugh! She laughed too, the honeymoon lady. But then the thing spiralled towards hysteria and I was left shaking my head and in trouble with HQ once again.

There is an ongoing incredulity in safari lodges about what to our western guests constitutes real and present danger. We guides tend to grow up barefoot and bareheaded and with a blithe disregard to the dangers of the sun. Going a little bit hungry and little bit thirsty and little bit cold and a little bit dirty is not much of an issue. Our window of discomfort is pretty large. As a result, we can be rather blasé about some of the things that worry our guests, such as whether they can drink the tap water, the possibility of contracting malaria, animals wandering through camp, the safety and maintenance records of the Cessna light aircraft they have flown in on, whether the salad has been properly washed and is the goat's cheese organic, what the actual, exact temperature is at any given moment, flying insects and swirling dust, prickly thorns and clinging burrs. A guest once asked me what my cholesterol ratio was at a time before I even understood that there were different types of it, and was astounded that I showed no interest in knowing the numbers. It seemed to me that it was something I didn't need to be concerned about. I still don't know what it is.

Despite the fact that they are safely ensconced in a wilderness paradise, served hand and foot and in our constant care, many guests are afraid of Africa. Sometimes, of Africans too. Particularly black Africans. On more than one occasion a guest has told me that they are relieved that I am white and English speaking because they have never met an African before and don't know how to react to one. The so-called Dark Continent is threatening in itself for many; sometimes the guests express the misunderstanding that all of Africa is a continent permanently beset by viral diseases (think Ebola and HIV-AIDS), vicious dictators and Muslim extremists, and that these factors are a true danger to the guests' safety. We casually – too casually, as I have come to discover – dismiss these trepidations as 'First World Problems'. The thing is, though, that as guides it is necessary to understand that, although these fears are of little significance to us, they are disproportionately important to our clients. We tend to forget that.

We Africans also usually move to a more gentle beat in a simpler world less conflicted by the tyranny of too much choice, therefore we are not as likely to be frustrated by the pressures of constant comparison. We have lower expectations of personal safety, comfort and convenience. It's not such an issue for us if we can't find a parking space right in front of the store door, or if our favourite show isn't available in HD or if the internet download speed is slow. It is all a question of perspective. I spend a lot of time in the first world. I see how those societies operate in a climate of high-visibility jackets and emergency sirens, but I was raised in a place where there are real problems such as poverty, poor education, bad governance, and water scarcity. I am one of the fortunate Africans, of course: I grew up well fed, clothed, educated and loved, but I am constantly confronted by the gap between poverty and privilege. Rich people's crusts are a feast to the poor. Poor people have different fears.

What educated, pampered, middle-class people (that's you and me) consider life problems are really just the side effects of not having anything more important to worry about. It's a privilege to get lost in the maze of modern life with its non-essential goals and minor problems. Without recognising it, we lose our sense of adventure and we grow up in a culture of subliminal fear. We live predictably and we live slightly scared. We have the prospect of a long and comfortable life ahead of us and we have time to plan for it. (Most Africans would take that great fortune any day, of course). First worlders tend to place too much emphasis on the *possibility* of danger, in 'what if' thinking. (By the way, that fear of failure and pain is what makes them successful. They don't run out of diesel, for example. They're scared of that happening, so they plan ahead: see *I Never Went For The School).* It's not that Africans are never scared; it's that they are scared of life-altering things, like drought and floods and baboons raiding their crops. Where a typical African villager, such as your safari lodge guide, will simply ignore discomfort and a surprising degree of pain (they have a deep and abiding faith in the tenet that 'all things must pass'), first worlders come from a coddled society. The difference is, in Africa, when the shit hits the fan, the real shit, we don't duck, we just wipe it off. Because there's more coming.

Take flat tyres for example. They happen all the time on safari. For the guide it is situation normal. You just get out, jack the car up, wrestle the flat tyre off and the spare one on, tighten the lug nuts, make a short pretence of dusting off (it's only dirt, none of that silly hand gel, thank you), and off you go. But for many guests it is a heart-stopping moment on safari. Many of them are genuinely scared. Not so much because there are wild animals about and they're off the car (some actually refuse to disembark, mind you) while the flat is being replaced but because this is the first time in their lives that they have ever even had a flat. They are bewildered. It is new territory for them. It was only when I bought a car in the UK and found that there was no spare tyre, no jack, no wheel spanner at all ("Oh no, sir, that's extra. But why do you want them?") that I discovered that if your car stops or if you get a puncture, you just call the AA and they come out and do it all for you. But there's no AA out in the Okavango Delta or the deserts of Namibia, and often no cell phone signal either, and it troubles people. It is an ingrained imaginary fear – there's no actual danger. And it is easy to become impatient with this attitude as a guide. It took me a long time to understand it.

But understand it we guides must. We may find the developed 'nanny states' of the first world just too regulated and safe and driven by a constant barrage of safety announcements about untended packages in public places, life guards, parking regulations, speed limits, CCTV cameras, fences, gates and barriers. We may think that there is such a thing as "too safe" and that life without a little edge takes the gilt off it. But we have to understand that there are significant benefits to severe regulation, especially in overpopulated countries, where there is no alternative if law and order is to prevail in a tight space. I find it interesting that public regulations in the UK are maintained chiefly not by the threat of police action but by the populace themselves: if you stop your car in the bike box at a traffic light, someone is going to tell you off, and if you mix your recycling your neighbour will probably (very politely) explain that it is simply not on. The implication when you cycle on the sidewalk and a stranger wags a finger at you, or if you put your stockinged feet on the train seat and the passenger next to you tut-tuts, is that you are an inconvenience and a nuisance and that you need to improve your social behaviour. It's both remarkable and impressive. We Africans tend to resist being told what to do, especially by our peers. We joke that we don't mind having the rules, but they are only a general guideline, that the red light on a traffic signal means 'go' and that the green one means 'go faster'. We chafe against regulations, and we regularly question their existence. Or ignore them.

Our approach to life isn't better, it's just different. A grazed knee elicits absolutely no attention, the solution to a headache is to drink more water, if you swam in the deep end and panic a little it is presumed that you have learned a lesson, and we're not that fussed about having regular mealtimes with a balanced diet of fats, proteins and carbohydrates (plus vitamins and mineral supplements).

In Richmond Park in London there are countless signs that warn against the dangers of the Oak Processionary caterpillar. Caterpillars! We kept caterpillars as pets. There are other warnings about Lyme's Disease, contracted via deer-borne ticks. Hell, I had tickbite fever as a five-year old, but here I am still. No-one wants Lyme's, it is bloody nasty, but seriously, if you're going to get it you will have to try very, very hard. I can't really take those warnings seriously – I find them patronising, but a poll of park users will show that people appreciate them and want them. Still, I'm happy to take my chances. Leave me alone!

You see what I'm driving at: the fear is imposed. But that doesn't mean it doesn't exist in the mind of the afraid. And until a guide understands the first world norm, he is apt to scoff at it. The safe and regulated world feels stultifying if you grew up wild and free in the era of no seatbelts and bicycle helmets and air conditioners carefully regulated to 21 degrees celsius. But if you didn't grow up as I did, well, I get it, our attitude can come across as a bit irresponsible and reckless. Worse, it can seem unsympathetic and even callous.

Which is why I got into trouble. The old Mombo camp was a wonderfully simple place. It has changed now, suffering a massive upgrade, and the air conditioners and plunge pools and gym and exceptional cuisine and elevated decks have become as important as the game viewing, but back then the camp ran on a hope and a prayer, and everyone loved it.

Every safari day concluded at the fire, and the ambience of a glass of wine and the soaring sparks under a cold bright sky never grew old. It was a time for the telling of stories at the settling of the day, a time to sit and grow drowsy as the night owls called and hope that a lion would suddenly start his booming roar across the floodplain. It was a time when the paraffin lanterns started to splutter and blacken their glasses, and when at last we humans, those most sociable and garrulous of creatures, tended to talk a little more softly as the crickets chorused and personal reflection took hold. It was a time when we could pay attention to our space and place, before the advent of the new social drug known as "blue-face"– the illuminated visage of folk on their mobile phones.

The lady from tent six, the honeymooner, reached down into the dark around the base of her chair, feeling for the plastic water bottle she had been sipping from. They were such a lovely couple, she and her husband, at Mombo for what we felt were the right reasons: wildlife. There was no silly fussing about bugs and bats and things that go bump in the night, just a comfortable contentment and an apparent pleasure in being in the company of us guides and managers. We always responded warmly to these kind of guests. Easy going, keen. Kindred spirits.

She raised the bottle to her lips and took a drink. A deep swallow. Then another. Suddenly she lunged forward towards the fire, gagging, the second mouthful spewing from her in a stream, soaking into the sand-filled tray that supported the log fire.

"Aagh! God! What is this? It's disgusting!" she shouted, retching and coughing.

No-one knew what was going on. She leapt to her feet, the director's chair crashing over behind her, holding the bottle at arms length, glaring at it suspiciously. We were all on our feet now, confused, alarmed, her husband trying to comfort her, but she shrugged his hand off angrily.

"What is this?" she yelled again, spitting repeatedly into the fire.

I took the bottle from her while her husband guided her to a nearby bench. A greasy feel to the plastic. I sniffed at the mouth of the bottle. Oh, shit! Paraffin! She's just taken two bloody great swigs of paraffin! What? *How*? I flashed my torch into the darkness where her chair had been. There was her bottle of water still, the lid fastened. Realisation set in.

Dammit man, Precise, how often have I told you not to do this? When you make the evening fire, I'm not expecting you to rub two sticks together like the Ancients and create flames from scratch, but you do not need to soak the wood in half a litre of paraffin to get the conflagration going. A small fire made from dry *Acacia* wood is adequate. But no. Precise has cheated again and used the lantern fuel to hurry the job. Not only that but he has saved some paraffin for tomorrow morning's fire in a disposable water bottle, and hidden the bottle just under the sand tray, right there where the guests sit.

I showed the lady what had happened. She'd finished gagging by now, and was washing her mouth out with water. Real water. With relief I noticed that she was smiling, and her husband was chiding her in a good natured way, how could you do that, I can't believe you did that, how on earth did you manage not one but *two* swallows of that stuff?

A bit of a laugh. Could happen to anybody. I told everyone how my uncle's favourite party trick was to hold paraffin in his mouth and spit it out onto a flaming match, creating a great ball of yellow fire, eliciting gasps of admiration from us kids and some disapproving clucking from a few older family members. In other words, a little paraffin won't hurt you. Time for bed. It all seemed okay.

But it wasn't okay the next morning. When I went at dawn to do the wake-up ("knock knock, good morning, time for game drive, see you at the deck for coffee"), there was a growl from tent six.

"There's a problem here, buddy." A very menacing tone. "My wife has been up all night with diarrhoea. She needs help." The guy was obviously under severe pressure.

"Okay," I said. "The best thing to do is, you guys just chill in camp this morning. This will pass. Drink plenty of water. I've got to go on game drive now but what else do you need? I'll ask the duty manager to check regularly on you throughout the morning."

I mean, what else do you do if you swallow paraffin, I thought. You lie down and it sorts itself out and then you get up again. Right?

"You're going to have to do a hell of a lot better than that, pal!" he replied. "She's been poisoned. We need meds." A pill for every ill.

"Medication? Sure, we have anti-diarrhoea stuff but apart from that, there's nothing else to do. Time. Just takes time. When my uncle swallowed some by mistake, he just drank beer!"

Not funny.

"We need a doctor."

First World Problem needs First World Solution. I was suddenly waking to this. Nothing's really happened, to my mind, but it's serious nonetheless.

"Right. Okay. I'll get the duty manager to radio Maun when the town office opens at eight and get the company nurse involved. No problem."

Backtracking. Not fast enough. And not enough empathy.

"Now. Radio her *now!*"

Whoa, that nice guy from last evening had disappeared. He really was under a *lot* of pressure here. Weak groans from within the dark tent. No 911 calls, no ambulance with rotating red lights out here, no white-coated doctor to pat your hand and say, "Take it easy, drink water, you'll be just fine."

"Okay, we have an emergency channel. I've got to go on game drive, the other guests are waiting, but the duty manager will get straight onto this, uh, emergency. I'm on it."

Which is how the very first incoming flight of the morning was carrying charcoal tablets. It seems counter-intuitive to ingest charcoal but it soaks up the toxins and is harmless to the system. And apparently they worked because, by afternoon game drive time, that honeymoon couple was back on form, chatting away and eating with tremendous appetite. Amazing what a little charcoal and hand holding can do.

And a well-timed, genuine, yet slightly obsequious apology.

24

THE SAND SAMARITAN

He never once spoke a word. It was surreal. The Sand Samaritan drifted in out of the wide open desert, changed the tyre, and walked off without looking back. Heading west, over the golden dunes towards the cold and distant sea. West, where no-one lives.

He wasn't even a Himba man. Those hardy people of Namibia's untamed north-west wilderness are nowhere prevalent but if you are going to encounter some local folk up there in that vast, wild space, you'd expect it to be a young man in a blanket minding his goats, a dark-skinned Himba, gazing without much interest as you roll by in your Toyota Hilux in a cloud of dust, the windows of the *bakkie* rolled up, the air conditioning on high and two spare tyres on the roof.

Two spares. Not one. The desert tracks are hard on a Dunlop, with flinty-edged rocks, and ruts that shake the sunglasses from your face, even with softer tyres running below one bar of pressure, and the saying goes that if you take two spares you'll not have a flat but if you only take one, you'll puncture twice. Murphy's Law, whoever he was. Oh, and don't forget the twelve-volt tyre compressor. No point in repeating the *Dunedin Star* disaster (see glossary).

No, this guy was a yellow man, a Nama, I think. They live mostly in the south of the country, but this fellow must have come from the Sesfontein area, where a tribal off-shoot have long resided. Even so, he was a very long way from home, and on foot, too. I tried to pay him as he was leaving but all he would accept was half a bottle of tepid water. He took it without a change in expression, drained it, and casually let the plastic bottle drop to the sand. I clucked my tongue, picked it up and when I looked again, he was walking away. Heading west. But not lost.

Andre Agassi, the American who won eight tennis Grand Slams, wrote that the loneliest place in the world is on the court. Just you and your tennis racquet and the baying crowd. He says he always felt alone, and utterly lost. He's from the desert too, Las Vegas, an oasis resort, but he obviously never broke down in a desolate place like north-western Namibia with only the cobalt sky and a quiet wind to keep him company. *That's* lonely.

This flat tyre had announced itself with a sudden hiss of air as the tyre-wall split and the air gushed out like the breath of a furious snake. I was alone, driving from Skeleton Coast Camp to the new Serra Cafema Camp on the Kunene river, the northern border with Angola. In those days, before a train of supply trucks created a wide and ugly meandering scar, the route was difficult to find, especially for a first timer. Chris Bakkes, who guided at SCC, had drawn me a rough map, literally on the back of an envelope, just as I was leaving.

"Head north, *ou maat*," he directed. "Don't worry about how far it is, it depends what route you take, they all end up at the Kunene river. It's going to take all day. Just head up the Khumib river, turn into the Rock Garden and after the spring you join the main track for Orupembe. But then you must look for a stick in the ground next to the road after the big sweeping right hand bend where the track starts to go through some drainage lines. I put it there a few months ago. Maybe its still there, who knows. Turn left."

I was nervous and I hoped it didn't show. I had two spares and a full tank of diesel but no satellite phone. We didn't have them then, and anyway that would have been a bit soft. But being lost is one of the scariest of human emotions. Ask any child at a fun fair whose parent has let go of its hand for a moment to pay for the candy floss and when the kid looks around, all it can see is a mass of tall people, not one of which is their father or mother. It is terrifying.

"*Ja*, and then you just look for this hill," Chris continued, pointing at the grubby paper. "It's a pimple from the south but pass it on the right after a few hours and it will get bigger and change shape and look like... this," he said reassuringly, sketching rapidly on the envelope. "And when you come to Green Drum, stay left. Straight up the Hartman's Valley. When you get near the river, you'll see Land Rover tracks to the camp. *Hou Noord en fok voort!* You can't miss it."

Oh, really? This from a guy who used to welcome his guests to camp with a cheery, "Welcome to Hell!"

But he was right. North, north, ever north, towards the winter solstice sun, and the landscape flowed slowly by, dunes to my left, small herds of grazing springboks, a few desert giraffes chewing the cud in the paltry shade of stunted *acacias*, and the promised mountain gradually changing shape to a gable as I drew nearer. That wonderful sense of adventure, the anticipation of new ground, of feeling like a pioneer, and a little fear of the unknown: a heady and welcome thrill. It's not for everyone. The whole day lay ahead, and the whole day was mine.

Then the left front tyre blew.

I wasn't lost. Not exactly. I didn't quite know where I was, but that's not the same thing. And anyway, I'd been lost often enough before. With safari guests on board, too. This time I was under no pressure.

Every guide gets lost. It is the nature of a safari guide to explore, but it's the last thing the guests who accompany you on a drive or a walk want to hear. So we don't tell them. We fake it till we make it. You don't have to know where you are to know where you're going to end up. Our clients come from a world of satellite navigation, instant access to that reassuring pulsing blue spot on their watch or smart phone or laptop screen. Their world, their values are about predictability and total safety. There's no edge, and they don't welcome it. The feeling of being lost strikes at the fundamental human craving for security;

nothing creates panic as rapidly as the knowledge that you do not know where you are. The guests depend on us guides to know the way (the clue lies in the name: guide!), to be perfectly confident of our position at all times, to be able to predict exactly when we will be back at camp. Of course, we can never be entirely accurate about timings (my standard response to, "How long before we get back to camp?" is "twenty minutes", a number that is not too soon yet not too long, and seems to answer most of the time). Even if we are not sure exactly, we know we will always get home, so we make it up. The guests always joke with slightly bitter humour about "African minutes, African miles" when we actually do get back to camp after perhaps 40 minutes instead of twenty, but I always tell them that I hadn't built into the equation the fact that I would find them a leopard on the way home. "That's how good I am," I tell them, and all is forgiven over the first gin and tonic of the evening.

We new rangers at Mala Mala Game reserve in South Africa used to get lost in the darkness all the time. There were a myriad roads out there. We would follow lions on the hunt into the darkness as long as we dared to, waiting for the head ranger's warning voice on the radio ordering us home (to the guests' chagrin – "We're here to see wildlife, not eat bloody dinner!" – they would complain, entirely reasonably) and having penetrated deep off-road into a block of land, it was usually our trackers with their spotlights that showed us the way out of the bush. The guests never recognised that the Shangaan man on the back who had been there year after year was flashing his light in the direction we rangers should drive, and our arrival back at camp was inevitably greeted with a chorus of, "Well, that was amazing, I don't know how on earth you find your way. *Incredible!*" What they didn't realise was that most of us got lost in the cities, driving around in endless circles, and quite regularly failed to find our vehicles in multi-story carparks. Different skills.

One late afternoon I responded to a Mala Mala leopard sighting west of Mlowathi dam in a heavily wooded area riven by drainage lines and small *dongas*. I was the last vehicle into the sighting. All the other rangers were leaving by the time I had located their Land Rovers by the sound of their engines as they forced their way over fallen trees and through thorn scrub. But it was my guest Bruce's last game drive and his first leopard, that jewel of the bush, the one that everyone wants to see. The one that Mala Mala has staked its very reputation on. My tracker, Simeon, shook his head warningly and pointed at his watch. I ignored him and followed the leopard, a petite young female, totally relaxed, quite okay with the sound of the engine and the crashing of the moving car. She took us into increasingly heavy bush until I could follow no longer. The sun had set. Time to get out of there. Find a road.

But focusing on the leopard while wrestling the heavy vehicle over tough terrain had completely disarranged my sense of direction. The trees were dense and tall and the light was fading rapidly. I couldn't see the setting sun so I had no idea where west was. No problem though, I had Simeon. I looked at him, trying not to let Bruce see me asking for help. Simeon shrugged. What? I thought, you're the flipping tracker Simeon, *you're* supposed to know! But Simeon was from Kirkman's Kamp in the deep south of the reserve; we had travelled far for this leopard, and this wasn't his area.

There's one thing you don't do as a ranger: you don't call for help. If you get stuck, you dig yourself out. If you get lost, you figure it out. It is *always* too soon to panic. It's not a good look. So I tried to retrace my incoming vehicle tracks as the light deteriorated, keeping up a lively conversation about the leopard and her history: her mother, where born, her territory, her favourite prey, which male leopard she had mated with. This didn't help my concentration. As I turned to talk to Bruce, I would glance at Simeon. Blank look. Shit. It was getting very dark. I switched the headlights on. Simeon's spotlight began to stab and search into the darkness.

We nosed through yet another *donga*, around a clump of bush, and came to a massive *Marula* tree. Dammit. We'd driven past that exact tree fifteen minutes before. Growing on the same funny shaped termite mound. Bruce had been quiet for some time. Now he asked:

"How long to camp?"

"Twenty minutes... to the road. Then straight to camp," I said with authority.

We smashed on. After a while we came out of another gully and... oh bugger, hang on, it's the same tree!

"Hey, um, Lloyd, didn't we stop next to this tree a while ago?" asked Bruce. Perceptive guy: most guests are lost from the moment we leave camp.

The game was up. Right, next strategy: full disclosure.

"Yes," I said quickly. "Same tree. Um, okay, actually, right now we are lost!" Then quickly, "But not to worry, I'm just going to climb that tree. We're back here because it's the tallest in the area. I know this tree." (This was a lie.) "I need to see the stars. As soon as I see the Southern Cross, I'll know in which direction to head, and then we'll be out of here in no time." (This I believed to be true.)

I was glad I couldn't see his face. Clambering from the highest tier of seats, I hauled myself into the tree, and there she was, Scorpius in all her welcome glory. As surely as she guided the early Portuguese navigators all the way down the west coast of Africa, she could guide me back to camp. Now I knew exactly which way to head to get to the nearest road, and it wasn't far, I was sure, just a few hundred metres. But as soon as I started to take the tortuous route around scrub patches and through drainage lines, I lost the constellation again under the tree canopy. Luckily, now that he was in on the secret, Bruce was in pretty good humour, joining in the spirit of adventure, anxious yet at the same time rather amused at my discomfort.

We came to the tree again.

"Ever read A.A. Milne? Pooh Bear tracking the heffalump," asked Bruce, now enjoying this immensely. Dammit, dammit, dammit, I thought. I'm going to have to use the radio. Dammit.

"62 Tony, do you copy?" I said quietly into the microphone. Tony had been the previous ranger at the sighting and was likely to be in the general area still. Or so I hoped.

"Go, 46. Having a little trouble?" replied Tony. He wasn't even *trying* to hide the glee in his voice. Dammit again. He'd been waiting for this call. He hadn't gone far. Probably stopped for sundowners at Mlowathi dam, his eager ear to the radio.

"62, are you still in the area? I need a rev and a light."

This was how we found each other in thick bush. We'd switch off, listen to another car gunning its engine, and make our way towards the noise. Or, at night, the other car's tracker would shine his spotlight upwards, sending a great white column of light into the sky, clear and obvious, a homing beacon in the gloom.

"Okay, quiet Bruce. Listen, please," I said.

Bruce immediately grasped the plan. And the reassuring sound of a Land Rover engine filtered through the foliage. Not too far away.

"Copied 62, thanks," I said, and started to drive my vehicle through the bush towards Tony's car. His light soon became obvious and to my intense embarrassment, as soon as he saw our rescuer, Bruce began to whoop. Even Simeon chuckled.

"Any time, 46. Mine's a Jack and Black." It was going to be an expensive night at the bar.

But when the left front tyre blew on a hot desert day in the Namib desert, I wasn't lost exactly, and I didn't need help. I had no guests with me, and I had time. I opened a bottle of water, took a long swig, and began to prepare to change the tyre. Spare tyre off the roof. Hi-lift jack off its cradle. Hand brake up. Loosen the lug nuts on the wheel.

And then the Sand Samaritan arrived. I was sitting sweating on the shady side of the vehicle, quietly thinking about where to put the lug nuts so that they wouldn't get sand on them, when like a pale ghost, he walked around the front of the car. I didn't even get a fright. He just came quietly and with purpose and took the wheel spanner from my hand.

"Hello," I said, perplexed.

He waved one hand at me, settled the jack in its slot, clicked in the pin, and began to lever the car up. He knew exactly what he was doing. I got up and looked around, fully expecting to see a flock of goats, a herd of cows, a travelling band of Himbas filing by. There was nothing. Absolutely no-one. Only the little desert whirlwinds and an endless expanse of waving, white-plumed Bushman grass. The yellow man pulled the flat tyre off the wheel hub and began to wrestle the spare on.

"Where did you come from?" I said, this time in Afrikaans, handing him the lug nuts.

Again, he waved vaguely, indicating somewhere between... here and... there. He worked on, efficiently. He dropped the car off the jack and began to wrench the nuts tighter now that the new wheel was anchored on the ground.

"I can do this, actually," I said, slightly embarrassed and deeply bemused. He looked at me, his eyes narrow, his face a mass of sun wrinkles. Carefully, he placed the wheel spanner on the road verge next to me, and rose. The work was done.

"Can I pay you?" I asked, in English, since Afrikaans didn't seem to be working. He made the sign of a smoker, except that he cupped his hand around the imaginary cigarette. *Dagga*, he was saying.

"I don't smoke," I said. "Sorry, man."

He pointed at the water in my hand. I gave it to him. He drained it, dropped the bottle, and walked away. I watched him go, heading for the waterless expanse of the Namib dune belt. He had no luggage. He had no shoes, or a hat. He seemed to have no needs at all. I packed up the car, fastened the flat tyre onto the roof-rack, replaced the hi-lift jack. When I looked again for the little yellow man, he was gone. I drove, wonderingly, north, as if in a dream that kept slipping away on waking. Where was he going? What was he going to do there? Why did he stop to help me?

The Sand Samaritan. Simply heading west. Not lost.

25

TAKE OFF, TAKE TWO

A single bead of sweat crept from beneath his peaked cap, made its way around the Bose earphones he was wearing, and continued down into the beard-stubble on his tightly-clenched jaw.

"Right, people, let's try that again, shall we?" the pilot said.

He was scared – he had to be – but it didn't show. Boy, this is going to be a brilliant story at the pilots' digs tonight, he was thinking. That was close!

I prised my pressure-white fingers from the dashboard, swallowed hard, and turned to look at the passengers. Wide-eyed and startled like me, hard-gripping the seat in front of them, not quite sure what had just happened.

With Gazza the Camel Guy, who had arranged the logistics for the trip, I had been walking with Charly and Lili in the Namib desert again, this time on a journey through the Palmwag Concession in north-western Namibia all the way to the Uniab delta, using the SRT (Save the Rhino Trust) patrol camels as our beasts of burden. They carried everything we needed: personal kit, food, water and camping equipment. Also among the retinue were a donkey, ridden by a senior SRT representative, and his dog, a scabrous old mutt, tough as nails, that looked like it was in the throes of scurvy. A typical kraal dog, mainly cock and ribs, scavenging for itself and wolfing down the odd casually discarded piece of gristle. The dog and donkey's primary job was to warn us of lions. Desert-adapted lions are nowhere common in that arid terrain, but they can pop up anywhere, and in an environment where food is hard to come by, a camel is a juicy option. Donkeys and dogs seem to be able to sense that lions are about, especially at night when the felines are on the prowl, so they are a pretty reliable early warning system (unless they also fall prey, which sometimes happened. Lions are clever too). Our week-long walk doubled as a rhino monitoring foray so several SRT men were there to assist us as camp-hands, cooks, camel drivers and to record any rhino activity they noticed: tracks, dung, more excitingly, actual live Black rhinoceroses. The money Charly had paid for this experience went straight to SRT to help them in their ongoing efforts in the conservation of the desert-adapted Black rhinos of Namibia.

But that section of the walking trip was now over and we were headed for Serra Cafema Camp up on the Kunene river for a little bit of luxury and some gentle day excursions. Easy going after the barren coastal plains and freezing fog closer to the Atlantic's Benguela Current. Nothing to threaten us up there. Well, except for the crocodiles, obviously. Which also eat dogs. And people. Willingly. But we'd be fine: our walking at Cafema would be among quartz-glittered mountains and through the yielding sands on the southern bank, not along the very edges of that water-worn wild river.

No; danger lay elsewhere. Long before we reached Cafema, as it turned out. Cows were the problem. They can be as lethal as crocs or lions. Not everyone knows that.

Camel Gazza dropped us around noon at the village of Purros. There's not much there: a shabby campsite, scattered tin shacks, some goat pens, a gaily painted school room donated by Wilderness Safaris (who managed the Palmwag Concession), the inevitable liquor store with a mountain of empty beer bottles shamelessly piled in broken ruin next to it, and occasional Himba villagers, the women mostly in traditional goat-leather clothing, their orange skins plastered in butterfat and ochre, lazing in the shade of stunted *Mopane* trees. Very little happens in Purros until the Hoaruseb river comes down in spate, at which time the young men of the village make some cash by helping to drag stranded tourists and their rented cars out of the muddy torrent. The same muddy torrent that they have only minutes before assured them is safe to cross. Naturally.

But they did have a handy airstrip there. It wasn't quite 'Purros International' but it was used off and on for years by the old bush pilots of the Namib. Just a dusty dirt strip on the southern bank of the Hoaruseb, it's south-western end abutting the village, bright green *Salvadora* Mustard bushes delineating its left hand edge as you took off towards the inland mountains, and a faded, tattered orange windsock bearing the logo 'Continental' about halfway down the runway.

The Cessna 206 bush plane is one of the most reliable and toughest aircraft ever produced. These days it has largely been replaced by the roomier 208 Caravan which carries more people and in greater comfort, but even now the 206 is still a workhorse of the safari industry and has over the years carried millions of bush lovers and their over-stuffed bags into remote places, bumping down on challenging landing grounds all over Africa in the harshest of weather conditions. When you travel on a 206, you know you are actually flying. It's not an easy aircraft to get into, especially for large people: there's no leg room, the air vents breathe rather than blow, the seats are narrow and the ceiling is low. Also, it tends to lurch around the sky like a puppet on a string on hot days. It's a bugger if you get the back seat because it reclines at a nasty angle that affords a view only of the passing clouds, and the fresh vegetables for the lodge are definitely going to end up on your lap. But it always works, it always gets you there, it doesn't break down and it's a hell of a lot better than walking. I love them: I feel like they are part of the adventure of safari, and the pilots seem to be having fun when they drive them around in the Big Blue.

On this particular warm May day, Camel Gazza got us nice and early to the Purros strip, and we waited in the shade of the Land

Rover, sipping iced water from the 12-volt vehicle fridge, listening for the telltale drone of an approaching aircraft. There were plenty of Windhoek Lagers in the fridge, which Gary had offered us, but we were anticipating some of those on a sundowner cruise on the Kunene later in the day, so it was just water and fruit juice for now. Anyway, you have to plan your liquid intake when bush flying; there's no toilet on a 206 so you just have to hang on grimly, and a bursting bladder is a particular kind of pain best avoided. Bokmakierie shrikes were still calling despite the lateness of the day, and looking towards the southeast from where I expected the chartered aircraft to appear, I could see other denizens of the air circling up there: a Blackchested snake eagle searching for reptiles, and, thermaling much higher, the larger shape of the giant desert vulture, the Lappet-faced. Gazza handed out nuts and energy bars, and we read our books, wrote up travel journals and talked a little about those incredible camels, how they had walked for a week without drinking at all, turning up their noses at perfectly potable spring water, yet consuming vast quantities of brackish lagoon water when they reached the coast.

Perfectly on time, as always, the little Cessna appeared, at first just a distant bumblebee hum, then a black midge flying low and fast over the grassy plain, then a fixed-wing bird in its white and blue livery, rocking its wings as it passed overhead, scanning the landing area, then lining up its approach and touching down in a rush, dust boiling up from the fixed tripod of wheels, the engine changing note as the pilot drained off the power and ran the plane down the runway, down the slope and out of our sight. He taxied back towards us, cut the engine, leaped nimbly out and doffed his cap.

"Hello everybody! The camel walkers, I presume?" he said, jauntily. "See any rhinos out there?" Sprightly lad, mid-twenties, keen as mustard. Simon. He'd flown us into Palmwag a week before. We liked his energy and his obvious delight in flying.

Our bags were ready for loading into the under-belly pod, and Gazza and I carried them to the Cessna. Simon, sitting on his backside in the white dust, manipulated them into the pod, shoving with his feet and pummelling them with his fist, forcing the cumbersome things past the annoying dust flange.

"Worst part of the job," said Simon with a grin. "When I'm piloting an Airbus one day, someone else will be handling the luggage."

He gathered us in the shade of the wing for the pre-flight briefing, brandishing a map.

"Okay guys, listen up quickly. You've done this before but I'm going through it again; standard procedure."

He explained the route too, tracing it on the map with a finger, then added:

"This is a bit of a tricky airstrip. It's got a bump in the middle, and it's rather short. Rather unique, actually. You probably noticed how I dipped out of sight on landing down the far end there? It's hot and we are loaded full so I will need the whole runway to get airborne. Don't be alarmed, I've done this before, but we're going to take off twice."

He smiled. We frowned. This obviously wasn't the first time he'd used that line, and he relished our reaction.

"We'll go off as fast as possible as I let the brakes go and then we'll get up for a little while off the bump, but we won't be going fast enough to stay up. So we'll land again, keep rolling and then I'll bring her up at the end of the strip. No problem."

I'd never used the Purros strip before and I couldn't quite tell just how much Simon was kidding. But passengers tend to be a little nervous in small planes and the pilots don't mess with their heads where safety is concerned, so affecting nonchalance (and I did trust the pilots' skills implicitly), I said:

"Great, thanks Simon. Cool. Okay everyone, let's get aboard. Serra Cafema awaits!"

I clambered in next to Simon in the right hand (co-pilot's) seat. Gazza stood beside the Landy, shielding his face from the prop wash, waving. Simon gunned the engine with brakes on lock, turned to check we were buckled up, gave us a thumbs-up, then let go. We shot down the runway, the engine howling as the propeller gripped at the thin noon air, and just as foretold, went airborne off the bump.

Trouble!

Across the runway, right about where we were due to land again, stood a small herd of cows. They hadn't been there when Simon landed so in the short time while we were loading they had wandered in from the river and were trailing across the runway towards better grazing. As time warped to slow motion, I noticed a horrified herder, a young boy, his blankets flying about him, still running down the strip-edge in the direction of the Land Rover, his animal prod-stick swinging from his hand, still hoping to warn us, but still below the ridge and out of sight off the start threshold.

I instinctively grabbed the dashboard lip to brace myself, not the brightest move in the event of a crash as my straightened arms would probably have been broken… but no crash came. And it wasn't because of a miracle. As cool as you like, with the Cessna gliding down but still under full power, Simon tipped the port wing up over a few cows, levelled the plane, flicked the starboard wing over some others, thumped the plane down, bounced it once, killed the engine, hammered the brakes, and we shot off the end of the runway, crossing a narrow road as rutted as a cheese grater, and came to sudden halt, our bodies jerking forward in the harnesses.

A short stunned silence descended. I looked at Simon. That single drop of sweat slowly descended past his ear. I looked back. Charly and Lili were sitting rigid, horrified. They hadn't seen the cows at first, seated as they were, low down in the back seats of the plane, but they'd certainly seen them flashing past their windows, right *here*, right under the wing, and felt the wild ride off the runway. They were old hands at this safari lark and had taken off from African dirt strips a thousand times before, but this was something new.

"Right, people, let's try that again, shall we? Lucky they weren't elephants, hey!" said Simon, calm and professional as you'd hope. Cool hand Luke. "We'll go for a record today, I think. Two take-offs, twice!"

No-one said a word. Simon fired up the engine, spun the plane around, and drove us slowly back up the runway. The herder had regathered his wits and was chasing the cows into the hills as fast as he could make them go. He turned and watched us taxi by, making a small apologetic gesture, a shrug and flap of the hand, nothing more.

As we crested the hump, we saw Camel Gazza still standing next to the car. He couldn't see the herd of cows, hidden away beyond the rise, but hadn't moved until he could figure out what had become of us. Simon spun the Cessna around at the top of the runway, stopped it, and called Gazza over to the little side window of the cockpit. Yelling above the din of the engine, he asked him to drive down to the hump to check for more cows. (Or elephants). Gazza mouthed "Okay," ducked under the wing, waved at us inside the cramped cockpit, and started to move towards the Land Rover.

"Wait!" shouted Charly very loudly through the perspex window at him, pointing at the car. "Just a minute. NOW I take a beer!"

26

GLYSSPS, OR MARTHAMBLES?

I shouldn't have done it. Not that particular day. I was just showing off to make a point, as I'd done a hundred times before. I drank the water.

The thing is, it's *good* water. The Namibian desert has plenty of sweet surface water that creeps through the rock and sand for millennia, and then seeps gently from the earth, creating a flush of vegetation that sustains wildlife of all descriptions. The old people, the wandering hunter-gatherers, and later on the tribal settlers, depended on these sources, as the animals still do today. Indeed, life in this arid place would be impossible without the springs. But you have to know where they are. Where the sweet waters are. Desert-adapted Black rhinos do. That's why we were there. We wanted to see one.

But now I was feeling pretty sorry for myself. Despite my humiliation and embarrassment, I felt even sorrier for Pastor, our guide. He'd dealt with many tricky safari situations before, but this one was unique. The guests and I were vomiting every few minutes and sometimes frantically scrambling down, almost hurling ourselves from the game drive car to squat behind it, leaving behind a hell of a mess on the road.

And, in my case, even my clothes. Pastor had run out of both ideas and platitudes by this time and was reduced to staring fixedly ahead, the poor guy, driving as fast as he dared across rough country, heading for camp, wishing the torment was over. Didn't we all, that day?

Health and safety. The African staff in safari lodges are always bemused by this. They say to me: "Why do the guests always ask us the same questions? Like, 'where are the vegetables grown? Can we eat the salad? Where does the water come from? Are there snakes in camp? And scorpions? Is it safe if there's no fence around the camp? Will we catch malaria here? What about the vehicles: do they have seatbelts? What was that noise outside my tent last night – a lion? I'm sure it was a lion! Why doesn't it just rip through the tent wall and eat us?' Why are the guests so afraid of so many things?"

To the staff, who have grown up hard-scrabble and often with little adult supervision, this camp symbolises ultimate luxury. No danger here, they're thinking. What's the fuss?

As I mentioned in 'First World Problems', it's a question of perspective. They don't realise that westerners are raised to be cautious, for their own safety. It's what keeps order in a first world society. It is the grease to those complex societies' wheels. The communal view as opposed to individual responsibility. Careful not to intrude upon each other's privacy. And westerners are taught to question the quality of food and drink. But Africans don't care about that stuff, much; they usually just eat and drink what is before them. They're people who don't ask where the water comes from.

But I realise that you can only know what you know. So I explain to the staff that almost all our clients come from a world where things generally happen on time and where health and safety and social responsibility play a very large role in their minds, where individuals expect and usually receive good service and care, where they mostly trust their bureaucracies to provide fresh food and clean water. I explain further that they live in a sanitised world generally free of bugs, disease, violence and wild animals. A world where all the basics are taken care of and much independent thinking has been replaced by systems that actually function.

And so when these tourists come to Africa, they're naturally uncertain and feel a little on edge. The world's media is not kind to Africa, often for good reason, and the headlines frequently do not make good reading. Our guests are not seeking surprises and they don't like the unexpected. They want what it says on the tin. It's a revelation to many of them how secure they actually do feel when they get here. It's a *pleasant* surprise. But it's natural for them to ask questions about drinking the water.

I don't like it when people are made to be even more afraid by safari operators. The safari industry is so scared of this litigious age that they spend too much time thinking about how not to be sued instead of how to give their clients a great experience in the bush. It is not surprising that we guides completely buy into the safety first approach. Since it is Europeans and Americans who mostly regard safari holidays as something worthwhile, we Africans simply must learn to appreciate their perception of what constitutes safety. Therefore, we provide holidays and build camps and fly aircraft and supply the food and service that at least matches and usually surpasses first world standards of safety and comfort. It is a marketing upward-spiral where we try to capture market share by catering to the needs of the client.

It is not always easy for a tribal African to understand why westerners worry so much.

And one of the things the clients worry the most about is the quality of the water.

So when I knelt down at the cool, clear rock pool that late morning in the Namibian desert in Palmwag Concession and cupped a handful of water to my mouth, it wasn't because I was thirsty. There was plenty of bottled water in the car. It was because I was making a point. Look, people, stop your senseless fretting: this wild water is beautiful to drink. I've done it countless times from pools and rivers across Africa and I'm still here, alive and very well, not wasting away from some hideous disease contracted from an infected desert pool.

And that's when the trouble started.

Dave, Ursula, Harriet and I had left very early that morning from Desert Rhino Camp (DRC) on a rhino search with our guide, Pastor.

"We're going to Zone Four this morning" he'd said. "It's far."

Far, bumpy and desolate. I groaned inwardly. I hate going to bloody Zone Four. You can't tell the guests that, though, you have to stay up-beat. The SRT (Save the Rhino Trust, a Namibian NGO dedicated to the protection of the last unfenced wild Black rhinos on earth) rhino trackers and the tourists that follow behind them in Land Rovers work certain areas in rotation so that individual rhinos, which are highly territorial, and therefore usually in a certain defined area, are not disturbed too often. Actually, in most cases the best-case scenario is achieved: the rhinos are not even aware that they are being watched. But Zone Four is far away, perhaps 40 km of hard, very slow, rugged driving over the rough basalt lava pillows that dot the eroded desert plain and hills, and the roads, such as they are, are barely more than simple winding two-tracks. It's all fun and games in the morning as you set out eager to get on the trail of a rhino or an elephant, and while you are buoyed by the expectation that you might even spot a great lion still roaming after a night of bawling to his competitors, but after the thrill of all that plus the bonus of sitting in undetected proximity with an iconic desert-adapted Black rhino, and then coupled with the drowsiness that follows a hearty bush picnic, the return journey can seem boring and infinite. Especially if you have to come all the way back from bloody Zone Four. I hate Zone Four.

I'd spoken to Martin, the SRT tracking co-ordinator, about it, before we left that morning. He'd patiently explained that we guests are invited to accompany the SRT trackers as they go about their daily research work, but that the priority lies with the work, not us. SRT follows a strict routine designed to monitor the rhinos accurately with the least possible disturbance, and therefore I did not get to call which zone we would go to. I knew this, of course. I was just trying my luck.

It was going to be a very long day. And hot. We'd have to stay hydrated. We'd have to drink plenty of water. Good, clean, safe, water.

"Is it safe to drink that water?" asked Dave.

"Well, yes," I said, "of course, it's a seep from a natural spring, filtered by the earth, pure and cool. It may taste a little different to what you are used to but that's because we do not recycle it, add chemicals to it, filter it through charcoal, and bottle it in plastic. Our water tastes like, well, water. Of *course* you can drink the water! Trust me, I'm a guide."

Hubris can hurt. It's easy to topple off a high horse.

Tracking wild Black rhinos out of DRC is thrilling stuff. The trackers go out in the cool dawn before the Bokmakierie shrikes have even begun their strident insistence that we should join them in the glory of an African dawn. They know their stuff, these trackers. They head straight to a natural seep in a drainage line and check in the mud for fresh *spoor*, the tracks of rhinos. Desert-adapted rhinos, a special subspecies known as *Diceros bicornis bicornis*, although extremely hardy and apparently impervious to heat, nevertheless tend to browse at night and then go to water in the early morning. If the trackers find *spoor*, it is likely to be fresh, just hours old, and they swiftly begin to follow the animal on foot and by Land Rover, watching the tracks, anticipating the likely path of the rhino, jogging on its path, cutting angles, eager to locate it. The game is on! When our guide gets the radio call, we follow eagerly in the trackers' wake, as alert and excited as bloodhounds, hoping for good news as it crackles from the radio: our quarry has been located!

That fresh morning we were lucky. The SRT men had gone out in the dark and found the three-toed footprints rapidly but they were far away from us: Zone Four, of course. We had some distance to cover to get there. Would the rhinos still even be there when we arrived? Pastor gunned the Landy. No stopping now for ordinary springboks, startled giraffes, or the little red steenboks that skittered away into the mustard bush. Go Pastor, go!

After an hour, we were drawing close to where the SRT trackers had reported the *spoor*. An inviting pool of water shone before us, couched in the red gravel, a mirage made real by its very wetness. The trackers were there, crouched at the pool's edge, talking amongst themselves, looking keen. It was a very warm morning now that the Atlantic fog bank had retreated under the threat of the hungry eastern sun.

"That water looks inviting, doesn't it?" I'd said. "Jump out, everyone, let's take a look at the tracks."

The imprints were perfectly clear, the edges of the *spoor* crisp and fresh, the back-pads shining like a mirror in the low-angled light. Fresh! This rhino had been here recently. A small rush of adrenalin. Excitement makes me thirsty.

"You are not seriously going to drink that, right?" repeated Dave.

"Sure," I declared. "If it's good enough for the rhino, it's good enough for me."

"Yeah but you also just told us that rhinos eat that spiky thing that looks like a cactus, what's it called, the *Euphorbia*, right? And it's amazingly poisonous to humans so... "

He trailed off, his meaning clear: you're not a flipping rhino, mate.

Even Pastor looked dubious. I was a bit peeved. Work with me Pastor, c'mon, we're both Africans, we bump fists and everything, you'd drink this yourself!

I scooped the water in my hands and drank. It was sweet and pure, and delicious. I'd painted myself into a corner now so I did it again, drinking deeply. I looked up at the trackers and noticed Martin, gaping at me, and pointing.

"What?"

He gestured in a horrified way at the top end of the pool. Droplets trickling from my chin, I followed his gaze. Something unidentifiable was lying in the water, something that looked like a wet pillow with the down scattered about. I couldn't make it out at all, so I got up and skirted the pool's edge to take a closer look. The SRT trackers were chuckling, and I noticed at last that not one of them had had a drink of this fine water. I approached the mess on the edge of the pool and suddenly recognised what I was seeing. A dead ostrich, obviously killed by a cheetah or a lion, as it came to drink, and its gory remains, at least a week old, lying in the water. The feathers were stripped from the carcass, lying in soggy piles on the bank, floating in wet clumps on the surface. What remained of the mangled, half-eaten body was lying in the water, silvery swirls of body oil gently drifting downstream. Straight to where I had just drunk my fill.

I froze, aghast. The clients were watching me in horror: they could see exactly what it was from up there on the car. Dave opened his bottle of clean, safe water.

"I'm sticking with this stuff," he said. Bloody guides, he was thinking, all the same, these guys, long on brio, short on sense. Idiot!

I brazened it out.

"There's a pretty strong flow of water through this spring. It tasted absolutely fine. I reckon I'll be okay, actually. C'mon let's go Pastor, we have rhinos to find."

But I was nervous. This wasn't quite how it was supposed to go.

The SRT men found their quarry quickly.

"Come," said Martin, explaining in his idiosyncratic English. "I beg you to improve your speed. These rhinos walk slowly, but they walk quickly."

It turned out to be three rhinos, actually, a mother and two calves of different ages, settled nicely in the limited shade of a clump of *Euphorbias* at a distance of just 100 metres, placidly snoozing, only their trumpet-shaped ears swivelling with the breeze, alert for potential danger even while they slept.

It was a wonderful sighting and a privilege to be in the presence of this endangered animal. It was doubly excellent because we had outwitted this beast in its own environment, tracked it, and now we observed it and photographed it undetected. We took our pictures and after 45 minutes we left them in peace, walking quietly away and leaving the rhinos none the wiser. It was deeply satisfying. Lesser mortals could have killed them as they slept. Lesser mortals do.

Lunch time. In the shade of a great *Mopane* tree some kilometres from the rhinos, we settled down with very cold drinks (beer and Chardonnay, just say the word!) to a surprising lunch: fresh garden salads, lasagne, home baked breads, imported cheeses and cold cuts, melon and fruit, even dessert. Life was good. Martin explained to us how the SRT goes about its work, while the trackers eyed the picnic with wolfish eagerness. Anything we did not eat they would get, and a lodge kitchen always looks after its own by preparing far more food than the guests can manage.

And then it began.

The Glyssps, as my grandfather used to call it. A deep rumble in my belly and a dull ache in my bowels. In the pleasure of watching the rhinos we had all forgotten about the ostrich water. Suddenly, my lunch felt like an unwelcome alien within, and my body began to reject it. In an instant I was on my feet, grabbing the toilet paper from the Landy console and bounding away for the sanctuary of a low ridge of rocks nearby. I was gone for some time, eventually emerging pale and wobbly.

"The ostrich water? No, I don't think so," I said weakly as I stumbled back towards the group, "Probably just something I ate."

Clearly I was deluded, however. We had all eaten the same thing. Before I was even able to rejoin the group I spun around and bolted, bent over, straight back to the rocks, retching (and worse) as I ran. My innards were in a knot and the pain was crippling. There was a stunned silence from the group and looks of profound distaste. Bloody guides, you'd think they'd know better, hey?

But now a strange thing happened. As I returned ashen and wan to the lunch circle, Ursula got up looking stricken, moved around behind the Landy and suddenly fainted to the gravel floor. Dave was there in a flash, supporting her, cooling her face and neck with water and a cloth, and carrying her into the shade. What had caused this? Ursula had not drunk the ostrich water. The magic of the rhino sighting was now quite forgotten in this confusing rush of sickness.

Ursula seemed to have recovered after a while. The trackers were busily bolting down the remains of the lunch. Soft white people, they were thinking, looking at me pityingly over their massive sandwiches. Marshmallows, they are. Pink and white on the outside, soft on the inside. A bit of sun, some dodgy water and they all fall over.

"Let's go, Pastor," I said, leaning exhausted against the vehicle and contemplating the rest of the day with grim despair. "It's a long way home."

It turned out to be the worst safari ride of our lives. Sweltering, bone-shaking, unrelenting. I had DRC way-marked on my hand-held GPS, and I miserably watched the kilometres ticking slowly, slowly, ever so slowly by. Periodically, the cramps came upon me and I yelled urgently to Pastor to stop, baling off the Landy before it could even come to a stop and bolting around the back of it with toilet paper in hand. After about the fourth time, the paper was exhausted, there were no more tissues in the vehicle, and I resorted to washing off with the bottled water. Consequently, that too was soon finished. Pastor radioed to camp requesting a special delivery: more toilet paper, more water... and for god's sake, hurry, hurry!

By now this shambles had become too much even for Dave's hardened stomach and he too suddenly began to retch in a bout of (presumably) unconscious sympathy vomiting. Ursula was lying across the seat, grimly hanging on, flushed and wet with sweat, and Harriet was sitting in the front row, trying to stay focused on the landscape. Anything but on the casualty ward behind her! I felt acutely embarrassed by all of this but I was helpless: I had never been this sick in my life. Pastor didn't know what to do to help.

"Drive, man, drive! Just get us home. Don't stop for anything!" I implored him.

And drive he did, hammering that rattling old Land Rover through dips, across rocks, down drainage lines, ignoring the wildlife. Once again, astonished giraffes and herds of springboks ran for cover before us. He wanted this over as much as we did. Africa's animals held no further charm for us that awful warm afternoon.

Eventually, a full nightmare later, and still some kilometres from camp, we rounded a corner to find a cache of mineral water and toilet paper in the middle of the road. The guide who had dropped it off was disappearing back to camp in a cloud of dust. There had been a lot of animated chatter over the radio in the Damara-Nama click language, and even in that dialect it sounded appalled. He wasn't waiting to see what kind of disarray we were in. Pastor slid from the car and fetched it, handing out blue plastic bottles of water, wearing a funny shocked look on his face. I was already off the car, pants down, squatting there in pain, and he gingerly handed one entire shrink-wrap of bottles around the back of the vehicle to me, trying not to look. I rinsed off, again and again.

The journey ended. At last. We dragged ourselves to our tents, shell-shocked and weary. I ordered gingerale and diet cokes, suitably shaken and de-fizzed, with ice and yet more water, to all rooms, and, after a long and very necessary shower, I lay down at last on something that wasn't squeaking and jolting. None of us were seen that evening for dinner and the splendid red sun, the croaking evening calls of the korhaans and especially the fine cuisine served for dinner, was lost on us.

In the morning I found to my immense relief that I was entirely recovered, except for a raging thirst. I walked quickly to the dining tent and discovered that my appetite had returned. My body had evacuated the toxins and I was perfectly well again. Wonderful! Large omelette with everything, please! And coffee. Also large.

Dave, Ursula and Harriet came in a short while later, also looking much recovered.

"What on earth happened yesterday?" asked Dave. "Why did we *all* get sick? You were the only one who drank the water. What did you call that? Glyssyps?"

I didn't have a clue.

"Well, *I* had the Glyssps. But you folk, I dunno, I reckon that was the Marthambles," I said, picking up a brimming jug of water and pouring them each a glass.

"Ostrich water?" I offered. "Trust me, I'm a guide."

27

SUDDEN JUSTICE

"I took him out," he said. "I'm only phoning to let you know as a matter of protocol. It's sorted."

"So... there's nothing I need to do?" I asked, bemused.

"No, no, it's sorted, man, I told you. Just thought you should know."

"So, I just want to get this straight. The guy is in jail now? No-one got hurt and it's over?"

"Guy? Guys! *Two* of them. Oh sorry, *ja*, I forgot to say, I had to take his *tjommie* out too. And, *ja*, someone did get hurt. *Them!*"

"Jesus! It sounds like a fucking war zone down there, china!" I said, startled.

"All quiet on the southern front now, though," he assured me. I could imagine his wide grin. "Don't worry, Boss, it's all good. Cheers!"

My mobile phone went dead, and I lay back on the pillows. The bedside clock showed a dawn hour. One hell of a way to start one's Saturday. Sue looked at me enquiringly.

"Everything all right?" she asked.

"I guess so," I said. "Now it is. I think. You know Danie down at Sossusvlei? The manager there? That was him. I'm going to call him The Sheriff from now on. Justice has been served."

Danie had walked into my office a few months before, a tough looking Namibian, an outdoorsman burnt brown by the desert sun, broad of beam, with a handshake that buckled one's knees, and long hair that gave him a Nordic beserker look. He looked capable, and had a relaxed yet determined demeanour that I found compelling. I was the Reserve Manager for a group of safari lodges in the Soussusvlei region of central Namibia, and needed a resourceful and self-reliant person who could manage the maintenance, the guests, the staff... and others, as it turned out.

Namibians have short weather-memories. Every drought is the "worst in living memory", the rains "arrive later every year" and they've "never seen the gemsbok looking thinner than this. Ever!" And I say: "The clue is in the name, people. Namibia. It's the only country in the world named after a desert. Reputedly the driest on the planet. So, yes, there's drought. There's supposed to be drought! Drought is the default climate here. Rain is unusual. Of *course* the gemsbok are skinny. That's their usual look. They're adapted for this. Fat gemsbok? Rivers with actual water in them? Listen, gemsbok in Namibia are *embarrassed* to be fat. River beds here *hate* having water in them. What's your point?"

"No man, but this year, *this* year, it's never been like this. All the rain fell on my neighbour's farm. I swear the rain stopped at my fence!"

"So there *was* some rain?"

"*Ja*, but... *ag*, look, you don't understand, *Soutie*, you come from bloody KwaZulu-Natal, man, you *okes* and your forests and waterfalls and all that green *kak*."

But this year the rains had come. Now the Namibians were no longer complaining about drought. Now it was the floods. The Sossusvlei Desert Lodge has originally, and with great inventiveness and regard for budget and use of local resources, been built out of bricks manufactured from local clay, baked on site. And in the heat of the desert, those bricks worked brilliantly. But the rains had come, the Tsauchab river was running high from bank to bank, and now those red bricks were dissolving under a relentless deluge, leaching steadily into the ground and leaving walls tottering under the weight of the roof beams and thatching. Urgent repairs were needed. As were *tog* labourers, temporary, casual workers paid by the day for the duration of the work. I was glad I had Danie down there: he revelled under these challenges.

He brought in Nama men from the tiny farming village of Maltahohe, one hundred kilometres distant. There was a reason those guys didn't have permanent jobs – they didn't want them. Most of them had small flocks of hardy sheep and goats roaming through the arid country outside of town, and lived on a hand-to-mouth basis. They gathered for preference on the veranda of the local liquor store, and many were not unfamiliar to the exasperated local constabulary. Full-time employment had little appeal, but the occasional boon of a week's work was usually welcomed. And these guys were tough and handy: they worked hard in a sweltering sun with little complaint, swinging shovels and pick-axes, and requiring little except a hearty meat stew with *stywe* pap once a day. Furthermore, they gossiped ceaselessly as they laboured, and were very funny. They spoke their local Khoekhoe dialect, naturally, but also an amusing Afrikaans *patois* that had us in stitches. The problem was, they kind of specialised in stitches.

They all loved a drink. They all had knives. They all loved a fight. And their entertainment usually proceeded in that order. This was followed very often by a hospitalisation and/or a period of rest and recovery in the local jail. Afterwards, there were usually no hard feelings. In fact, it wasn't at all unusual that the aggrieved parties were brothers, cousins, even father and son. And the police knew them all.

So in the midst of the storms, Danie drove a Land Rover to Maltahohe to fetch men off the veranda of the bottle store. He chose the two that looked the most sober (meaning that they had run out of drinking money) and cautioned them:

"*Manne*, one week of work, all board and lodging included, but NO DRINKING! I don't want any shit from you. Got it?"

"*Ja meneer*," ("Yes, sir") they agreed meekly, and climbed in. They probably just wanted to get out of the damned rain.

But the Namib desert makes a man thirsty, even when the water falls and the puddles form, and when darkness comes, what is a man to do? One life; live it! And as it happened, Danie's teenaged daughter was visiting him at the lodge at the time. And it wasn't very long before a quantity of home-brewed *witblitz* found it's way down the throats of the Maltahohe men. And those Nama mouths began to talk. And the talk was of Danie's daughter. There was some lewd chatter, a bit of drunken suggestion, a mite of licentious prattling, and the daughter reported it to her dad.

The Sheriff promptly stepped out of his office and summoned one of the Maltahohe men, who wisely, faced by a giant, potentially crazed desert viking, denied everything. The matter might have been dropped right there, despite abundant evidence of the abuse of illegally obtained alcohol, for Danie was not an unreasonable man. However, the injudicious actions of the second Nama man ruined everything. Drawing a thin blade from his pants, he rushed at Danie, crying out for vengeance against the allegations made against his *compadre*. This was not Danie's first fight, and he was a sober as the proverbial. He easily side-stepped the flying Nama, tripping him up with an adroit flick of a leg, and kicked the knife from his hand. Then, with the greatest of ease, he grasped the small man by the throat and held him up against the wall while the Nama's legs kicked uselessly in mid-air. Danie was just beginning to explain to the man the error of his ways when the first Nama, now emboldened by liquor and the bravery of his friend, decided to engage in the action. He, too, pulled a rudimentary knife from his waistband. Danie saw a look in the dangling man's eyes, and turned, just in time to avoid a slash of the blade. Dropping victim number one, Danie cracked the second attacker on the cranium with a mighty fist, then spun around and did the same to number two. Both men immediately declined further engagement, and sat there numbly in the mud, their eyes spinning and their senses addled.

"I think that will be all, thank you, men. I will now drive you to the Maltahohe police station where I will personally hand you over to your old friend, Sergeant Witbooi. I will be pressing charges for assault with a deadly weapon, of course, so that you get a full week instead of a mere overnighter. And I will not be paying you for any work you have done here."

Which he did. And having done so, he phoned me the next morning to report on his actions.

Having digested the news and drunk a coffee, I phoned Danie back an hour later.

"Listen, Danie, well handled and all that. But now I'm wondering, what the hell are we going to do about the bloody clay walls, man! Desert Lodge is melting into the sand while you are busy fighting the Gunfight at OK Corral, and we need labourers."

Danie chuckled.

"*Ag*, not to worry, Boss. When I got to the police station, there were two other guys walking out of the cells, those two that I fired for drinking *last* week, so I employed them instead!"

28

HARD CHOICES

This guiding game is all about people. Social interaction. Banter and jocularity best mixed with a healthy dose of empathy and sincerity. We're entertainers, and dream-makers. A guide is professionally limited if he is deeply knowledgeable about the environment yet hopeless with people. Ours is not the province of researchers and ivory-tower academics. The guide is the key holder to the safari experience, the one that unlocks the knowledge. It is always the *people* that make the difference to my wilderness experience. The rhythms of the bush are far more predictable than the humans that come on safari to get a feel for them. And boy, do you meet some memorable people.

But, Tim. Tim was something else. I'll never forget Tim.

Most of the folk you meet on safari are pretty much like you and me, perfectly interesting in their own way and often intriguingly quirky. Part of the fun of guiding is that you just never know who is going to pitch up, and you need to be ready for all-comers. One evening at Damaraland Camp in Namibia, for example, I found myself sitting at dinner opposite an astronaut. He hadn't actually done the

Neil Armstrong moon walk but he'd been up there, orbiting around and around the earth in that claustrophobic little tin can, and he held me enthralled. At Chitabe, Okavango Delta, there was a Welsh guy who owned a miniature train; one of those small steam engines that he actually sat on as it chugged around his estate, pulling a string of wagons behind it. It was all he could talk about. You might think the train would be filled with delighted children, but no: he professed a distaste for kids, and simply rolled around the tracks on his own while his wife, no doubt, shook her head at him through the living room window. She didn't sit with him at dinner that night at Chitabe: taking a break from trains, and him, I expect. On another occasion at Serra Cafema Camp, northern Namibia, I discovered (after three days!) that the really pleasant quiet woman in the drawn-down baseball cap was an Oscar-winning Hollywood actress, travelling under a pseudonym. She looked different in real life. Less made-up. Less photoshopped, too.

I suspect that I have guided people who shape or inform the world at a macro level but in the earlier days of my work there was no Internet. I don't mean no Internet in camp. I mean, no Internet at all. So there was no facility for instant electronic information, no googling of celebrities and names as the camp managers do now. We were very cut off from the outside world, and we didn't mind much. We only used first names with the clients: it was pretty casual in the safari camps. That's how they usually wanted it, too; it was refreshing for them to be just 'John' or 'Jane', no honorifics. Most (but certainly not all) of the more famous names that came on safari were happy to escape attention and I was always conscious that this was time-out from the media for them, so I seldom quizzed them about how they fitted into their versions of the world. Of course, the Look-at-Me ones told me who they were anyway.

But this guy! This Tim. Few people have added as much colour and fascination to my day as he did that morning. His story was startlingly different. Once he finally got around to telling it.

He had travelled alone to the original Pafuri camp in the northern Kruger Park in South Africa (before it was washed away a few years after this story in a Thousand Year Flood that left most of the furniture floating downstream amongst the hippos in the Limpopo River). I met him on one of those sultry evenings when the hawk-moths spend all night trying to get a sip of your red wine and the unabating electronic pinging of the fruit bats drives you mad. I was sitting by myself at the bar when Tim bellied up to it. We exchanged pleasantries over drinks and peanuts. A pleasant guy this, I thought immediately, but tired looking. He said he was a journalist with *Time* or *Newsweek* or one of those prominent periodicals that people relied upon for news before the advent of that new species – 'the people who walk face down, glued to their devices' – and he said he had just arrived in South Africa by way of China.

"China?" I asked, surprised.

"Oh, I was there to get some information from someone I know so I can write a piece for the magazine," he replied. And then after a hesitation, "It was rough, man."

I was surprised to be taken into his confidence. After a short while I said:

"Rough? Why?"

"Complicated story... actually I haven't even filed it yet," he said, waving a dismissive hand in my direction, looking distant and apparently regretting his disclosure.

My cue was obvious, so we talked desultorily about other things. He was, he said, in South Africa to research probable government collusion with the Vietnamese in the rhino poaching epidemic but I could see his mind wasn't really on it. Something had just happened to him in China that obviously weighed upon him. He was that distracted that an elephant could have walked into the bar and inhaled the peanuts from the dish at his elbow and he would barely have noticed. He was drinking too quickly, too.

After a while he lit up a cigarette and I left him there to brood while he swirled the smokey Bourbon through the ice cubes.

But the next morning at breakfast, to my surprise, he walked directly over to my table looking quite cheerful and he seemed open to conversation. I suggested we take a stroll out of camp along the Levuvhu river, ostensibly in search of the rare Fishing owls that were rumoured to roost by day in the upper reaches of the giant Sycamore figs that lined the high banks. I suppose it was a lovely morning, with nyala scattering ahead of us and crocodiles slipping quietly into the water at our approach, but I sensed I was about to learn more about this man so I barely noticed any of that.

Not far from camp we stopped in a small grove of Fever *Acacias* and settled comfortably on a fallen branch. Tim didn't appear to be troubled by the flies that buzzed annoyingly around our heads. He sat for a while watching the river, then he blew through his lips and with a shake of his head, started to speak.

"Lloyd, I couldn't sleep last night. Too many sounds outside the tent. Elephants or something. Some animal walking about in the grass. Man, this place is so *noisy* at night time. I think there was even something on my roof. Anyway, so I ended up writing my China report. It's been in my head for days now. I was lying there listening to mosquitoes and the words suddenly popped out. They've been stuck and this place has freed them. Or maybe it was the whiskey. You wanna hear one hell of a story?"

My heart leaped a little. I nodded without speaking.

"Okay. You been to China?"

"Yes. The usual tourist stuff. Forbidden City, Mao's mausoleum, the Great Wall, Peking Duck, bloody dreadful local wine. We caught the train from Beijing to Shanghai, which was cool."

"So you went to Tiananmen Square."

A statement. All tourists to Beijing do.

"Sure, it was sort of impressive," I told him. "In a big, flat kind of way."

He smiled and lifted his sunglasses. I could see his eyes. They were grey.

"Okay. But there's another face to Tiananmen. I've met it, and it's scary. I had a friend called Wang."

"Had?"

"Yeah, I reckon so. Had." He paused, then: "Funny thing, though, this piece came out differently to what I was expecting. I've never written like this before. It's not the usual opinion piece.

It's more of a… I dunno… a first person drama."

Gazing out onto the rippling river, slowly wiping his glasses, never once looking at me, he started to speak:

It's a windy evening on the Shanghai Bund, and growing dark. I'm smoking. Pretending to.

I doubt I'm fooling anybody.

I see him emerge from the crowd, suddenly a face I know materialising from amongst the dark-suited hard-striding businessmen and gaggles of tourists swarming by. Of course I'm expecting him but even so it's a shock, and I jump a little. He comes to stand close to me and gives me that old grin, and then as quickly the smile is gone.

"If it's not from the heart, it's nothing," he says.

The wind tears the words from his mouth. It's what we used to say to each other. Back then, at college, when we were… back then. Before he chose a different destiny. He's only been out a week, and he looks haunted and hollow.

I'm sitting on the railing along the edge of the embankment, one leg hooked over the metal, and the wind-spray from the dirty old river is wetting my shoes. He's squinting sideways at me, head cocked over a bit, in that familiar way. I hand him a Camel and a lighter. The flame stutters and he drags on the cigarette with practiced ferocity, then rolls it into the corner of his mouth. The familiarity of that habit pierces me. The anonymous crowd swirls around us, all the languages of the world mixing into an excited hubbub. I feel like I'm in a movie. I feel like I should be the guy behind the newspaper, the guy in the raincoat. In reality, I feel vulnerable, exposed.

I swing my leg down, and we both stand with our backs to the incongruous European architecture, facing into the breeze, towards the creeping water. I want to embrace him, to hold him for a long time, but I dare not. We're supposed to be two strangers sharing a smoke. We *are* strangers to each other, these days.

There is silence for a few seconds.

"Been a while, buddy. You okay?" I ask. Of course he's not but

I don't know what else to say.

"Sure. You?"

"Uh, yeah. Sure. I'm on holiday, remember? I'm museum-ed out. And I've seen enough Art Deco buildings to last me a lifetime. I've even been to the Friendship Store!"

Wang doesn't smile. He's all business. Urgent.

"So you came. Thanks, Tim. Listen, you only get to do this once, so get it right, man. Can you get it out?"

Demanding. He was always spare with words but he's so... abrupt. He's changed. *They've* changed him. I become defensive.

"How do you mean?"

"I'm just saying this is serious, you know, and you will never get to come back to China afterwards. The story is mine but it's gotta come from inside *you*, and it's gotta be real."

He's still got that beguiling hybrid Chinese-East Coast accent after all these years. I would have thought he'd lose it, in that place.

"Hey dude, I'll get the docs out inside a bag of tea or something, don't worry about it!"

I'm trying to keep it light but I just want him to keep talking. I've missed him and I want to hear his voice. It's only now I realise how much. He passes the cigarette lighter back to me. My hand shakes as I take it and he briefly holds my wrist to steady it. His fingers are bony. He's so thin.

"Keep it," I tell him. "Been a long time between smokes. This stuff can kill you, you know."

He grimaces. He knows I'm thinking about how things were between us, about where he's been since June 1989, and he knows I'm afraid. But he knows I know I'm all he's got. I'm more welcome in his world than he is himself these days (not for long), and he needs me. I pull my jacket hood over my head because of the wind but my glasses are already spotted with mist. It's so cold. He cups the cigarette in the palm of his hand. It glows in there, living against the breeze. A point of light, of hope.

"Okay," he says. "Sorry, Tim. I trust you. Just do what you do."

He spits onto the pavement, downwind, that Chinese thing they all do, and feels in the pocket of his coat, dragging out a fat envelope. He stares at the river very briefly, and then shoves the packet at me. I quickly put it in my bag.

"It's all there. I wrote this twice. They confiscated the first copy. Two extra years. Not easy to let this go."

"It'll be okay, Wang. I made you a promise. "

It's false bravado, and he knows me too well to fall for it.

"I know. Still."

The wind tugs at my shirt collar. It's fully dark now, and wet, but people still brave the streets, walking head down against the weather. Minding their own business, unmindful of any life beyond their own. He suddenly looks into my eyes, as if searching for further assurance, and shrugs. What choice does he have?

"You'll see this in print, Tank Man. Now the world will know who you are."

"Yeah. Sure. It's not about me, Tim. People need to know what goes on here."

An unexpected memory of manicured Princeton lawns and sun-bleached benches crowds out the bleak Shanghai riverfront. Two young men, students in The Land of the Free, talking, laughing, relaxed. Touching. Different planet.

"So now?" I ask.

His prison haircut is still growing out, and he doesn't fit the civilian clothes they gave him. He wears them like sacks hung out to dry. He evades the question.

"Thanks for doing this, Tim."

I persist.

"Now, Wang? Where do you go? What's the plan?"

A sudden desperation overtakes him, and he grabs me ferociously, hurting my forearms. Surprising strength from this small man. Straight from the heart. More strength than I will ever have.

"Fuck it, Tim! You *know* what! *Aluta continua*. What *else?*"

I briefly met his family when I got the message to meet Wang. His mother, a tiny bird of a woman, bowing and nodding in the presence of the big, white, round-eyed man, scared of me and the consequences I can bring. Children in the back of the house, with frightened black eyes. No father; eliminated in the Cultural Revolution.

"Go," he says fiercely. "You gotta go. This is dangerous."

I give him the rest of the cigarettes. As I move to hug him, he retreats down the railing.

"They could be watching, Tim. Just go."

"Stay out of trouble, Wang."

It's a despairing and clumsy thing to say. He's chosen his fate. He chose it when he left the Princeton lawns, when he came back here with a Masters in politics. And stood in front of a tank.

He starts to say something to me, then quickly touches my hand and his eyes show fleeting tenderness at last. It is all he affords himself. It is all he can afford me, despite... well, that.

"If there's anything... I mean, we could try to... " I begin, and then stop, helplessly.

Wang is gone. He's walking away. Walking away from me, again. A taxi honks at his small form as he crosses the road but he doesn't look up. The garish golden arches of a McDonalds illuminate him for a few seconds, and then he's gone.

There is so much pain in my chest I can barely breathe.

It was very quiet amongst the fever trees as Tim finished, as if all the creatures of the wild had stopped to listen and were totally present. As if suddenly nothing was more important than this moment. I didn't say anything.

After some moments a Green pigeon made its curious descending trill, and the spell was broken. Tim's gaze changed and he fixed me with an intense stare.

"We all have to make choices and we all change the world," he said.

29

DEAD WEIGHT

You learn as you go, they say. Experience is the Great Teacher, and sometimes to your great surprise you actually remember the lessons. This time was a PB: I learnt and remembered three lessons all at once. Three handy tips I hoped I would never need to put into practice. God, what a night!

Firstly, if someone asks, "Do you know First Aid?" in the most casual and, "Sorry to bother you at dinner, sir," manner, you can bet that something is brewing. Don't be fooled by the off-hand approach. Expect the unexpected.

Secondly, just leave them on the floor. Once they're down, they're down.

Thirdly, crucially, don't lace the fingers together.

Palmwag Lodge, Kaokoland, northern Namibia. A long time ago it was a rudimentary lodge, still an outpost on the long and dusty road to the Kunene river with only the shabby clay-brick castle up in Sesfontein north of it if you wanted a beer and to refuel your safari vehicle. Palmwag Lodge is a true oasis, with scores of tall Fan palms rustling their leathery leaves in the cold westerly that blows in off the Atlantic coast and Palewinged starlings keeping up a constant fluting whistle as they fly in little groups down to the water. A miracle of a place, as all oases are: permanent water, cool and clear, and a dense bed of reeds and bulrushes even in times of the most severe drought. Remarkably, fish, little Redtailed tilapia, and frogs too, find a place to live there in that harsh arid environment. Elephants, sometimes lions, always leopards, walk by night among the tall reeds.

The gathering place for parched travellers is the Pool Bar. A pocket-sized green lawn, a small plunge pool and a thatched *lapa* where the lager was always plentiful, and usually bitterly cold, though the sun is always hot. It is a convivial place.

Philip, the lodge manager, and I found ourselves eating a cheese burger and chips there one evening. At a distant table, a group of four German FIT's (fully independent travellers, self-driving in a rented 4x4 Nissan "Softbody") were enjoying dinner, too, quaffing half-litre tankards of Tafel Lager, swapping travel stories and chatting affably amongst themselves. I had just finished presenting a ten day guide training course at Palmwag, and was relaxing at last, the work done. Sometime during their meal, apparently, one of the German men suddenly got up from the table and walked off in the direction of his tent. He must have waved away his concerned companions, no doubt saying, "Not to worry, I'm fine, I'm fine, I'll just go and lie down." Philip and I were talking about the guide training, and didn't notice him leaving. The bar area emptied as it grew late. Eventually, only the three Germans remained.

After a while, dinner done, one of the Germans approached us.

"Excuse me, do you know First Aid?" he asked politely.

"Yes," we said. All the lodge staff received regular on-site training. "Can we help you?" I continued, surmising that someone in the party was suffering from one of the usual heat-related maladies such as headache, sunburn or dizziness.

"Our friend is feeling not so good," he said slowly in German-English. "Would you mind to have a look at him?"

I thought he was talking about one of the two companions he had left at their dinner table, all of whom looked perfectly relaxed and unconcerned to me.

"Of course. Which one of them feels unwell?" I asked.

"No, no, it is our friend who went to the tent before. He said he needed to lie down because he was feeling, how do you say? Nauseous?" the German said.

"Oh, okay. Let's go," I said immediately.

Phillip went via the lodge office to pick up the First Aid box and I led the guests past the reed beds and along the dark path towards the guest tents. It was a spectacular night for stars, the sky inky-black and the celestial display a thing of awe. One of the Germans mentioned this to his colleague, and my understanding of Afrikaans, a somewhat related language, enabled me to deduce his comment, so I stopped to show them the Southern Cross, and how to work out where south is. No-one was in a hurry, and while we waited for Philip to catch up with the box, one of the Germans asked me to point out Scorpius too. When Philip arrived, we proceeded to the tent where the ailing German had gone to recover.

I mounted the steps, Philip close behind, and found the tent entrance zipped closed from within.

"Hello," I said. "Excuse me. Hello?"

No answer. The three Germans had congregated on the small veranda behind me but were making no attempt to get into the tent. It was odd. I called again, louder, and finally:

"Rolf. Rolf!" one of them said urgently. Still no reply. Something was amiss.

I pushed the canvas flaps aside, unzipped the insect mesh screen, and peered in.

Rolf was there all right.

Dead.

He was a very large man indeed, and his body lay face down on the coir mat, head twisted to one side, his lips purple, blood coagulated from a deep gash on his nose. Small white pills lay scattered about on the floor and across the bed. I quickly stepped out, allowing the flaps to fall closed. Whoah! Higher Grade problem here.

"Hang on, hang on, folks. Just wait there, please." Then quietly and with a nod towards the tent door, "Phil, take a look." His face in the dim glow of the paraffin lanterns showed that he had already guessed.

There is no easy way of telling someone that their friend is dead, but I was particularly concerned that Rolf's wife might be one of the ladies in the little knot of people on the veranda.

"Is Rolf's wife here?" I asked. They shook their heads. No, she is at home in Germany. Okay, good. Well, not good maybe, but that helped. I drew breath. I had done this once before, at Xigera Camp in the Okavango Delta, Botswana, when a radio message had come through asking me to tell a woman that her aged mother had passed away, and that tourist had taken it very calmly indeed, thank goodness. But what words do you use?

"Please wait here for a moment," I requested. I needed Phil's corroboration. I needed to be perfectly sure.

I ducked into the tent once more. Philip was on his knees, testing the man's pulse, checking for breathing. He said quietly:

"This guy died a couple of hours ago, man. We're too late. It looks like he died of a massive heart attack while standing up. Check here: he was trying to get his pill box open. He might even have choked on his own vomit. Whatever. He's gone."

"And this?" I murmured, indicating the blood on Rolf's face. But I could see: it was a flesh wound, a gouge where his nose had struck the bed post as he toppled over. Non-fatal. I touched the man on his forehead: cold, cold, cold as ice. A horrible kind of cold.

I stepped outside again. None of the Germans had tried to enter: it was very strange. Did they know? Had they sensed this turn of events?

"Folks, I am very, very sorry to tell you this. Your friend is dead. I think he has had a heart attack. He has been dead for a few hours." I could not bring myself to say his name. Rolf. I'd only just heard the name. He'd never been Rolf to me.

Short and straight. How else? Not one of them said a word but the lady sat down suddenly on a veranda chair. The others stared at me blankly. Then one stirred himself, the man who had asked for help.

"Rolf has had heart bypass surgery. Last year. He is on medication for this. Nearly he did not come on this trip because of this problem. Now... kaput!"

Well yes, exactly. Kaput. I could scarcely believe how rational they all were, and was deeply grateful to them for being so phlegmatic about it. Was this holiday supposed to have been Rolf's swan song, his final trip before an easy retirement in a picturesque mountain village in the Alps? Safari can get very weird indeed sometimes. Expect the unexpected. There was a hurried consultation on the veranda.

"We would like to see the body," said the man. The body. No longer 'Rolf.' The body.

"Not yet," I said. "Sorry. Procedures. We need to call your Embassy and the police, and make some preparations first. Come with me to the Pool Bar; the assistant manager will take care of you there. We need to inform the authorities. Then I will call you."

They obediently followed me. Bugger the procedures, there was time enough for those. It was the middle of the night anyway. It was just that we couldn't let them see Rolf in this state. We needed to clean him up, wipe off the blood, decongest his mouth and nose, and try to create the illusion of dignity. Phil had set to work by the time I returned. We'd both done service in the South African Defence Force: this wasn't our first body.

"We need to get him onto the bed," he suggested.

Dead weight. Suddenly I understood exactly what that meant. Rolf was corpulent, and slippery from blood and mucus. We simply could not pick him up. We'd have to clean him *in situ* first. And there was no way we could call for help. It would freak out the staff, and the other guests must not be alerted. It took some time, a pile of damp toilet paper accumulating on the floor, but at last it was done, and we began to heave and hoist and roll the body onto the bed. The guy was heavy. At one point as we struggled, my exertions led to a squeaking fart. The tension broke and we got the giggles.

"I think I've just pulled a *poep*-string," I said, stifling a laugh and replacing a lolling dead arm on the bed just as another limb escaped my clutches and sagged heavily onto the floor.

Eventually, Rolf reposed upon the bed, looking serene and clean.

Except for the mouth which sagged open, exposing yellowed teeth and an unnerving view straight down past his epiglottis. I tied a bandage around his head to keep the jaw closed. Just like on TV. We placed a lit candle on the bedstead, cleared away the debris, repacked all the pills and summoned the Germans from the Pool Bar. They trooped in silently and sat around the bed, touching Rolf's arms and hands gently, talking quietly. We left them to their mourning.

I called the German Embassy. It was now well past midnight but nevertheless, with calm efficiency, a woman took the names of the group and the deceased and asked the circumstances, then requested me to get the body to the nearest morgue. They'd handle it from there, she said, and would also inform Rolf's wife about what had happened. She was magnificent to deal with. Magnificent, because I could anticipate what response I was about to receive from the next call I needed to make...

The Kamanjab police. The closest Charge Office and morgue. A little farming community at the end of the tarred road, 120 km away. At first there was no reply. I rang again. And again. Finally, a grumpy voice answered. I explained.

"You must get the deceased here. We cannot come there. No fuel for the car," the disinterested duty sergeant informed me.

"So we can move the body, then?" I confirmed.

"Bring it. Bring the body to Kamanjab." Click.

We told the Germans the plan. They had decided to curtail their holiday but wanted to escort the body as far as the morgue. At five in the morning, before any other guests were stirring in camp, Phil and I log-rolled the corpse, now stiff with rigor mortis, onto a wooden spinal board, wrapped it in a blanket and plodded with it (dead weight, again) to my *bakkie* where we secured it with straps. The Germans followed behind in their rented car, the extra passenger seat an eerie reminder of their loss, as we drove up and over the Grootfontein Pass and through the jumbled granite *koppies* towards the rising sun. Every time we hit a bump in the road, I looked back apologetically. There was Rolf, inert under his grey blanket, uncaring, a not-person. It felt just a little creepy having him back there: yesterday this time he had been a sentient being, excited about his Namibian safari, enjoying the company of his friends; now, he was just rigid dead weight.

At the Kamanjab police station, the duty sergeant raised a bleary face in surprise as I pushed the door open, letting in the sound of morning and the early light, rousing him to unwilling action. The three Germans settled down on a narrow wooden bench against the wall, patient and respectful, while Phil waited in the car with the body.

"Oh, yes, the dead man," said the sergeant as I explained. "You need a Case Number. You must make a statement, and then we will take pictures of the body. To check there has been no fools play."

"Fools play? Oh, foul play," I said. "Sure, officer. I typed out a full statement last night to save you time. I just need to sign and date it for you. The body is in the *bakkie*. Should we move it to the morgue before the weather becomes hot?"

"No." Flat and final. The voice of petty officialdom exercising its power, sheltering behind regulations. "The statement, first. I will question you, and write it out myself."

"But... "

No buts. The policeman grubbed around in a drawer for a short pencil, scratched about for the correct statement form, quite literally stuck a tongue in the corner of his mouth to facilitate concentration and began to take down my statement in excruciatingly bad English. I suggested that he simply copy out my typed statement but once again was rebuffed. Rolf, outside in the warming sun, was ignored until the all-important paperwork had been completed. After an interminable 30 minutes, the sergeant pushed the scrawl towards me. It was barely legible and written in that curious lingo that the locals affect, called 'Namlish', a startling abuse of the original language. There was no way I was going to bother to make corrections: it seemed okay in the essential facts, however they were spelt and explained; it was growing hot out there, and Rolf urgently needed to be moved into the fridge.

"Yes, yes, exactly," I said, and signed it rapidly.

"Now we must make a copy," said the sergeant, grabbing another sheet of paper.

Oh my god! Visions of this poor semi-educated policeman slowly blunting another Staedtler HB flashed before me, another tedious wait while officialdom took its wearisome course... but then mercifully he got up and switched on an ancient copier hidden under a pile of tatty files. The Germans, having leaned forward at this news, now sat back on their wooden bench, deeply relieved. I breathed out. The primary tip for surviving in Africa is to remember that Africans have more time than you do, whether there is a body in your car or not. Chill, dude, I told myself. Except it was Rolf that was supposed to be doing the chilling.

The sergeant pushed the paperwork into a tray marked "Today" and, completely failing to heed my own advice I thought, "Great, let's do that, let's get on with today, shall we? Let's get those photos done and get the body into the morgue, matey!"

Ferreting about in a cupboard, the sergeant now produced a very old looking SLR camera. He switched it on, and looked dubiously at it.

"The battery is flat," he announced. "I shall examine the corpse manually."

Leaving the bemused Germans within, we proceeded to the *bakkie*, where Phil unfurled the blanket to reveal poor old Rolf to official (manual) scrutiny. The sergeant took a long dispassionate look.

"This man is totally dead," he announced. "He needs to go to the morgue. Come!" And he disappeared without further ado around the back of the Charge Office.

Yessir, that's the sum of it, I thought. He *is* dead. I think you will find that is what I have been telling you since I called you at midnight. Phil and I looked at each other, shrugged, replaced the blanket and dragged the spinal board from the vehicle. With the Germans watching through the open door, we shuffled around the corner, bearing their friend away for ever. The sergeant was waiting at the entrance to the morgue, pointing through the door. We staggered in, struggling to keep the board level, and hoisted the body onto a stainless steel body-table. The policeman flung the blanket off, looked once more at the corpse and said:

"Lucky. We have one shelf left. There was a knife fight yesterday in the township so the other two shelves are already full. But you must go outside and wait."

Lucky for whom, sergeant? Us? Rolf? For the body that was Rolf. What if all the fridge shelves *had* been full? It didn't bear thinking about. And why should we wait outside? We'd been with the body for nine hours now, we might as well see this through. We hesitated, confused.

"Out!" he commanded.

Phil and I retreated, mystified, to the veranda outside, but the door remained open.

CRACK! I jumped with fright. A short pause. CRACK!! It sounded like pistol shots. What the hell was happening? We nervously peered in at the door. The policeman was busy sliding the body into the fridge. It was a tight fit. It seemed that the sergeant had more empathy than I had given him credit for because he glanced up and said:

"Next time you bring a body do not make the fingers so."

Next time! I hoped there wouldn't be a next time! Phil and I gaped at him.

He laced his fingers across his belly so that his elbows extended out like wings. What?

"Because when the body gets hard later, the elbows stick out. So," he said, demonstrating. "And then the body, it will not fit into the fridge. And then I have to break the arms open at the elbows to make the arms straight to make the body fit. It is not nice."

No Sergeant, you're right, not nice for anyone. Not even non-sentient Rolf.

You learn as you go.

30

MOUNTAIN OF FIRE

This is a place I cannot stay away from. I go there almost every year. Once, up there, a cobra spat its venom at me, covering the side of my face with its toxic juice, and on two occasions I have entirely run out of water, saved in the first instance by dint of digging periodically all night in a cave floor for a slow seep, and on the second when an equally parched but observant fellow climber noticed a flight of buntings rising from a concealed, scum-covered rainwater pond.

But every time I scramble up that great jumble of rough-edged rocks, I think constantly of Lalu. And Heiner.

You should see Namibia's Brandberg Mountain, its rose-coloured granite glowing in first light! Have you had the joy of seeing it under the full moon? Don't wait too long. It is a *magnificent* mountain, unspoiled, breathtaking. The Brandberg, the 'Mountain Of Fire' – *Daureb* in the local Damara people's language – is a 30 x 20 km massif which dramatically pops up out of the desert plain, so the view from anywhere up there is one of *distance*: all the way to the sea on the west, 100 kilometres away, with its attendant Atlantic fog bank clearly visible, and all the way to nothing in every other direction.

Some mountains have paths to follow. Not this one. With the Brandberg you choose a ravine and you scramble, rock hop, boulder and climb all the way up as the slow-cooled rock-crystals tear at your fingers. It is very taxing work. But attaining the highland meadows is so worth the effort: in a good season, streams of icy mountain water run through them, and there are large endemic *Acacia* trees, squat peeling kobas succulents with leathery green leaves, giant bifurcated aloes, and masses of wild flowers, as well as the evidence of klipspringers, leopards and little wild hares. And Kaokoveld rock dassies, small rabbit-sized creatures that creep about in the shadowy clefts and crannies of the scorching rock, making their curious bird-like screeches in the evening hours. Black eagles wheel against a cobalt sky and whisper-sweep along the precipices; or perch, aloof, on stoney pinnacles – their watchfulness make me think of Tennyson and his waiting, sharp-eyed prey-bird. Is there a better feeling than walking in the mountains with the sound of a high chill wind amongst the crags?

Once, Bushmen, or San, the 'people', the only people then, passed by here. Hunter-gatherers who came here with the rains to eat the wild berries, and perhaps to think, and maybe just to look at the view. And to paint. The caves are a riot of art, overlapping, with no apparent respect for the previous artist's work, and featuring a wide range of styles. These people were travellers and carried their images in their minds: there are paintings of lions, elephants, rhinos, antelopes... and in one great cave, a ten metre long python curls across the tall open face, always warmed by a setting sun. On the floor, if you are observant, are found stone tools created from a rock not found on the mountain, carried there from a distant source. And the *spoor* of a leopardess, perfect in its form. The Brandberg is very hot, and it is very cold, yet even so, these people chose temporary residence up there on this mountain island, far from the lowland plains dotted with springboks and herds of galloping Mountain zebras. Their paintings are ethereal and hard to fathom. They celebrate totem animals such as giraffes, and honour the falling rain in paintings portraying the bursting asunder of pregnant, flat-bottomed clouds. These were not careless doodles.

This is a spiritual place. Why did these people paint? What message were they trying to portray? Where did they go in their minds when they did this? What hopes and plans and fears did they have? Did they have expectations of the future?

I guided a small group of friends, including Lalu and Heiner, up the Brandberg, ascending by the Hungarob ravine. Hefting heavy packs, we struggled over two days up that giant 130 million year old inselberg to lofty Konigstein, the highest peak at 2580m, and signed our names triumphantly in the summit book. As the Bushmen did with their paintings, we too left our mark. But the point of the mountain is never quite that: it is about being in a place of wilderness, with good people. Nowhere is the walking easy. There is no even ground up there. Having attained the top, and then descending in diminishing light over the rocky ridges to the pleasure of the meadow, we camped, spreading out our sleeping bags on the yielding gravel of the dry creek bed. That night the southern sky wheeled slowly overhead, the great planets moving inexorably toward the western rim and the reddening morning, and in the fresh day the cawing of the Pied crows called us to rise and witness a distant dawn.

Through the long evening, as the ancients might have done, we chatted about our futures. Lalu and Heiner had arrived in Namibia by driving a huge red fire-engine of a truck across Africa all the way from Germany, but when they reached Namibia they simply stopped travelling and set up home. The serenity and welcoming emptiness of the desert sometimes halts people in their tracks. Yet, despite their many African adventures, they had hitherto never climbed the Brandberg, Namibia's iconic landmark. Now we were putting that omission right.

The next day was one of those long, waterless days on the Brandberg. We had expected at least some remnant water in the shadowed overhangs at Long Pools, but they were bone dry. I took stock, measured our collective water, and divided it up equally with the admonition that we still had at least six hours of steady descent in the hot and broken country of the Gazab Shlucht in order to reach the base of the mountain. But that was not where we had left the car. The car was parked around the mountain where we had commenced the hike, at the bottom of Hungarob. One thing at a time, I thought. This will be okay. I was feeling very fit and full of bounce so I rationed my own water, about a litre, taking only the merest sips, and arrived eventually at the bottom with most of it remaining. I ushered the group over to a small *Acacia* tree, its branches bravely forming a little patch of shade, pulled out my small water bottle and placed it in the centre of the circle of people. No one wanted to be the first to take a drink.

"Do not leave this place. Sip the water very slowly. I am going to run to the car. It's about ten kilometres, and there is no path, so it will take me some time. I will be absolutely fine. Wait for me here. DO NOT LEAVE THIS PLACE!" I commanded.

Lalu was my Pilates instructor, whom I had met earlier that year while training for the 2006 South African Iron Man Triathlon. She was short, strong, athletic and damned fast, and while I had struggled along mid-field in that race, she had passed me several times on the looped course, finishing third woman that day, and encouraging me enthusiastically each time she came by. Later, she had assisted my wife, Sue, in rehabilitating a fractured spine by means of swimming pool therapy. Lalu was caring, expert and positive at a time that was very scary for all of us. Climbing the Brandberg, I got to know her boyfriend Heiner too, and he was a class act, a gentle bear of a man with flowing brown-blond hair, permanent golden face stubble and a relaxed manner that invited friendship. There was just no ego about him. Lalu and Heiner: so in love, so good together.

So, given her athletic prowess, I reflected as I set off for the car (and its twelve-volt fridge full of iced drinks and water), shouldn't Lalu be the one doing the rescue run? No. I was fit, and I knew what I was about. Lalu, being short, had really struggled coming down the mountain that day because so much of the descent requires hopping from rock to rock burdened by a cumbersome pack. Where Heiner and I could sometimes lower ourselves using arm strength, Lalu could not because her feet would not reach the ground. She had taken strain that day, and champion triathlete though she was, it was up to me to get to the truck.

Plus, I could read the bush signs. This was my gig. I was carrying no water, and I wasn't about to pass up the opportunity to drink some, so when I saw the deeply grooved path and scalloped hoof marks of Mountain zebras leading into the mountain up a narrow ravine, I knew exactly what that meant. These equines had passed here on their way to water. It meant a diversion but it was worth the chance. And pretty soon I found it: a beautiful mountain pool, deep, in a small gorge, sullied on the edges where the zebras had drunk but clear and cool in the middle where they could not reach. Quickly, I soaked my shirt and hat, drank my fill, drank again, rested a while, drank a third time, then jogged away, back into the deadening heat but full of zip. I was happy.

From there on, it was quite easy going to the car, bar a few tumbles over shrivelled thorn bushes (mere flesh wounds!). Never has a cold Coke tasted as good. I gunned the *bakkie* back to the waiting point. They heard me coming and there was plenty of cheering when I nosed the Toyota Hilux and its valuable cargo under that little *Acacia* tree.

Okay. So we went up a significant mountain, got to know each other, got very thirsty, and came back down. What makes this a story, then? Where's the peril? Where's the happy ending?

Brace yourself. There's a reason I think about those two people when I climb the mountain. I am paying homage.

In late 2008, two years after our climb, Lalu secured sponsorship to go to the Iron Man event in western Australia but, a few days before the actual event, she was accidentally run down in the street in broad daylight by a drunk driver. Her life was changed in a split second. She was stabilised and, after many months, was flown, still comatose, in an ambulance aircraft to Germany, where Heiner joined her, and where he takes care of her to this day. Lalu suffered extreme physical and brain damage, and remained in a deep coma for seven years. Although she is now making a gradual recovery, she will never compete in triathlons or climb a mountain again. Indeed, she can barely stand. Heiner's life has changed utterly too, of course... but he is there, with Lalu.

One day, you're up a mountain, revelling in life and the joy of being vital, the next, confined to a bed or a chair until you breathe your last. Those were not the plans we discussed on an alpine meadow at night on the Mountain of Fire.

The Brandberg has me in its grip and I will always return to walk through its inviting valleys and amongst the rocks that dwarf me. But to share the experience is vital: you want to talk about it, become re-energised by it in retrospect, and, for that, you need companions who understand, who speak your language. People who love the challenge and mountain equally, and together.

People who love each other.

The Brandberg to me, now, always, is their mountain.

(For Lalu and Heiner, with love.)

31

MEAT LOAF ON A SATURDAY

I can hardly believe this. I'm nabbed again! Last week it had been on highway B1 at the police road block just north of Windhoek. The trailer I was pulling did, in fact, have a new licence but I had left town in a hurry, placing the paper disc in the glove compartment of the Toyota Hilux, meaning to put it in the trailer's metal holder later. I showed the licence certificate to the cop, who glanced at it, then diligently wrote out a ticket anyway.

"What are you fining me for, officer?" I asked with barely disguised exasperation.

"Failure to display," he answered.

Is that even a law?

But *this* is, definitely. This time I'm bust, fair and square. It is numbingly cold when I get the Hilux stopped, and slide out. The music blares briefly from the over-stressed speakers and then mutes as I slam the door. Two things need taking care of right away. Firstly, I desperately need a pee. And secondly, a traffic cop has just stepped out in front of my truck, his hand raised to stop me. From where did he materialise? He'll get run over, doing that! I'm on the B1 highway again, the Great North Road, this time just south of the town of Tsumeb, and the dawn is only just beginning. Before approaching the policeman, I walk around behind the vehicle and take a long and welcome piss into the fragrant milk bush that always grows along the disturbed road verges. The steam is rising, and catching the first rays of light. (You can find art in anything, really). That's July in Namibia for you, though. Funny how people think that desert countries are always hot. But anyway, Constable Shikongo is on duty, apparently, and he's caught me. For speeding. He's dead right; I was absolutely flying.

It's been a good ten day stint delivering training to the guides at Mushara Lodge, just outside Etosha Game Reserve, and I have been tee-totalling that whole period. Just to see if I can do it. I did, but I doubt I'll do it again; it seemed unnecessarily abstemious, and there's something fundamentally flawed about saying no to a large glass of Robertson merlot when they serve you the eland steak and pepper sauce in the outside *boma*, and a Fierynecked nightjar is carolling away as it greets the chilly evening. So I'm ready for a bit of a party, and my friends in Windhoek have told me to meet them at Joe's Beerhouse for one of those famous towering burgers on a skewer and a few large steins of Tafel Lager before the rugby kicks off. Natal Sharks against the Blue Bulls. There's every chance we're going to give the Bulls another hiding, and I don't want to miss it. So I'm in a hurry. I haven't seen a single other car this dark morning, the road is straight and long and empty at this time of the day and I have been gunning the Hilux south in delicious anticipation.

Namibia is a big country. Long, actually. It seems that wherever you're going, you're always heading either north or south, and for a long way. Namibia is also rated (and who knows who compiles the statistics?) as the country with the worst drivers in the world. I'm not so sure about that, having been to Paris, Kampala and Bangkok, but I'd definitely go with "The Most Impatient and Without Regard to Anyone Else's Health and Well Being" award. There are only just over two million people in the whole place and they are all in a mad rush to get to nowhere as fast as possible. The B1 road north from

Windhoek to Oshikango up on the Angolan border is called the 'Death Road'. This title is chiefly owing to the drivers of the thousands of mini-van taxis, aggressive young men who are paid per passenger, and who overload their death-traps with poor unfortunates who are too scared to complain about the appalling driving. No bus leaves until it is chock-a-block full, people's faces squashed up against the windows, their brightly coloured plastic luggage piled on their laps or tied haphazardly on the roof of the taxi. The joke is that no bus in Namibia is ever full. Never mind that red safety sticker on the door proclaiming 'Licensed to carry ten seated passengers ONLY'. These guys drive very fast and extremely randomly. So, when one of these taxis hits something – as they do very frequently: a cow crossing the road, a pedestrian misjudging the speed of an oncoming vehicle, or worse, another taxi – it results in tragic chaos. Funeral parlours make good business in Namibia, and they literally line the B1 in the northern parts of the country, alternating with *cuca* shops selling quarts of Black Label lager. Go figure.

There are multiple road hazards. Taxis. Cows. Donkeys. Warthogs. Kudus. Pedestrians. Cyclists wobbling across the road. They are all on the road edge or the road itself, and represent a clear and present danger. And, today, I'm in a hurry too. I have over 600 km to travel, so I've made a very early start before the crazies take to the road. The problem is, Constable Shikongo is out even earlier than I am. It's a real surprise.

The traffic cops in Namibia are not known for being early risers. Or for paying much attention to their duties. There are roadblocks on every road coming into the capital city, Windhoek, and in many other places, manned by a large number of uniformed police as well as some in mufti who swagger around with cigarettes in their fingers trying to look important. Ostensibly, the roadblocks are there to check for stolen vehicles, weapons, and animal products, particularly fresh meat. Also, in these dark days for the wild elephants and rhinos of the country, ivory and rhino horn. The bored policemen are perfectly happy to allow the vehicles to queue up in scores, edging slowly forward while the cops saunter around the foremost vehicle pretending to check things before laconically waving the driver on with a grudging "Proceed". If they are in a bad mood because some white guy – it's usually the white guys – has given them some lip about hurrying up, they take even longer. But it is perfectly easy as a matter of fact to drive through the roadblock without doing much more than slowing down. You just have to choose your time and weather carefully. Very early, for example. The cops won't even emerge from their snug kiosk. Very late. Same thing, straight through. Too windy, too cold, too hot: all good times to travel. A wave of the hand – "Proceed." Sometimes their heads are actually down on the desk in the little charge office, and they don't even see you pass by. Raining? Not a chance they'll come out. The thing about dealing with bureaucracy in Africa, and anywhere, is that you just have to be cleverer. Timing is everything. And remember the Golden Rule: they have more time than you! So either box clever (you know where the road blocks are, after all) or zip your lip, smile and be friendly, and take a good book. I recommend *War and Peace* for longer trips. Because the more impatience you show, the more aggression you display, the more you roll your eyes and sigh and look at your watch, the longer you are going to be kept waiting and inconvenienced. If you do that, you will find that the sullen policeman now wants to inspect the trunk, or that suddenly your indicator lights are not working, or that you don't have a Public Driver's Permit, or you're missing a document called something like a 'P-94' that you didn't even know existed. And maybe it doesn't.

But Constable Shikongo has blindsided me. This is no permanent roadblock. The cunning fellow has set up a mobile gun camera on a long inviting straight, and he has flagged me down. I finally finish pee-ing and walk to where he is waiting beside his little red VW Golf with the blue and white police decals on it.

"Good morning, sir," he says very politely, his breathe pluming. "Unfortunately, you were driving 149 kilometres per hour."

"Good morning, Constable. Yes, I was," I reply reasonably, spreading my hands apologetically. "When you stopped me, I looked at my Sat Nav and that's exactly what it said. Your machine is working very well."

Shikongo is astonished. He's expecting a protest. Most guilty drivers put on an amazed face and insist on inspecting the speed camera reading, as if that makes them innocent. Shikongo is young, professional and very keen.

"Yes, sir, 149. It is too fast," he says firmly, as if he still expects me to dispute it.

"Very fast," I agree. "29 kilometres faster than the speed limit. I am very impressed with my truck. I didn't know that I could make a Three litre Hilux Double Cab Raider go so quickly on a flat road. Downhill, maybe, but not on a flat. I call my car 'Three Litres of Throbbing Diesel Power'. Good name, hey?"

The constable is flummoxed by this friendly approach. Suspiciously, he pushes back his cap and rubs a hand up his face.

"Eish, sir, exactly... where have you come from? Where are you going?"

It's a standard police question. They always ask it. You can name pretty much any destination you fancy at this point. How would they know?

"Constable, it is very early. I'm glad you stopped me. I left Mushara – do you know Mushara? Outside Etosha?– in the dark and I was just thinking I needed to stop and pee. And have some more coffee. I didn't want to try to pour my coffee – look, here it is, in this flask – while I was driving, because it is too dangerous. Accidents can happen."

Shikongo nods, looking a little confused. A law-abiding citizen, he's thinking... except he just violated the Highway Code by speeding. What's going on?

"Would you like some coffee? What time did you get up? On a Saturday, too! Constable, I am sure you are the only policeman on duty in the whole of Namibia this morning. Here," I say, shoving a plastic mug towards him. You can hardly see the surface of the coffee, it is steaming so wildly. "Careful, it's bloody hot."

The policeman hesitates. I can see he thinks that something fishy is happening, and he is weighing up whether this amounts to attempted bribery. Actually, I'm not being patronising, I really am impressed that he is on duty – frankly, we could do with a bit more of that in Namibia – and the coffee is nothing more than a friendly gesture. Shikongo takes it, and sips cautiously. He'd like it sweeter but he knows these white people are all health conscious about sugar-spikes and other funny stuff.

Conversationally, I ask: "What is the fine for doing 29 km over the speed limit, Constable?"

He puts the mug carefully on the hood of his Golf, and reaches through a window to the back seat to extract a bulky red file. Flipping through a few plastic leaves, he runs a thumbnail down a chart and politely announces, "2500 Namibia dollars, Sir."

Shit! I almost drop my coffee, and my jovial mood begins to evaporate. It's all very well fessing up and being friendly with the fuzz but hang on, two and a half thousand bucks?

"What!"

"Yes, sir, it is incremental as you get faster. They have recently upgraded the fines. Eish, it is a lot of money," he adds apologetically.

Upgraded? Is that what they call it?

I have never paid a bribe and I do not intend to do so now. I knew full well that I was speeding, and on the B1 especially, we would all do well to slow down. But I am wondering if Shikongo is expecting me to offer one, now that the rubber has hit the road. I look closely at the file he is holding, and I see there is another lying on his car seat, a green one, marked 'Rural'. Taking the red one from him, I look at the cover. 'Urban.'

"Hang on, Constable," I say. "This is the wrong file, isn't it?"

The policeman frowns and looks at the cover. His face changes.

"Oh my God! Sorry sir, excuse me!" He's flustered.

He takes up the green one, and checks it. He's an earnest young fellow and I have never had a traffic cop apologise to me before. Normally, they're passive-aggressive, the cops: the hated spoilers in the national game of 'Let's get there as fast as possible, of course I'm a good driver, it's everyone else who is rubbish.' It's the same rationale that young men use when they go to war. 'It won't be me who dies today.'

"The fine is actually not so much, sir. It is 1000 dollars," he announces happily, taking out his charge book and pulling a cheap ballpoint from his uniform pocket.

I'm not so happy. Even so, I won't bribe him, and to his credit, Shikongo doesn't look like the type who will accept one. He's young. If the government doesn't pay him properly and on time, though, that will change. He will have no choice if he wants to feed his family.

Well, I've been Mr Nice Guy thus far, and with no intention of subverting the law but now is the time to play the Joker card. To appeal to the policeman's sense of humour, sympathy and altruism. And to apologise. After all, 1000 bucks is a lot of beer money, and Tafel is a very fine lager. I wrap them all in a single quick explanation.

"Constable Shikongo," I say reasonably. "Sorry I was driving so fast but I am a man on a mission. I have been working very hard, training young Namibian guides for the safari industry, and I need to get to Windhoek by lunch to meet my friends. So I left early to avoid the traffic, the road is totally open, not a vehicle in sight, and I was so excited about things that I got a bit carried away."

Shikongo hesitates. Lifting the pen he says, "Yes but why were you driving so fast? You don't need to drive so fast. You'll make it."

I gesture towards the Hilux. The windows are closed against the cold but the sound of loud music, though dimmed, is obvious. The car is rocking to the sound of 'Bat out of Hell'. I take the constable by the elbow and walk him to the car. As I open the door a blast of sound stops him dead. 'Paradise by the Dashboard Light'. I don't turn the volume down.

"Do you know who this is?" I shout at him.

"No sir!" he bellows.

"It is Meat Loaf!" I yell. "Do you like it?"

He looks unsure about this. Am I talking about food or music?

"This guy," I shout, pointing into the car, "he likes to sing loudly. Very loudly. I like him a lot. Do you like music?"

"Yes, sir," he roars back.

"Me, too. I like loud music when I am driving. I know all the words. I sing with the music. Especially when I am going to meet friends for lunch and watch rugby. Especially when I have a long way to go. And this music is road music. This music is not slow music. It is fast music. This music is too fast to drive slow. So I can't drive 120 kph when I am listening to Meat Loaf on a Saturday. It is the fault of the music!"

Constable Shikongo gently pushes the door of the Toyota closed. The music is muted again to conversational level. Not his cup of tea, Meat Loaf, obviously. He looks relieved. He tugs his uniform jacket straight.

"Okay sir. I will let you go with a warning only. But you must change your music, sir! You must listen to music that makes you drive slower. Please listen to slow music."

And with a smile he waves me into the car.

"Extend ahead," he says.

32

BODY BAG

There's a soporific hum in my ears as the Cessna drones west from Dar es Salaam to Ruaha National Park in southern Tanzania. I'm dozing fitfully in the co-pilot's seat with my head bumping uncomfortably against the smeared perspex side-window when the pilot taps me on the thigh and holds his mobile phone up and nods at it. I take it from him and look at the small cracked screen of an outdated Nokia but my reading glasses are in my bag and I can't make out the text. I shrug. What?

He looks meaningfully over his shoulder at my guests, then leans towards me and half-shouts above the din of the engine something that sounds like, "Unexpected passenger!" Eh? I put on the co-pilot's headset so I can talk properly to him, and speaking into the closed-circuit microphone I say, "What's up, dude?"

"Just received a text from company HQ," he tells me. "There's a body bag at the airstrip that we're landing at. Some guy got smashed by an elephant this morning. Need to fly him to the morgue."

Oh, I see. Bloody hell. I thought he was going to tell me something mundane and operational such as: "We're going to have to land and refuel en route because there's been no AvGas delivery to Ruaha."

"So?" I ask.

"Do you want to warn your guests?" he asks. "Could be upsetting."

"Don't tell me the body's just lying in the airstrip reception hut in full view? For god's sake, man! Are you in comms with them on the ground?"

"Yes."

"Well, tell them to shift the body out of sight! We'll disembark and push off and, after we've gone, *then* you can load the body bag."

"Okay, but what are you going to tell the clients? Everyone will be talking about it."

"Leave that to me. Not a word, chap. I need better information about this."

Thirty minutes later, we're on the ground and heading for camp through the parched savanna landscape. It was perfectly serene at the strip, outwardly normal, although I did notice several green-clad rangers hovering near a ramshackle hut close by. I'd warned our local guide not to say a word. He was pregnant with bad news – "It was at our camp!"– but, finger to lips while the guests were pre-occupied with boarding the Land Rover, I'd told him to contain himself.

It's a funny thing about the safari business. The first truth about truly competent guiding is that it is heavily personality-driven. Great destinations and excellent wildlife need to be interpreted. The guide makes or breaks the trip.

The second truth is about safety: if people are scared, they can't enjoy the experience. Only once those two factors are in place follows bush knowledge and the exposition of wildlife behaviour. But the safety thing is intriguing: people want to feel secure about the water, the food, the animals, the political situation, the weather, the aircraft, tropical diseases and a dozen other worries, and yet, actually, they just love the thought that danger lurks close by. It thrills them to be shaking the hand of people who have survived crocodile attacks, who have suffered from malaria and tick-bite fever, who have endured epic mountain walks without water, who have stood down lion charges, who can find their way home in the dark when the sun goes down. Safari clients want to hear those stories (that's why I wrote *Africa Bites*); they just don't want to be *in* them.

And there is a curious fascination about death at the hands of wild animals. What conversation it engenders! What excitement it creates! When somebody gets run over by a bull buffalo at Victoria Falls, or a Grizzly bear snacks on a lone salmon fisherman up in the Yukon, or a half-tamed lion in some drive-through safari park in South Africa reaches in and extracts a witless tourist who disregarded the "Keep the windows closed at all times!" signs, it makes the news worldwide. It's on YouTube in hours. It's a social media sensation. And you'll be amazed to hear that, bizarrely, it's good for business. It puts Africa and safari on the map for a while. It displaces Brexit and North Korea and the Crimean annexation from the headlines for a brief while. Remember Cecil the Lion? Weirdly good for business; catastrophic for Cecil and the professional hunting fraternity.

I don't lose guests to fatal wildlife misadventures. I have never met a guide who has. But we are all aware that our clients are in the unexpressed thrall of the beguiling edginess, slight though it is, of an African safari, that they thrill to the thought that without us they could just possibly, maybe, perhaps, have a too-scary experience. We all know the statistics, though: you have more chance of electrocuting yourself at home with a toaster or being ironed while jaywalking by the Number 65 bus to Kingston than you have of being hurt by a wild animal. But you never think about your usual manageable daily risks. Scary exotic wildlife, though: that's different.

Passing slowly by herds of peaceful elephants gently tending their young and playfully splashing in the shallows of the Ruaha river, we dust-cloud into camp. The manager greets us in the carpark with ice-cold facecloths scented with lemon grass, and a pinched expression on her face. I descend before the guests can do so and quickly murmur to her:

"They don't know. Say nothing yet. We'll talk, okay?"

The manager reminds the guests that they are in an unfenced lodge where wild animals are free to wander at will. She tells them to enjoy watching the wildlife but to be aware that these are not tame animals. That they will come close because they trust us not to bother them, and that we need to respect that. Preliminaries handled, the guests go to their rooms and I sit with the manager. She's outwardly calm, but distraught, suffused with a combination of frustration and controlled anger. I'm expecting that it will be a local ranger or staff member that has been killed by an elephant; some calamitous encounter in the last darkness of the night.

In fact, it's a *guest*.

She walks me to a spot on the river bank not above fifty meters from the main guest area and immediately I see the evidence. The ground is severely scuffed, grass is de-rooted, and there are still faint pink traces of blood on the sand.

The manager's eyes become wet with the horror and she speaks in a sudden torrent.

"Right here. A young Spaniard. Killed right here, this morning, *in camp! In front of his wife!* They were on *honeymoon*. I told him not to get so close. I told him! I thought he had listened to me but, when I wasn't watching, he went back and he carried on taking photos, and when I looked again... it was a female elephant with a calf. A lovely old female. We know her, she's always here. Was."

"Was?"

She bursts into tears. "The Wildlife Department guys came and chased her out of camp and shot her with their AK-47's. And they shot the calf too! I heard the shots. The whole thing was so horrible. And the wife speaks no English. Can you imagine?"

I can't.

"The elephant kept mock-charging him. The dining room staff were screaming at him and the elephant was trumpeting but he just stood there taking pictures! The ele kept warning the guy but he just stood there. His wife was in hysterics too but he just *stood* there. And then eventually the elephant came up the river bank in a rush and knocked him down with her trunk and leaned over him and stabbed him with a tusk and then stood over him, squealing. It wasn't the ele's fault. And now she's dead. *He's* dead."

I don't know what to say to her. What words suffice? The shock is coursing through her. She is outraged at the man's naïveté, at the death of two innocents, at the awful, unescapable immediacy of dealing with the dead man's poor wife. It's been a truly horrifying morning for her, and suddenly here *we* are now, fresh new safari clients, eager to have a wonderful time, to watch elephants living pure and unfettered and trusting lives.

"Look, I'll tell my guests, okay? It's not your responsibility," I say gently. "They'll be fine. Get on with what you need to do and don't worry about my people. I've got this."

Before lunch, I sit my guests down and, without any drama, explain to them what happened. We walk to the site of the tragedy and I interpret the marks on the ground for them. Professional, dispassionate, no drama, a quiet voice, no moralising and no latitude for gossip and finger-pointing. I don't even remind them that they need to be aware of the fact that they are in the presence of potentially-dangerous animals. They're respectful and awed. This, here, now! And truth be told, they're just a little titillated by it. Another Africa story, a story at first-hand. Blood on the tracks! *We saw it.* We were there!

Habituated animals. Not tame animals. Lions sleeping right next to the game drive car. Elephants strolling by as you eat breakfast. Hyaena cubs sniffing at the wheels of the Land Rover. A leopard lying relaxed on a horizontal tree bough only metres above you. The habituation of wild animals is a deliberate, controlled and time-consuming process. It means that, after a period of time, they will choose to live their lives in trust of people. They become used to the fact that we elect not to interfere with them. We neither harm nor help them. We're just a neutral presence that they learn to tolerate. It makes no difference whether we are there or not, their behaviour is just the same. And that keeps working – provided we don't change the rules. Our behaviour must be consistently benign. Furthermore, if we do impinge upon them and they take exception to it, we need to honour the warning signals they give us. They'll not simply hurt us willy-nilly. They're bigger, stronger, faster and better armed than us. They could kill us if they want to. But they do not want to: they almost always run away, or repeatedly tell us that we have violated their space. They bark or growl or trumpet or lower their horns or bristle or make fake rushes at you. And eventually, eventually, if we ignore these fair warnings, if we abuse the relationship of trust we have agreed upon, they have no choice but to defend themselves.

And then we end up in a body bag at the airstrip.

33

ANOTHER KIND OF NORMAL

His kids behind him on the game-drive vehicle are cringing but they're not going to let him see that. He's The Boss, the clear and unquestioned head of a South Korean family. His teenaged daughter is particularly embarrassed, flinching when I look over her father's shoulder at her. It's hard not to laugh at their reactions. I'd love to, but it would be damned rude, and, anyway, I'm so appalled at what he's just told me that there's nothing actually funny about this.

"Oh yes," he says in his idiosyncratic English, "You bring back from market, hang by feet from tree, and beat with stick. Make soft, skin come off easy."

Jamie Oliver should think about a recipe book for preparing dog. It wouldn't be a big seller in the UK or America, but it might be a winner in Korea and China. Maybe Owamboland in northern Namibia too, although there all they do is roughly dismember the dog and chuck it into a 200 litre drum of vigorously boiling water, with handfuls of salt.

I've been to the Beijing food market. You can get virtually anything there; that's a generalisation that is actually true. Living creatures, beasts and fowl and fish and things that crawl and slither, crowded into small wire baskets or glass tanks or plastic buckets of murky water. Perfectly normal, whatever the Western taste may be. You have to try to suspend judgement, but it's very hard to do. And there are plenty of dogs available, poor scrawny hounds with beseeching eyes and pathetic little wags of the tail. "Pick me, choose me, take me home." If only they knew. The stomach turns. And yet...

We Westerners are more than content to eat industrial-scale produced meat. Beef from cattle crushes; poor dumb force-fed cows standing in their own shit, eating fish meal and being injected with growth hormones. And it's the same with battery chickens and pigs, but as long as it is all cleanly presented at the supermarket with no blood and a nice piece of parsley on top, we're fine with it.

But dogs?

We'd gone out that early morning from Dumatau camp on a day that promised much. The Painted dogs (better known as Wild dogs, a name that confuses the uninitiated, who think I'm taking them to see some feral German Shepherd dogs, or something) had been seen the evening previous, looking lean and hungry but since there was no moon to see (and hunt) by, they had settled down for the night, and, fortunately, quite close to the lodge. I was in no doubt that they'd jog-trot that morning at first light, and we intended to be there to watch the social greeting ceremony initiated by the leader of the pack – the alpha female. It's a wonderful ritual to witness, the post-rest interplay of dominant and subservient dogs leaping and twisting and allo-grooming and twittering like a cage-full of excited parakeets, followed by the sudden and definite lope of the alpha as she sets off in the direction that she thinks that food is likely to be. Painted dogs are a threatened species these days, severely and mistakenly persecuted across Africa for their depredations on domestic stock, but they do need explaining to guests.

"Dogs? We've got dogs at home. No, sir, show us lions and elephants!"

"You'll see when we get there," I say. "And if they hunt, why then, you're in for the ride of your life! Most exciting spectacle in the African bush."

The prospect of blood always thrills people. Boxing, MMA, WWE, NFL, and rugby... they're all legal fora for satisfying our human propensity for violence. Watching Formula 1 racing and MotoGP. Round they go, round and round. Pass the popcorn. But wait! A crash! YES! *That's* what I'm talking about! Woohoo! Put it on the big screen in slow motion...

We quickly found the Painted dogs where they'd been left the night before. Sure enough, they chittered and played for a while, and then set off towards the river, a profitable place to hunt, full of impalas in restless red herds. We followed the pack at a distance as they gauged their chances and then, suddenly, it was on! The dogs dived in, scattering antelopes in every direction, the impalas alarm-snorting sharply, bounding prodigiously, high-jumping over *Guarri* bushes and fallen leadwood logs, creating confusion, leaving the dogs unable to choose an individual victim. It was hard to know where to look, with multiple dogs streaking past the car, their lithe forms flattened in the chase, white-plumed tails streaming behind, ears back and white-yellow teeth exposed in the adrenaline-fuelled pursuit. And they missed. They got nothing! Nothing at all.

No blood. Still, it was extremely exciting and the guests were ecstatic. Safari drives are always wonderful but usually rather gentle affairs, admiring recumbent lions, watching herds of grazing zebras or a skein of geese flying low over the river, determinedly going... somewhere. An Amarula coffee and rusks while Red lechwes splash through the shallows. But, now and then, a safari drive shifts suddenly towards exhilarating and those are the stories that end up in books such as this one. This morning was one of those, but now the Painted dogs, still hungry but utterly spent, were resting all around the car, panting hard, and the impalas had regathered safely but warily along the tree line.

"Wow, that was fun!" I said breathlessly. "There're only a few thousand of these dogs left in the wild. It's a real privilege to see them."

"We eat them," announced the Korean man.

I paused, startled. The local guide, Joseph, sat bolt upright. Behind The Boss, his daughter, a high school student in the USA, opened her mouth to say something, then thought better of it. Her two brothers, both at Ivy League universities and also therefore more sensitive to western cultural norms, looked embarrassed.

"Yes, I know dogs are on the Korean menu," I said carefully. "But not these. Not African Painted dogs. They're highly endangered so... "

"All dogs," said The Boss firmly. "We eat."

His family grimaced. I decided to go with the flow and ask him about it.

"Oh, send cook to market, bring one back. Hang from tree... "

"Gosh," I said, trying not to sound censorious.

"Very delicious. Tender!" he assured me, complacently.

I've had my fair share of meat pies in my life. Ostensibly, they were beef, or chicken. Once, in Australia, kangaroo. But who knows? The joke in Windhoek, Namibia, was that when the Chinese restaurant opened up in the suburb of Klein Windhoek, the issue of roaming street dogs and feral cats disappeared. I've even eaten bear, in Slovenia. I didn't know I was doing it and I simply could not figure out what I'd been given ("Try this, very good, traditional Slovenian meal," I was told) until they translated the menu for me. I felt a bit ill afterwards but that was psychological – guilt will do that to your digestion. So I'm loathe to point fingers; I'm sure dog is pretty good. Better than oysters anyway. I don't get oysters. They're just like massive gobs of mucus, no matter how much lemon juice and black pepper and Tabasco you lavish upon them. *Sies!*

I changed the subject as the drive progressed but it wouldn't stay changed for long. Every time I pointed out a new species of animal or bird (or even, on one occasion, a huge Monitor lizard), the Korean man wanted to know what it tasted like. It was extremely annoying. Why can't wild creatures be wonderful intrinsically? Why can't they just *be?* Why do people insist on measuring them by how good they taste? And I'm not only talking about Asians here – all nations do it. "I'll bet that Guinea fowl tastes good in a red wine marinade." We humans love blood, and we're preoccupied by food. We're still hunters and gatherers, under a thin veneer of civilisation.

Later that afternoon we went on a fishing trip, a gentle chunter down the Linyanti channel where we angled for the fat river bream that laze in the ample shade of the water lily pads along the banks, hiding from Fish eagles. The Korean man hooked a fish and dragged it flapping on board. Unpocketing a clasp knife, he flipped open a blade with a finger nail. Once again, Joseph was horrified.

"Hey, mister, wait! What are you doing?" he asked urgently.

"Make fillet," said the Korean man. "Eat now."

I interceded.

"No, no, no, this is a national park, you can't do that. You have to put it back. 'Catch and Release', that's the policy. Sorry."

The local guide nodded energetically and tried to take the fish from The Boss, who held on to the squirming bream.

"What? Why? We eat, we eat. Many fish here."

A short tug of war ensued, which Joseph won, gripping the intended victim firmly, even protectively.

"Okay, okay," conceded the Korean man, opening his hands to Joseph, "I take only one fillet. One side of fish only."

Joseph raised an eyebrow, shook his head in disgust and tossed the rapidly asphyxiating fish into the stream. He fired up the Yamaha outboard engine and took us straight back to camp, deeply disgruntled.

At dinner that evening, the Korean man told his family about the incident. There was much sympathetic shaking of heads as The Boss outlined the deep injustice done to him. After dinner his daughter drew me aside and said, "I apologise for my father. He's old fashioned. He doesn't understand."

"No problem," I replied. "We Africans are fantastically skilled at wiping out our own wildlife. Look at what we're doing to elephants, rhinos, pangolins and hundreds of other species. It's just that this game reserve is a place of sanctuary. Tell me, do you eat dogs?"

She looked down, a little ashamed but said, "Yes, in Korea, when I'm at home. I like it, actually."

"Okay, well, most of the people I guide like to walk their dogs, not eat them. But, by the way, here in southern Africa, we eat worms. *Mopane* worms. I've had them. Not so good to my taste but millions of people love them."

"Yeugh, that's *disgusting,*" she said, aghast.

"Not here it isn't," I said, "Here it's just another kind of normal."

34

DIMINISHING RETURNS

Dammit. Dammit, and dammit again. Not for the first time, I've failed to heed my own advice. Guests seek leadership from their guides, that's why they have them in the first place. Leadership, knowledge, companionship. And sound advice. Advice such as: "Mind your fluid intake today folks. It's a long flight on a small plane, and there's no toilet on board."

It had been a frenetic morning getting everyone from the Halzburg Hotel in Windhoek to the international airport for a dawn take-off. Brent had suddenly mislaid his passport, it was hard to find a receptionist awake enough to take a credit card payment, and the transfer driver arrived late, looking rumpled and ashamed. He looked even more dismal once I had finished my, "Really? So this is how the best safari company in Namibia operates? Unbelievable!" admonishment. I was properly disgruntled. In my defence, the sparrows hadn't even started to chitter and chirp yet and I hadn't had coffee. But then I found the fancy Italian cappuccino machine hissing in a corner of the hotel and I set to. I forgot to *not* drink coffee. And I love coffee. I don't know what the long term effect on my adrenals is going to be but I'm very fond of the java.

Now we are airborne for Maun in Botswana, thirty minutes into the flight, and I notice with horror the stirrings of bladder pain. What! Oh shit, I can't believe this, we still have two more hours of trampolining about the warming May Kalahari sky, and I need the toilet. Imminently. The guests are all slumped in the front three rows of the Cessna Caravan, dozing or reading their Kindles in the gathering light. I move quietly to the back row and settle nonchalantly into a seat. The pilot senses the weight shift in the aircraft and glances back. I give him a beaming smile and he responds with a thumbs-up, then returns to his instruments. Okay, Mr Solution-driven guide, what's your plan here, I think. The pain is increasing rapidly. We all know the pain; it is a very particular discomfort, and the mind begs for relief. A silly old alphabet rhyme invades my disturbed thoughts: "A for horses, B for mutton, C forth Highlanders, ...P for relief." Not funny.

I'm always reminding the guests to stay hydrated. Sip, people, sip water, it's hot. Most adopt my advice. There's a price to pay for the exaggerated health information on Embassy travel advisory websites about consuming three litres of water per day. At that rate, you'll need a 'loo with a view' because you'll spend almost your entire safari holiday with a distended bladder. But constant sipping is good. The problem is that very many safari guests have never had a bush wee. It's easy for men because, when they get to the letter P, they can hop off the game drive vehicle, pluck out their 'picnic attachment' and stand splay-legged to one side of the road, making the usual time-honoured urinal jokes about "this is where the big guys hang out". For women, it's much more awkward. It's not only painful to squat down (and there are some elderly ladies who might never get back up again!) but they find it unhygienic and embarrassing, sheltering behind the Land Rover, making obvious puddles on the road. (I always wonder what the animals think when later they wander by, sniffing at these territorial markings. "Dunno what species pissed here but it reeks of ammonia! Best we watch our step, this one smells dangerous.") So, sometimes women simply refuse to bush wee at all. As a stoic lady once told me,

"Lloyd, it's porcelain or nothing", and many women will choose to endure hours of pain, quite spoiling their game drive, grimly hanging on in waterlogged misery until we return to camp. Anything to avoid the ignominy of a safari squat and the aggravation of grass seeds in their knickers. Still, it's a trade-off that bewilders me. Maybe I just have a low pain threshold.

Right now, I'd donate a kidney for a bush wee (well, it's the kidneys that are the problem here, after all) but unfortunately there are 10 000 feet between me and the ground and at least a further 120 minutes of pain. More, if you know immigration at Maun airport: the toilets are on the *far* side of immigration, and the queue is interminably long if you've touched down in the wake of South African Airways out of Johannesburg. It's a disaster of an airport for people who drink too much coffee.

And then it strikes me! This is going to be okay, actually! Relief floods through my fevered brain; I'll kneel down behind the seats in the luggage space of the Cessna, and pee into an empty mineral water bottle. Of course! No-one will see, they're all slumbering like winter bears up there in rows A, B and C, and the pilot is preoccupied with flying the plane and talking nonsense to his buddies on the company traffic channel. Cool! Quietly I get up from the seat. I know what to expect. There will be a big cooler box at the back of the plane filled with plastic bottles of water, so I'll simply open one half-litre bottle (surely that will be large enough?), dispense its contents into the cooler box, then refill it with my urine, and tuck the bottle into my carry-on luggage, out of sight. I'm liking this plan. A lot.

I glance into the back of the Caravan. No cooler box. *What?* There's water though, a dozen shrink-wrapped bottles, tiny little 250 millilitre things, barely of use to man or beast. No, man, there *has* to be a cooler box. There's *always* a cooler box. Please let there be a cooler box! There isn't. Crap.

I sit down again. Plan B. What *is* Plan B? I'm feeling weak from that old familiar pain that you get towards the end of the first half of a rugby game when the alcohol has done its best work but your bladder is screaming at you. You don't want to miss a single second of watching the Sharks mauling the Bulls for the second time this season, but you know the stadium's urinal queue is going to be very, very long indeed. Caffeine and alcohol. Those two have a lot to answer for. They occupy far too much of the mind.

I resign myself to an experiment. I'm going to have to empty a bottle. Just one. By drinking it. It's a risk I'll have to take. How fast does water turn to pee? I don't know. One hour, maybe? I suspect it happens faster, but I consciously fool myself: okay, drink 250 millilitres, then fill the bottle with urine, at least that way you stay even. In theory, the pain will remain at the same (barely manageable) level. It makes scientific sense, but I'm not certain. In any case, I have no choice: I am in proper pain now, and I can't do the "porcelain or nothing" thing. I guess I'm an instant gratification kind of guy. Everyone is still dozing up front. Well, there's a first time for everything. I unscrew the bottle cap, and sip gingerly. The water doesn't go down easily. I'm not in the least bit thirsty, and it is deeply counter-intuitive to take in liquid when your mind is hollering, "Not *in*, fool, out; OUT, OUT!" But I get it done. 250 millilitres of temporary respite awaits.

I kneel behind the seats and set to. Careful now! The plane has reached cruising altitude, so it's smooth, but you never know when a maverick pocket of discordant air is going to disrupt your aim. And the bottle opening is small, man! Be quick, people are going to turn around and say, "Oi! What the *hell* are you doing back there, Camp?" It looks flipping dodgy. I get stage-fright, and nothing happens for ages, but eventually I feel the acid burning down the pipe and a weak dribble emerges. Then the flow increases and the pressure becomes alarming. The little bottle fills rapidly. No spillage, thank the gods for small mercies – hold the joystick still, captain (the pilot, I mean, what were *you* thinking?) – but there is an unexpected complication: foam. Frothy piss, at least half the volume of the bottle, and I've got to stop. It hurts to cancel the programme in mid-stream, but I have no choice. I cap the bottle, tuck all away, and surreptitiously examine the result. The pain in my bladder is quite unabated, and there is no more than 125 millilitres of actual liquid in the stupid bottle. I'm going to have to let the foam settle, and do it *again*. Dammit. Dammit, and dammit again.

The eastern earth meridian is showing bright and yellow now, and the guests are soon going to be waking, and tucking into their breakfast bags. I don't have long. Should I drink a second bottle? I can't face it. I just *know* that this is a case of diminishing returns. You'll make it worse, pal, I tell myself, and it's already bad. Okay, let's fill just this single bottle, and call it quits. One more go. Kneeling again, I gingerly top up, and secure the warm vessel in my backpack. For the remainder of the interminable flight, I curl up in my seat and hang on in awful self-condemnatory silence.

The Cessna touches down in Maun. No SAA flight. Hooray! Oh, wait. Aagh, typical! We've been told by Air Traffic Control to park about as far from the terminal building as is possible. I stare hatefully at the lollipop man waving us in with his day-glo paddles. Hurry up! Can't you see there's a problem here? And then the pilot needs to cool the turbo down, so I sit waiting in agony while the bloody propellor spins to a stop. Immediately, I'm out the door. It's not protocol and the pilot is astonished, but there's no time to explain. Never mind the steps, chap, I tell the approaching apron assistant, and I leap down to the tarmac, my persecuted bladder reminding me of my folly as I hit the runway, and sprint-stumble awkwardly to the edge of the tarred surface. The guests are watching, agape. It's not the first time I've guided them, but they've never seen this happen before. Fumbling at my flies, I let go. It's a particular kind of pain, and it's a particular kind of relief, too. And it doesn't stop. It smarts all the way down the tubes, and it goes on and on and on. Dimly, I think, matey, have you learned a lesson here? Don't be doing this again.

I re-join the guests with a wan visage and a sheepish grin, and the assistant ferries us over to International Arrivals, a pokey little hall with torn wall posters extolling the wonders of the Okavango Delta. A self-important official is crammed into a wonky chip-board cubicle, fingering his stamp and glaring at these tourists who have dared to ruin his day. Out of pure spite, he tells me he needs to conduct a random hand-luggage search. "Whatever, dude," I think, and unzip my backpack. Mr Immigration reaches in and extracts a small mineral bottle, a small, *warm*, bottle, filled to the very brim with... orange juice? Oh crap, I've forgotten about that.

"Hey," says Brent, "where'd you get the juice? I didn't see any of that on the plane."

"Brought it with me," I say in what I hope is an assured voice.

"No liquids through Immigration, sir," says the official to me sternly, peering at the bottle and giving it a suspicious shake. "You'll have to drink it right now, or I'm going to have to confiscate it."

I pale, and my facade slips a little but recovering quickly, I tell him:

"Keep it pal, it's all yours. Enjoy. I can't possibly drink another drop."

35

VANILLA GUIDING

The boots were in a box on the desk when I walked into my office that morning. Tough buffalo leather with a soft impala-skin tongue, and chunky impossible-to-wear-out rubber soles. A generous toe cap for feet that prefer no shoes at all. Courteneys, legendary Bulawayo-manufactured safari shoes, hand-stitched and sturdy, like the Zimbabweans themselves: they just go on for ever, despite everything that is thrown at them. Actually, it's a bad business model, really; you just can't wear Courteneys out. I've been wearing mine for twelve years now, and the only change has been the laces and some occasional polish. They're ugly things, boxy and wide, with no modern pretences like contoured arches and ergonomic shaping, but they're very comfortable. I love them. I've led walking safaris all over Africa in mine: I'm sure the grooved treads harbour even yet mud from the cloud forests of Bwindi, sand from the Namib dunes and clay from the Lugenda river in Mozambique.

Lewis sent them to me. They're not cheap, and he couldn't actually afford them, back then. It's a gesture I will never forget, but I wasn't surprised he sent them, because Lewis is a rainbow guide. His character is bright, his style is multi-coloured and his attitude is golden. There was a short note inside the left shoe that read simply, 'Thank you.'

If you want a multi-faceted, quite possibly a life-changing experience on safari, you need a guide like Lewis. You want a big personality, confident and with opinions, hungry to listen and to learn; a story-teller and a person hugely eager to introduce you to the resonance of the wilderness. You want someone with a ready laugh who is his own person, not a drone. You don't always get that. Far too often, unfortunately, you end up with a vanilla guide: a hint of flavour, nice yet somehow rather unsatisfying, leaving you wanting more.

Safari tourists settle. I wish they wouldn't. They all too willingly accept sub-standard guiding in the lodges. Usually, this is because they don't know any better. Everyone lives in their own reality. So the guests will choose to believe that their sightings, their safari experiences, are the best ever, the 'most unique.' It is necessarily so because it validates the spend, the effort, the travel, the choice. No-one is going to go home and say it was 'so-so.' So we all play the game, guides and guests, that this is the finest safari ever undertaken. And there is nothing wrong with that. It's natural. But could it have been even better?

Vanilla guiding. It is truly astounding what some guides can get away with and just how much their clients will put up with. It amazes me what excuses the clients will make for vanilla guides. It's because of an understandable but unconscious patronisation. They don't mean to be condescending but sometimes the guests feel sorry for the guide. They forgive the vanilla guide for not knowing as much as he should. They let the guide off for being a bit late for activities. They pity the guide who can't afford binoculars – and yet, really, who trusts a guide that has no binoculars? That's like trusting a mechanic with no spanners or a doctor without a stethoscope. They frown when they can't properly understand the guide's accent, but are too embarrassed to ask him to repeat himself more than once. They smile indulgently when the guide nods off in a warming sun while parked at a wildlife sighting. They shrug when the guide cannot produce even a basic map of the area, and when he claims that he has no bird identification book because it was left out in the rain (by himself!), and can't afford a replacement. They will accept a certain degree of slovenly personal hygiene, occasional sullenness and even rank unsafe driving. And here's the kicker: they will, despite all this, tip the guide generously upon departure and tell him what a great guy he is.

Why do some safari guests tolerate insipid performance? They don't accept incompetency at home, surely? Back in Europe or the USA, a sloppy effort from any supplier is not rewarded by cash and a pat on the back. The problem, of course, is that this positive reinforcement of lacklustre guiding encourages a plateauing of standards. Vanilla guides are more than happy to comply with lower expectations. That's how most people are in *any* industry. We're a lazy species. So sometimes guides need a prod. And the prod is most effective when it comes from the guests.

We guides have an important ally in the process of transformation and dream-making. The wilderness itself. The wilderness speaks to our guests and captures them in its mysteries. Watching wild creatures in a place where the hand of man is almost non-existent very often effects a personal transformation and our job then is to interpret, to facilitate, to share the nuances of the stage upon which we are so lucky to work.

But... it is the magic of the wilderness that is also the very reason that vanilla guides can get away with spiceless performances. The bush experience is so dramatic on its own that it can carry a lazy guide. It can make him look better than he is. And so the clients actually *don't* always get full value for money. But they don't realise that. If a guide takes them to a pride of lions on a kill, or a pool where hippos yawn widely at you all afternoon, maybe a river where a herd of elephants drinks while their youngsters splash each other in the shallows, perhaps a forest where baby gorillas tug on the ears of the great silverback, the experience is wonderful and everyone is delighted. Job done! The guide can sit back now. Right? Wrong! *Anyone* can do that. It's what you do on the way there, the interpretation of the sighting, what you do afterwards, the way in which you add perspective and analysis and story, that sets you apart as a guide. A great guide sets the scene, creates the drama, reveals the moment, and leaves the clients hanging, anxiously hoping, for more. He doesn't just pitch up, watch and push off. He's a magician. He's a ring master. And he loves it!

From whence arises this inadvertent patronisation, this settling for lower standards? It revolves around privilege, and luck. The guests look at their own lives, and acknowledge their happy circumstances, and feel grateful for their lot and a bit sorry for the guides who don't have these advantages.

Remember, I'm one of the *lucky* Africans. I have a lot of things going for me, by pure good fortune. I grew up white and middle class in apartheid South Africa and therefore I was given an excellent education. My cultural heritage is European which means that I tend to eat meat and three veg, listen to rock music, read novels set in England and America, watch Netflix and value the same basic things as my guests, such as rapid service, attention to time and detail, and crucially, an appreciation for the environment and wild places. I didn't really choose that: it happened *to* me. But what this means is that it allows me easily to share conversations with my clients and appreciate their needs, and be comfortable in *their* countries.

And until about twenty-five years ago, all guides in Africa were essentially like me. Young white men, tremendous wildlife enthusiasts, very eager to simply be in the bush, almost anywhere, with almost anyone. We were the ones at the wheel, the jeep jockeys. It was all we wanted to do, and we really didn't care if the money was no good.

It's changed, though. It *had* to change, and we white guides had to change too. These days when you stay at a lodge in any African country, it is almost certain that you will have a local man driving the safari car. Occasionally, happily, you might get a woman. (That's the next necessary guiding revolution; overcoming the cultural assumption across Africa that it is a job that should be done by men only). But these new young guides are under subtle pressure from the industry to work in the way that the older white ones work, and that can be a problem, a cultural hurdle. Why should they copy the old-timers anyway? Once a new style and a tradition of excellence amongst local guides is established, when their kids look at them and think, "That's who I want to be, an excellent safari guide, like my dad", the problem will mostly vanish. For the present though, too often the guiding standards are poor, and the guides are getting away with it. They are not being held to account by the guests.

Most African guides are quite new at this. Many of them are not yet very good, and distressingly lacking in genuine enthusiasm for the wilderness. But the clients forgive them because they think that the guides are doing really well despite their limitations, despite their upbringing, despite their lowly economic status, despite their history. So what if they don't know what that bird is called, or who won the Stanley Cup or the fact that they can't pour a gin and tonic? True. So what? The guided experience still works provided that the local guide understands what he *does* have.

And that is authenticity. He has a story. He doesn't just talk about herding the goats and keeping the cheetahs from eating them. He *was* the herder. He doesn't just talk about using the root of the Camelthorn tree to make a potion that inhibits coughing. He actually does that. The local guide doesn't have to repeat second-hand information about the elephant-human conflict when it is his own crops that are being destroyed by elephants every year. That's where their strength lies, not knowledge of international politics and what's hot in the West End.

But he has a challenge nevertheless – he needs to keep growing. What conversation (after talk of wildlife has been exhausted) does he have when he sits for dinner with the guests that night? When the talk, as it always does, turns to COVID-19, Brexit, the American political fracture, NFL football, *Breaking Bad*, champagne versus prosecco, the Myanmar mess, fracking and oil pipelines, global warming, the first test at Lord's and plastics in our oceans, well, then that local guy just wants to go to bed. It's not his fault. It's cultural. He had a different education. But something might get lost in the guided experience when he can't have those conversations. The bond between the guests and the guide might never fully develop.

But let's assume that a local guide has indeed created his unique style. Is there still a problem? Unfortunately, there can be.

It's that many guides shelter behind their lack of opportunity and use it as an excuse to openly solicit their guests. The guests get played, and it is embarrassing to watch. One shameless guide I heard about persuaded his guests to pay for his dental work. There are too many conversations that go something like this:

"Nice binoculars," says Elvis. "I wish I could afford some but my kids' school fees are so expensive, and I have to take care of my aged mother."

"Nice sunglasses," says Elvis, looking at his own battered plastic ones bought at the supermarket. (In fact, Elvis never actually wears sunglasses, but *your* Oakleys will sell nicely in town when he goes on leave.)

"There's no coffee in the game-drive basket this morning , so you'll have to drink tea," says Elvis. You hate tea, but okay. (Elvis forgot to check before departure, and now he's blaming the kitchen staff).

"No, I don't know anything about smaller animals," says Elvis, "They didn't teach us that." (So, not Elvis's fault then? And who are 'they'?)

Really? You folks really okay with these lines?

"But the guide is such a nice young fellow, he has four children in the village, he is so earnest and polite and caring, he's trying so *hard...* ," you say.

You're being played. You've got a vanilla guide; he's letting us all down, and you're not getting your money's worth. That sympathy tip you're about to hand him? You really ought not to, you know, it's the old 'three cups and a silver ball on the pavement' trick, and you think you know which cup the ball is under? Fooled ya!

There is too often a strong mercenary element to achieving the guide training. For many young guides, it's a job. Just a job. Where's the passion for the wilderness? Generally, however, it seems there is indeed a positive correlation between those who further their qualifications and the quality of their guiding. Human nature being what it is, though, there are always a few whose actual guiding bears no resemblance to their actual ability, were they inclined to apply it. Will versus skill.

Increasingly, happily, however, your local African guide is likely not only to be very good but also genuinely passionate about conservation and his way of life. And people like me are now the private guides who accompany the safari group and work alongside the local guide. We value the local man: he knows where the animals are, what happened on the previous drive, what the best route to a sighting is, where the best picnic site is, where the most relaxed leopard is likely to be resting today, what the chances of seeing baby hyaenas at the den are. Sometimes the local guide, the best ones, despite the limitations of an unsophisticated background, can indeed carry the show on his own.

A truly vibrant guide. Like Lewis. If you get Lewis, you get lucky.

Luck? It's a perplexing phenomenon. Some say you earn it. Some say you make your own. Lewis did.

I had been running guide training courses in Namibia for Wilderness Safaris for several years. We had a real issue in the noughties: suddenly, lots of lodges, and no staff to run them. I saw my opportunity and asked the boss if I could set up a guide training programme. I'd been a high school teacher in a different life, and the two passions easily combined: helping people to move beyond their present, and being in the wild places of this planet. A dream match-up for me. To his eternal credit and my eternal benefit, the boss agreed.

We needed dozens of guides, they needed to be local Namibians, and we needed them fast. The marketing guys had got a long way ahead of our ability to deliver a fine service, and standards throughout were poor. We were depending on the bush experience to carry us, but that couldn't last. I got to work.

Immediately, my ideals were dashed. I had naively expected a rush of environmentally-minded aspirant guides, people eager to work in the bush, the kind of people who save up for their first pair of binoculars, who keep lists of new birds, learn to identify desert butterflies and chameleons, turn over rocks to find scorpions, the type of people who animatedly told stories and asked the guests a thousand questions about their worlds. In other words, people like me.

A hundred people pitched up at the office in response to my newspaper advert. City folk. I gave them all a basic species identification test. They barely knew what a sparrow was, and almost none of them even had a driving licence. You see what I mean about growing up privileged and lucky? My parents took me to game reserves twice a year. Game reserves, magnificent chunks of wilderness, set aside for white people, back then. And they taught me to drive a car *because we actually had one.* I had a foot up into this business. But these kids were just desperate. I chose thirty to go on a free entry level guide training course at Freidenhau dam, outside Windhoek. Only three of the candidates were whites, and two of those were farmers' sons whose main interest in wildlife was how to make *biltong* out of it. But at least they had a driving licence.

And the start of every course, every time, went like this:

"Why do you want to become a guide?" I asked them all.

"Because we need a job," they said.

"Yes, but why have you come on this particular training course, this *guiding* course?" I persisted.

"The food is free," said one, without a hint of embarrassment.

"What do you know about guiding and the tourism industry?" I asked, startled and annoyed in equal measure.

"You drive around and you show the white people elephants and lions and they tip you in dollars and when you go on leave you can buy Levi's and a cell phone," said another.

"You do know that you will have to work very long hours in all sorts of weather? You will have to fix cars in the workshop, wash dishes, dig holes, move rubbish and unplug sewerage drains. And the guests will expect you to know everything about the bush?" I pointed out.

No response except averted eyes. There wasn't a single conservationist amongst them. No genuine passion for this job. I did detect some personal ambition, however, along the mercenary lines of, 'I will be a trained guide so you will have to pay me a lot and give me the wealthiest and most famous guests who will tip me generously'.

"Okay," I said in despair. I mean, what can you do? – you have to work with what you get. "You want money? Okay. If you pay attention at this course, if you really, really show me that you want to learn about being a guide, if you get good at this, only then will you work with our guests. And then they *might* tip you, if you're good enough. But here are the numbers. Real numbers, okay? You're going to have to work bloody hard because of the initial 100, I chose 30. You. Of you

30, I reckon I might choose five to work for us. Of those five, perhaps two of you will pass probation. The other three will almost certainly be fired for being drunk on duty, or for theft, or for coming back late from leave."

More averted eyes. But these *were* real numbers. My boss had reminded me that the secret to keeping my head above water in the safari training business was to learn to control my disappointment, and it was heartbreaking to see some of our staff members, really good people, suddenly given access to drink and vehicles, throw it all away through alcohol abuse and the 'borrowing' of cars, often simultaneously. What youngster doesn't go crazy on booze and wheels some time? But it just happened so damned often! And young guides died.

It was only through persistence and a lot of such courses that we trained up the guides we needed, and when we sent them out after a series of knowledge-based courses, they were still raw. Vanilla guides. Not their fault, of course but I'd hoped for so much more enthusiasm. I was concerned that the quality of guides I was producing was too poor, that they were too wooden and robotic, going through the motions, just doing it for the money. And then, one day, a light shone through the gloom.

The receptionist phoned and said that a Zimbabwean man wanted to see me, that he had been waiting since early morning, he wouldn't take no for an answer. Please would I see him? I sighed and told her to bring him through. A young man came into my office, cleanly shaven and in a smart shirt, took off his hat, shook my hand firmly and said in careful English:

"Sir, I have heard from friends in my country that you run guide training courses. My name is Lewis. I very much want to become a safari guide but there are no jobs in Zimbabwe, and no free training. I have come from Victoria Falls to ask you to train me and, if I manage, to give me a job."

Victoria Falls is 1400 km by road from Windhoek. That's the same distance as driving from New York City to Orlando, Florida, fuelled not by gasoline but by hope alone.

"How did you get here, Lewis?" I said, struck by his humility, openness and obvious self-reliance.

"I have a friend who works for the Inter-Cape bus service, sir. I can get to Windhoek anytime. It is a long way but if you can offer me training, I will come every time. I will never be late. I will pay attention. I will work hard. I will not let you down."

I knew instinctively that every word was true. You just know. I decided immediately. Anyway, I have a soft spot for the Zimbos, I can't help it. Great people. Except for their government.

"Lewis, listen, I will give you all the training you need. All the way up to advanced level. But, I'm very sorry, I can't offer you a job. We are employing Namibians only. That's the company policy. When the time comes, I will speak to the Wilderness Safaris guys in Victoria Falls, but with that crazy government of yours the safari business is struggling there, and Wilderness Zimbabwe aren't employing guides at the moment."

Lewis made a face, but then he smiled.

"The training will be enough," he said quietly. "Thank you, sir."

Through that year, and the next, Lewis made the journey to Windhoek seven times. Seven times he arrived early. Seven times he came top of the class. Seven times he went back to his country without the prospect of a job. Seven times as I shook his hand goodbye, I wished he was a Namibian. Lewis needed a job. But it was more than that: Lewis was a true conservationist, and a people's person. Lewis had the potential to be very, very good. The safari industry, the world of wildlife preservation, needed guides like Lewis. Zimbabwe needed Lewis.

In the meantime, I ran the courses and created guides. Some flourished and took the opportunity to make a career, some became vanilla guides and did the bare minimum, and some, too often ones with character and colour – potential rainbow guides – blew it completely in a haze of alcohol and lassitude. Slowly, we made progress and the lodges began to deliver guided experiences that equalled the brochure hype.

In the February after Lewis had completed his training, we had a meeting in Victoria Falls to discuss guiding programmes across the countries that Wilderness Safaris operated in. Lewis was as ready as I could make him, as ready as he had made himself. I spoke to the Operations Manager for Zimbabwe.

"We're not employing," he said. "In fact, we're downsizing. If people leave, they don't get replaced. The others just muck in, take over the work. There are no jobs. Each worker is supporting an entire family on a single salary. Sorry. Your guy sounds good, and I know Wilderness Safaris Namibia have already spent a lot of money training him, but still, that was your budget, not ours, and we just can't take him."

"Just meet him," I implored.

The Ops man agreed. I called Lewis.

"Nine o'clock, Elephant Hills hotel. Over to you, my friend."

Lewis got the job. I got a pair of Courteneys. And you, dear guests and lovers of Africa, got a brilliant guide.

36

VVVIP

It drives the camp managers bonkers, and it sets a lodge guide's teeth
on edge. And it seldom works.

'VVVIP' in red, underlined, italics, bold, the works. The message
on the booking sheet sent from company HQ means, "Be very, very
nice to these particular guests. Our business, our *jobs*, depend on these
people. Treat them with kid gloves. Make a special effort. We need to
look *great* on their website."

This means a special hand-crafted welcoming note in the room, a
complimentary bottle of wine (not the cheap house stuff), and some
reluctant obsequious schmoozing from the camp managers, who resent
being reminded about how to do their job. A meeting is called with
the guide. The Chosen One. "Don't let us down, this comes all the
way from HQ, do you understand how important it is to make the
right impression?"

"But," protests the guide, "I treat *all* my guests as VIP's. They're
all special."

Which is bollocks. In the roiling dust and shimmering heat of a long summer as the peak safari season progresses and the people on his car come and go, all the guide can think of by the end of his stretch of duty is how much he is looking forward to eating KFC and watching bad television and just for goodness sakes to be left alone. His attention wavers as fatigue sets in. People inspire, but they make you tired too. But in principle he is correct. Why would a guide treat any guests differently to any others? They all pay the same money, they all want to see the same things, they all sit on the same car and take the same walks and eat the same food. As a matter of professionalism, a guide tries to do his best for everyone. But he can't.

He can't, simply because it would be unnatural. It's a job where you are dealing with people, and human dynamics are always complicated. The reality is that we respond differently to each other in different circumstances. All of us, for example, have had a very competent waiter that served a fine meal in a cool and professional way. No reason to complain. Yes, everything is fine thank you. Great, enjoy your meal. Good night out, home by nine. And then we have also all had a waiter who made our night. Same service but the meal was *fun*, and the atmosphere was delectably charged with banter, repartee, perhaps some cheek. The waiter had character. Chemistry. Actually, yes, we will have another bottle, what the hell! And when your bill comes, maybe you find that the wine has been comped. The waiter had fun because you were up for it. You turned what might have been a mundane evening for him into an entertainment. But it didn't happen at the table right next to yours, even though they had the same waiter. You, the patron, controlled the tempo of the evening. Why would guiding be any different?

You don't all get treated the same. Especially VVVIP travel agents. Tricky lot, travel agents. They promise plenty of future business to the company and they travel on reduced rates but are unlikely to be treated any better than a usual paying guest because the guide's point of view is, "No, just because you're getting this cheap doesn't mean you're better than the other folk on my car. And stop throwing your weight around, this is *my* office." Small-minded, short-sighted, yes... but that's how it can be sometimes.

You don't all get treated the same. Because, guess what? Quite often, in fact, you get treated *better* than the average guest. A guide can do the equivalent of comping your wine too, only he does it in a different way. The guide can go above and beyond for you, if he takes to you, if you stand out, if you're there to have fun. *You*, the client, control that.

That's what happened with Enoch. A walking safari with Charly and Lili, once again, this time in the Linyanti region of Botswana. We had already completed four days of hiking up the length of the Savuti Channel and were supposed to be met at the old *Mopane* bridge over the channel by Enoch, but Enoch had gone missing. An embarrassed lodge manager met us at the bridge and transferred us to camp, promising that all would be well, we would have our walking trip all right, he would find us another guide, Enoch was unfortunately "delayed." Reading between the lines, the powerful likelihood was that Enoch was in fact still in Maun, drunk. I had been concerned about this happening because Enoch's reputation preceded him, but he also had a reputation for being a phenomenal walking guide, extremely good with guests, amazingly knowledgeable and hugely entertaining. Anything but a vanilla guide: a brightly coloured firework if anything. I was really looking forward to working with him.

But he wasn't there. Dud firework. We got on with the safari but – lo and behold – that evening (I could easily imagine the radio calls to Maun, the frantic scramble to search the town, wash and shave him, get him onto a Cessna to the reserve) Enoch walked sheepishly into the firelight after dinner and introduced himself. I was very angry and intolerant at being let down but Charly and Lili set a more mature tone, welcomed him, and I soon got over myself. Onwards and upwards. Plus, Enoch and I were sharing the guides' tent so the sooner the atmosphere between us improved, the better for everyone. Enoch was anxious to make amends, and asked what we were hoping to see. Lions, I told him, we have been unlucky in the item of lions this trip. Lions, on foot.

In the night a lion roared, that deep distant moan that at first you are not sure you have heard, an elemental sound that makes you sit up as you try to figure out where it's coming from, and how far away it is.

"It's The Boss," said Enoch from deep within his blankets. "Ten kilometres." He hadn't even bothered to sit up to listen. "North-east, near the Baobab Pan."

I looked at my watch. It glowed green: 3h30. Pitch black outside, and a chilly breeze blowing.

Twenty minutes later The Boss roared again, his grunts tailing away into the frigid May air. He was answered immediately this time by another lion, another male, calling out the eternal nocturnal challenge: "Whose land is this? It's mine, mine, mine."

"Heading east now towards Ibis Island," came Enoch's muffled voice again.

At half-past four The Boss really let go, and his rival shouted back: "It's mine!" Closer, now. God, what a thrilling sound, the noise rolling in waves towards us.

"Let's go!" said Enoch, suddenly hurling his blankets aside. "I'll meet you at the main area." And he was gone though the tent door in a second, dragging a beanie onto his head, his torch probing the shadows as he trotted to the garage.

Now, here's the thing. Okay, Enoch had ground to make up with us, but it was damned cold, damned dark and damned early and there wasn't a hope that there would be any coffee about. But no other guide in camp was going to rouse his guests at this pre-dawn hour. They'd almost certainly find those lions anyway but only once the sun had taken the edge off the gloom. The Boss could wait until coffee and rusks had been taken and everyone had settled comfortably in the game drive vehicle, tucked up with hot water bottles on their laps and wearing wind-proof ponchos. No rush. But also, no adrenaline rush. It was about to be just a standard safari day for them, and their guests. They were under no compunction to find The Boss silhouetted against a red and rising sun. Enoch was going to pay the price for this, however: his fellow guides were going to be under serious pressure from their jealous and disgruntled guests. Special treatment, you see. How come we, only us, went out in the dark? But Enoch was also genuinely excited to do this and he had enough experience and character as a guide to disregard the peer pressure. I was still dragging my Courteney boots over thick winter socks when the headlights of his Land Cruiser flooded our tent with yellow light. Charly and Lili were already on board, looking dazed but keen.

"Come on, come on, let's go!" commanded Enoch.

We drove, fast, under a brilliant deep purple sky, cutting out way through thick stands of tall turpentine grass that smelled of kerosene and blocked any view. There was no roaring now, or if there was it was muffled by the sound of the grass swishing loudly against the sides of the car. Enoch drove swiftly, unerringly, and then suddenly stopped, killing the engine.

"Listen!" he said.

The Boss was at it again, bellowing, and a pair of Egyptian geese from a distant pond rose hissing and honking in alarm and hurtled blindly into the night. How had Enoch heard the lion against the growl of the engine? He was good.

"Two kilometres?" I ventured, and pointed. "That way?"

"Three," said Enoch. "*That* way," and gunned the engine.

The early light that makes you feel just a little bit superior to the slumbering masses began to create forms from fantasy. In a clearing in the depths of some open woodland, far from any road, Enoch suddenly stopped again, leapt from the car and grabbed his .375, beckoning us to follow. A small herd of zebras galloped away. People! On foot! We followed Enoch to a prominent game trail, an elephant highway created by the passage of huge feet moving towards the lagoon. He crouched and, using a stalk of grass to point with, outlined some marks on the ground.

"Very fresh. Ten minutes. He likes this path. I know his feet. The left front foot has a toe missing, can you see? That way."

Ten minutes! He's just *here!* We knew what to do. Without a sound, we trailed behind Enoch, who was completely at ease, walking quickly and confidently on the path, looking around without concern. I kept just behind him, watching the tracks. Enoch was the master tracker but to me the tracks seemed to be getting old too quickly. A little less crisp on the edges, and several of them already had the imprints of the first foraging turtle doves on them. We were striding faster now, almost trotting, and I knew were getting further behind the lion. His tracks were spaced apart, long paces: this lion was hastening to confront the intruder. I clicked my fingers to get Enoch's attention.

"We can't catch him," I said in a low voice, a little out of breath.

Charly and Lili understood the situation, and looked disappointed. Enoch on his own might have run the lion down but to jog on a lion's tracks as fresh as this, with clients, is dangerous. The lion could easily stop to listen, to taste the wind, hear us or smell us, and go into hiding in long grass near the track...

"We will see him," said Enoch without explaining further. He leaned his rifle against a small shrub, cupped both hands around his mouth and made a far-reaching strangled noise, raising and lowering the pitch, the squealing distress call of an animal in trouble, an animal in the jaws of a predator, bellowing in the knowledge that its life was just about over. The noise curled out through the woodland and died away in a series of echoes. It was creepy.

"A baby wildebeest dying," he announced. "Come quickly, up there. He's coming!"

We retreated rapidly up a giant termite mound, a centuries-old castle created by multiple generations of the insects and settled ourselves behind a fallen knobthorn, a bastion of a tree that gave us sanctuary. Enoch hung his rifle on a branch.

"No talking," I said unnecessarily. "Absolutely no noise, no movement, please."

Enoch made the call again. We stared down the path. Nothing. A little late-to-bed Barred owlet hooted once or twice, and then suddenly some Bush squirrels started up their alarm chattering. Enoch stared into a grove of *Crotons* for a long minute and then announced casually:

"A leopard. It has come to find the dead wildebeest. But it saw us and it has gone now."

What! We swivelled on our backsides and scanned the green foliage. No movement at all. And then a noise caught my attention. The sound of an animal running through tall grass, the fronds parting before him, getting closer, fast, straight towards us. And there he came! The Boss, at the gallop. I grabbed Lili's arm and pointed. Enoch picked up his firearm and checked the safety. He was smiling. The great lion ran straight towards us, straight down the elephant path, straight out of the red, red sun, his massive head held low, his mane flaring, backlit by the brand new day, the sound of his pads perfectly audible, little clouds of dust exploding at each footfall in the soft light, his shoulder blades rising and falling with each stride. We held our breath. It was absolutely thrilling. On foot in the presence of this great beast, a great beast on the hunt. He knew that wildebeest was here, close by, he didn't know what had caught it, but he was going to find out, and he was going to take it. Take it all.

The path ran twenty metres past our termite mound, and we sat as statues. The lion was intent on his mission, and he knew exactly where to go. He swished past without seeing us at all, jogged on to almost exactly where Enoch had made the first distress call, and stopped. He looked around, raised his head, sniffed the wind, circled a little and stood there looking confused. His total concentration was on his potential prey, and his prey was mysteriously missing. No-one took pictures. No-one moved. We sat.

After a while, The Boss decided that he must have been mistaken. No blood, no smell, no wildebeest. Could he tell we had been there? Surely? What about our smell, our tracks? But he gave no sign. He never once looked towards us. His chest stopped heaving and then he slowly made his way down the path, his rival quite forgotten, and disappeared into the woods without looking back.

We sat for a while longer, in awed silence. Then Enoch beckoned and we quietly moved away in single file, making our way back towards the vehicle on a different route. Still no-one spoke. What to say? What words describe that? We climbed onto the Land Cruiser and suddenly, feeling safer, everyone started to talk in a rush. An excited babble. This was not our first safari but my god that was epic! *Ex africa semper aliquid novi.* (Out of Africa flows something new.)

We drove directly back to camp. It seemed too mundane to be looking at herds of impalas after that. And we needed coffee. The other lodge guests were just leaving on game drive. They looked at us inquiringly as we tumbled from the car, our hair all over the place, the men unshaven, the ladies with their pyjamas sticking out from under their heavy jackets. Those folk were going to have a very good day. They were going to see a great lion. But our day had already been made.

You don't all get treated the same.

37

EXCEPT WHEN IT ISN'T

In the interval between main course and dessert, the safari camp's choir, dressed in its distinctive 'Nelson Mandela' button-up singing shirts, troops into the dining area and parades itself in a ragged line before the dinner guests, and I think, 'Oh god, here we go again, I flipping *hate* this stuff.'

Whichever camp you're in, it's always the same act. The troupe mumbles and giggles amongst themselves, dithering about and shuffling into line, apparently looking for someone to take the lead, seemingly arguing good naturedly about which song to sing, then someone sings the first line of a song but the rest of the singers don't like it and so the words die, the audience laughs as they are expected to, and eventually the lead singer, usually a chef of large proportion (good, good, never trust a skinny chef), starts to ululate and suddenly the entire ensemble are away, clapping and stamping and swaying, and almost always doing it beautifully.

What voices! What rhythm! What harmony!

Yes. But what a con.

Does the choir really want to be there? Sometimes, yes. Sometimes, they take enormous pride in their show and are manifestly practised and their exuberance is unfeigned. The choir enters inter-camp competitions and they take it very seriously indeed. Not always though, and sometimes they can't be persuaded to perform either, unless they are paid to do so. It's always made me feel uncomfortable, the way the lodges put these folk out on display. It's become the norm, the expected thing to offer as evening entertainment. It's often boring too: the same lacklustre masquerade but with different players, the same songs ('Amarularularula') and once they do get going, the songs go on and on and on. Dining room service is temporarily suspended so tough luck for you if you were hoping for a glass of wine because your waiter is now the baritone at the back of the choir. The guests are tired after a long day in the game reserve and three or four harmonious songs would be truly lovely but now they're unstoppable, the choir, and every singer has to take a turn at leading, and then the bloody conga line starts and you feel judgemental and disapproving and a right wet blanket if you don't participate, but your daddy dancing is typically bad, and the entire thing is tedious and awkward.

And then the tip box comes out. Not subtly placed on the Reception counter but wantonly presented, circulated amongst the guests like the collection plate at Sunday church, but guess what? The takings are meagre; the guests don't have money with them because their wallets are in their rooms, so now they're self-conscious about appearing to be mean, coughing and staring into their empty wine glasses as the box passes them by for the second time. The shift in the mood of the choir becomes apparent. To them, this is a commercial opportunity, wasted. But they're not cross with the guests who don't know better. They're grumpy with the managers, who find this crass exploitation of a captive audience acutely embarrassing, and who therefore have not informed the guests that they might want to bring some cash to dinner. The managers are caught between a rock and hard place: the lodge is pre-paid, fully inclusive, the guests have deliberately booked it so that they do not have to concern themselves with payments beyond the initial lump sum, and to ask them to dig their wallets out for dinner goes very much against the concept, the very ethos. But the choir doesn't see it that way. They know that these overseas guests are well off, relative to them. What's a couple of quid going to cost the tourists, really? That's all they're asking for, for heaven's sake! But the managers not only seem to apologise for this gross trap, they're apparently actively obstructing it.

It's overdone: the banging on the drums and the antic capers. Once, long ago, it was wonderful. The choir sang because they wanted to please the guests, to give them a window into their culture, their pride in their tradition of entertainment with song and dance and stories at night. But then Mammon intervened and altered the wholesome nature of the event. Guests started to tip the choir, which was fair enough and appreciated, but the singers quickly identified the songs that the guests best responded to, the ones they could clap and dance to, the ones with sing-along choruses. Often, these were hymns, recognisable and easy for guests to join in with, and the traditional folk songs took a back seat. So it became boring. Sometimes as the choir files in, I take a whisky and go and sit outside in the dark. Then the noise simply becomes pleasant background, blending nicely with the sound of the night crickets and the tinkle of melting ice in two fingers of Glenmorangie.

And yet, on occasion...

On this night, at Tswalu Kalahari lodge in north-western South Africa, the choir is comprised entirely of children, some as young as five. Now they're using the *kids* to pluck at the guilt strings of the tourists, I think with horror. But then these youngsters start to move and sing and I nearly fall off my chair. They're amazing! They're brilliant! It's fresh, its energetic and these youngsters move differently somehow, stamping and shaking in precise rehearsed sequences the likes of which I have never seen before. And they really seem to be enjoying themselves too, no fake smiles. They're practised and proud of their skill. What is more, there's not a tip box in sight. I'm transfixed by their performance. I hear myself laughing and my foot is tapping and for the first time in ages I don't want the dinner entertainment to stop. And I am reminded how I used to feel when I watched a choir sing around a fire and I think, this is like then, this is magical! It is so lovely to be surprised, to be delighted. That's what we strive for on safari but like in every industry, new ideas are quickly replicated. Cold face-cloths when you disembark from the car. Bread rolls baked on the grid before your eyes. Pizza Friday. Jam jars that are actually solar lights. Surprise bush breakfasts. Everyone starts doing them. And they're great because for the guests, of course, it is *all* new.

And I muse upon the words of a colleague who once reminded me, when I said that I was unutterably bored by the choir, that, "It's not what you want, Lloyd, it's what the *guests* want." (Thanks Fox).

But *do* tourists know what they want? And how do they distinguish between the authentic and the phony, the tired parody? Do they admire the mime artists on Circular Quay at Sydney Harbour because they think that is typically Australian? The Zimbabwean wood carvers in Victoria Falls: are those curios really made right there, by that guy? Llama wool hats in the Cusco town market on the way to Machu Picchu: not made in China, I hope? Plastic opera masks in St Mark's Square, Venice, flogged by African migrants. What actually represents local culture and how do you access it? How about feeding the pigeons below Nelson's Column in Trafalgar Square? Isn't that traditional somehow? Or how about... taking pictures of ochre-encrusted bare-breasted women selling carved corkwood spoons on the pavements of Windhoek, Namibia? What's real?

The Himba people are not even from Windhoek. Traditionally, they herd their cattle and goats a thousand kilometres away in the desert areas of northern Kaokoland. If you venture far off the beaten track you might find them at their temporary villages, the pubescent boys watching over the flocks and the women dressed as they have for centuries in goat skins and necklaces of ostrich egg shell, their bodies smeared with a paste of butter-fat and ochre powder, living simple lives. It really is amazing to witness.

And then sometime in the noughties, an entrepreneur, either from amongst the Himba themselves or more likely a percipient tourist operator, said to them, "Hey guys, great plan, how about you set up a model village not too far from the road where we can always find you? It's such a pain selling an authentic tribal experience when you suddenly bugger off and we don't know where you've gone; everyone's disappointed, and its bad for business. So how about we build a replica village and then you hang around there all the time with the kids and the dogs and the goats. Make things to sell. We'll bring tourists and you'll make a fortune."

And lo, it came to pass. And not just in one locality, either. You will now find these villages in such unlikely places as the gates to Etosha National Park. Worse, these ostensible pastoralists camp out in the streets of the capital city, and even more astonishingly, in the foggy coastal damp of Swakopmund for goodness sake, trading 'authentic Himba curios', underdressed by western standards with their breasts uncovered, and charging ten Namibia dollars for a photo. I don't blame them for taking advantage of the tourists' desire to see them: the Himba are an ancient and intriguing group of people, and anyway, who is to dictate to them how they choose to make a living. But it feels cynical and exploitative and I cannot abide it. And there are an increasing number of tourists who refuse to do these visits, who will not participate in the farce.

But happily my blanket reservations were abolished recently; the exception proves the rule. I went to the Hoanib Valley Camp where I was guided by Frank, a local Himba man, who took us to the very place where he was born and introduced my clients and me to his family. This was no facsimile cattle-post. There was no pretence or posing for the camera. Frank spoke without a commercial agenda about his life as a young fellow chasing cheetahs away from the goat flocks, and why the Himba knock out the top incisors of their children when they reach puberty. About the daily struggle for water in a parched land, and the dowry-cost of getting married. About drought, and night lions on the prowl, and the heartbreak that elephants cause when they demolish the water reservoirs. It was stupendous. It was refreshing. It was utterly real.

But the cash culture. We did that, we safari people. We create an industry and make promises to potential clients about showing them traditional cultures, and we fulfil those promises in a somewhat authentic fashion. It may well be that the Himba welcome it. No one can deny, for instance, the Navajo their guided cultural tours in Monument Valley, or stop the Maasai on the lip of the Ngorongoro Crater from demonstrating their vertical jumping dance, or indeed prevent an Okavango bushman from selling his spear to a tourist for one hundred lousy bucks, the very spear that he inherited from his grandfather. But it feels cheap.

And so does the damned singing.

Except when it isn't.

38

FIFTY SHADES OF KHAKI

I kept this story till last. But some of you spotted the title on the Contents page and came straight here, didn't you?

We used to call them the 'clip-clop' girls. It was because of the sound their shoes made on the bare cement floor as they followed their Flehmen-faced guide down the passage of the singles quarters to his thin-walled, spartan bedroom. It was a strictly nocturnal noise, often followed by hoarse whispering and stifled giggles. Back then, guiding was a boy's world, a young man's world, and there was plenty of good-natured sniggering and poking of each other in the ribs the morning after the tell-tale noises had been heard. Don't think, though, that the muffled tittering was always made by likely young lasses. Some of those muffled noises were surprisingly mature-sounding. You played the ball where it lay. Back then.

"So, um, khaki fever, is that a real thing? Sex on safari, I mean, like, does that happen... a lot?"

It's a question that arises sometimes, cautiously raised, in the manner of one who really wants to know but worries that it is an indelicate thing to ask.

A lot? I'm not sure about a lot, but yes, yes, absolutely it does. Guests and guides: well, they're all human, aren't they?

In my book *Africa Bites*, I wrote about other inevitable guest questions, primary amongst which are, "So, what's the most dangerous animal out here? What's the scariest thing that has ever happened to you?" The trite answer, and I have sometimes resorted to it, is, "Us. People. *We're* dangerous. And scary."

We are, too. It is hardly ever the wildlife that surprises me. The animals behave according to reasonably predictable patterns. But some people on safari! They can be weird. There's something about the African air that can change them. The wilderness awakens the senses. It's arousing. Like alcohol, it changes perspectives and lowers the defences. The genie pops out of the bottle. Sometimes as a guide you just don't see it coming. And sometimes you do. And if guides are of the mind, they can take advantage of it.

I think of Linda. In those days we described a safari holiday as one for the 'newly weds and the nearly deads.' The demographic has changed a lot now, a more even spread of ages, as middle-class wealth has spread in America, Europe and the East. But Linda was neither of those: she was middle-aged and had kept herself in fine trim over the years. When she and her husband stepped out of that little plane at the airstrip, her predatory eyes lit up like the morning sun as she spied Sean, the khaki warrior, waiting there, nice and upright next to his green Land Rover with the yellow sticker on the door. Sean's eyes widened too. God, Linda was a stunner! The atmosphere immediately crackled with sexual tension, and the game was on. Played by safari rules. If he chose.

Sean quickly discovered that Linda was adroit at finding ways of getting rid of her husband, a meek guy, and no doubt perfectly aware of what was happening, but he'd obviously been ignoring his wife's indiscretions for years. So when she suggested that he looked tired and might benefit from an early night ("You go ahead, darling. Sean and I will have just one more little drink here at the fire"), he timidly went off. When Linda thought that a private game drive with Sean was a good idea because her husband was getting bored with "all those leopards and things, I mean, how many of them are there out there for goodness sake!", he complied.

You think you know how this story pans out, don't you?

You're wrong. Sean managed Linda coolly and professionally, paid attention to her husband and spent as much time with him as Linda would allow, and, when she left the game reserve, she took her unrequited sexual urges with her. No 'clip-clop'. But of course those stories often did have a different kind of ending.

Things could get awkward. A guide called Jared nearly fell prey to an aspirant Black Widow spider (you know, those arachnids that mate with their partners, then kill and eat them) on her honeymoon. Her *honeymoon*. When he recognised the species and recoiled, rejecting her advances, she complained bitterly on day two (of four) to the manager that Jared was an inconsiderate guide, that his bush knowledge was poor, that he drove too fast, that he missed all the good sightings, that he was ignoring her (he was!), that he was in general a discredit to the game reserve. Unfortunately, the reserve management took her at face value (as they must with such a complaint, but even so, they displayed an alarming lack of impartiality) and the poor guy was immediately required to attend a disciplinary hearing. Since the guest had booked both a privately guided vehicle and private dining, there was no one to testify to Jared's innocence except for the husband, and it was brutally clear that he had no intention of getting involved. Eventually, mercifully, the case was dropped but Jared was so incensed by his treatment by both the vindictive Black Widow and the reserve that he went on leave and simply never came back. Beware the rapacious spider.

As in many businesses, there is a company policy on standards of conduct in safari lodges. Or not. Or not? Well, some safari companies in fact do, and did, not bother with the bits of paper that tried to regulate the social (read 'sexual') behaviour of their staff, relying instead on individual responsibility. I would say that that approach almost always worked. The fact is that contracts attempting to regulate human activity may serve as useful guidelines but they are nothing more than that. Human nature will always play out (and all too frequently find it's lowest point, like water) and even the most sensible of guides will sometimes stray from the accepted norms. Especially when a guest arrives seeking a bit of khaki.

One place I worked at had the unofficial policy of: 'We know it happens. We know *why* it happens. So, if it *does* happen, be discreet. Otherwise you'll get fired.' These days most licensed guides are required to sign a national Code of Conduct, and their training courses inevitably include a section where 'inappropriate familiarity' is heartily discouraged, along with other stern guidelines such as 'no solicitation from guests', 'treat travel agents like gold' and other Boy Scout stuff you don't think you actually need to be told. But whatever happened to 'use your common sense', 'discretion is the mark of a gentleman' and other inherent pearls of wisdom that are usually learned through osmosis? It's pretty obvious: if you are enamoured of just one guest, you are certainly not paying attention to the others. And that is not on.

Take Jennifer, for example. She came over from Scotland, travelling alone, and boy, was she on a mission. I don't know if that was her intention or the genie just unexpectedly came roaring out of the bottle, but, on the very first game drive, she got to work on poor Barry. He was a good looking lad all right, and pleasant in a rather serious sort of way, but naïve, straight out of university where it seems that he had done nothing except study his zoology textbooks and hide away from girls. The fairer sex was a terrifying creature to him and he could barely bring himself to talk even to the pretty young women with flouncy ponytails that managed the reception desk and curio shop. These girls were chosen for their looks as well as their administrative skills as a matter of unspoken policy, and they were lovely. Those criteria are sexist and would not pass muster these days, but that was how it was. As described earlier in this book, I myself was fortunate to have the 'right' skin colour, accent and schooling to get my guiding job. That's all changed. The lodges are now filled with all sorts of guides – women, men, multi-lingual, multi-racial, multi-national, gay and straight. It's not only a young white man's job anymore, and the diversity is fantastic.

Barry knew his stuff. He was one of those anorak guides, unstoppable on a plethora of obscure subjects such as migratory butterflies and the feeding behaviour of little known swifts, and he was seldom deflected by the inevitable inquiry of, "Yes, but where are the lions?" Reading textbooks was one of Barry's skills, reading social situations, not so much. But Jennifer didn't mind that. Because she could read *Barry*. He was clay to be moulded.

My goodness, she set about him. The first game drive was a shared one with other guests, but by the next morning she had had a word with Reception, paid an extra fee, and she had Barry to herself. They were quite late back to brunch that morning, and Barry had a dreamy and wide-eyed look about him. We guides all smirked and clapped him on the back and he looked very pleased with himself. By day two, his grin had diminished to something more tight-lipped: he wasn't liking our jokes anymore, and, by day three, (after Jennifer had extended her stay by another night), he was looking decidedly distressed. The poor man was worn out. Jennifer had turned out to be too much of a good thing, and he had a slightly desperate, trapped air about him. I saw the look Jennifer gave him when he dropped her at the airstrip, though: she wasn't done with Barry.

So, when Barry checked the booking sheets a few weeks later and saw her name there again – sole use of vehicle – he went pale. The manager noticed his frightened look, took pity on him and gave him leave for that period. I assume the manager let Jennifer know that Barry wasn't available, but that didn't stop her; she had the fever. Another guide, Kevin, who had been on leave when the Barry episode happened, was slated to guide her. When Jennifer alighted from the Cessna and Kevin walked over to meet her, she had a mean and hungry look about her. We hadn't warned him, of course. Poor Kevin.

Khaki fever. It is very real. But what is it? What is this malady that so often grips people when they come to the wilderness? Why do perfectly normal, sober-minded people often find a renewed sexual appetite in the bush? Why is it that their guide sometimes becomes an object of sexual desire? Not every guide is handsome, articulate, witty, gun-toting (many guests like that) or even available. *Au contraire*, many are smelly buggers that wear their uniforms without enough pride and have no sophistication about them whatsoever. Some are simply society dropouts whose only refuge is the bush. They don't even always *like* the guests. Yet they are desirable to many of them. I think it is because they're different to the people that the guests meet in their daily lives. A bit exotic. Just a little bit... dangerous?

I'm told that there can be something about a man in a uniform.

Safari is about adventure. Safari is about things beyond the norm. Safari is about perceived *danger*. It is about a small window into another world, a place where you want to dip your toe into, just your little toe and not for too long, and feel the thrill of things beyond your ken. If you have been on safari, you'll know that in addition to the usual inside one, almost every tent or room has an outside shower too. Very few people have taken a shower outdoors before – indeed, many fear to do so. But, on a warm day, when they step naked outside and face the wilderness, with birds in the trees overhead and an elephant idly strolling by, on a warm day when afterwards the breeze dries their skin and they stand there quite exposed, watching a crocodile sun-basking on the sand bank right below the tent, why, that is delicious, energising, thrilling. It is sensual. Not necessarily overtly sexual. Deeply sensual.

The people who build safari lodges know this. My boss once told me that every room must be totally private from every angle of view so that a couple would be able to make love in any and every place in the room and veranda without being seen (or heard) by the neighbours. He knew what sells. Ever seen the glossy brochures advertising a safari lodge? There's always a beautiful girl in the infinity pool, invariably naked, with her back to the camera, with a colourful drink close at hand. Safari is certainly sensual. Tingly.

The very rawness of the wilderness is an aphrodisiac. Everything about it reminds us that once we lived in caves and scrabbled for a living in competition with other animals, living in fear of predators that were faster and fiercer than we were. It was very edgy indeed, and we had to be clever to survive. We're not that far removed from that time; we remain elemental. We recognise that if we go out in the dark on safari, we could be in mortal danger from lions and hyaenas. If we venture into the swirling brown stream, a crocodile, undetected and sinister, could snatch us. If we poke our head into the den of the sleeping bear, beware! Despite our technological advances, we remain vulnerable in the wilderness. And on safari we actually feel that. It is simultaneously thrilling and scary. It's not for show that the guides escort you to your room at night, usually armed with a rifle. No wonder they warn you against walking anywhere except on the pathways, and to stay indoors at night. You're safe... but you're in danger. Ooh, that feels *good*.

And nothing can be more elemental than the heady stew of sex. The promise of romance, albeit temporary (dipping the little toe), the adventure, excitement and a little peril. Leaven all this with a youthful and keen young fellow, thicken with hormones and flavour with alcohol, and your stew is cooked. It is very easy to over-eat. Usually it's the short-term 'nudge-nudge, wink-wink, what goes on safari, stays on safari' type of affair, and most people understand the rules, and expect nothing more. But sometimes these trysts develop into permanent arrangements. Sometimes those arrangements actually last, too. Actually, surprisingly often if I think of my friends who have married their clients. Go Jack. Go Belinda. Go Chris. Go, you good things! I never thought it would last!

Larry guided an Italian honeymoon duo at a lodge in the Sabi Sands, a couple who were obviously in love, smiling into each other's faces, always holding hands like teenagers. A lovely, happy couple. So he was very surprised to receive a Facebook message nearly twenty years later from the lady, inviting him to 'friend' her. More than that, to come over to Rome and stay with her. She had had three children in the interim but was now divorced and wanted to 'see if the old magic was still there'. Larry was gob-smacked. What magic? Absolutely nothing had happened between him and the lady. It had been nothing but a fun safari and he had liked both her and her husband. What message had she perceived from him? None that he had deliberately put out. Yet apparently khaki fever had struck. As I say, expect the unexpected. Bizarre. Larry did not reply, he did not go to Rome, and eventually the messages from his 'Latin lover' stopped clogging his inbox.

But I have seen cases where the guide did take up the invitation to go and live abroad with an infatuated client. It almost always ends badly. It's different over there in the first world. Khaki fever diminishes as memories of the African sun dim and the guide's tan fades, and, to him, the birds seem to call less stridently at the break of day, the beer tastes bitter and there's something wrong with the *braai* meat. It's an old saying: you can take the guide out of the bush, but you can't take the bush out of the guide. Not a proper guide. Not a guide who went to the wilderness because he was drawn to it. Not unless he finds a way to get back to Africa frequently.

A guide ought to understand mammalian behaviour. You'd think. But they sometimes get caught out by clients who know the game, who prey upon the instincts of the guide, who are out for some malicious fun. Peta was one. She was a rich-kid, spoiled, young and very beautiful, and she loved to tease. Peta played the game with practised skill, and I watched her cruelly lead Deon, her guide, straight into the pit. Her father, the exasperated man, watched it happening, too. He was obviously repelled by her behaviour and wore an apologetic look. I don't know where the mother was: divorced, I think. I saw Peta's dad talking to Deon in a confiding way but Deon really thought it was love, reciprocated. If the silly bugger had only paid attention to Peta's behaviour with other guests and guides, he would have recognised that he was a pawn: she was flirtatious, vain and coquettish with every man there. But Deon was smitten, and promised that he would visit Peta in Europe on his very next leave. I really think he thought they were going to get married, that he would have a life abroad with money, connections, comfort, that he had found a life-love. Foolish man: he cried quietly when he read the only letter she sent him after she left. "Do you really think you're the first guy to have fallen in love with me? Get a life."

Guides, too, can be feckless, ruthless and hard-hearted when it comes to the effects of khaki fever. Sometimes they play. But sometimes they get played. Sometimes they're the bug. Sometimes they're the windshield. Broken hearts dot the safari trail. It works both ways.

There are safari guide's wives (and perhaps husbands these days) who fear and hate khaki fever. Especially if that is how they procured a husband themselves. They understand its workings, its natural and almost inevitable consequences. It must be very hard to see all the photos posted on Facebook at the end of a safari where your husband is at the centre of every champagne and sunset picture, an adoring woman with her arms looped across his epauletted shoulder, laughing, possessive, grasping... and your husband's response is always, 'Oh, khaki fever, part of the job, you know how it goes, nothing happened.' Perhaps not, pal, perhaps not, she's thinking. Or maybe, she's thinking, because you are human, because no one is immune to flattery and attention and a good old ego boost, because you are a sexual being, maybe something *did* happen. Maybe it happens *every* time. Maybe it doesn't matter. To you. So maybe I can't be married to you anymore. Because of that, and because you're having more fun than me, stuck at home with the kids as I am, doing their homework with them, dropping them at ballet and cricket practice, going to PTA meetings without you. So maybe, since we're on the maybe-train here, you should change jobs, and be with *me*. Just saying.

But he probably won't because he probably can't. He's a guide. He would wither in town, and without the attention he gets as a guide. He needs the bush, and the thrill it brings. The thrill of being the key that unlocks the magic of the wilderness to people. The conduit that allows people to reconnect to their very souls, to the elemental parts of the human condition. He can only be himself. He chose this. But there is sometimes a price to be paid when it comes to relationships, and I have seen it happen countless times.

As well as creating African journeys, I give guide training courses these days, mostly to young black men. And an important aspect of the training is this: be bloody careful how you greet and say farewell to clients on a daily basis. It is a matter of etiquette and custom that African guides have trouble with, and they ask about it all the time. It's confusing, especially to guides who have not had the advantage of international travel.

Once we have got past the basics of learning the firm (not limp... ugh! But many African people shake hands that way, it's cultural) handshake for both men and women on first greeting, we move to ongoing physical contact. By the time the guide has been with the clients for a few days, has shown them leopards and rhinos and elephants nursing their young and buffalos seeing off a lion attack, has poured them fine wine and perhaps demonstrated his outdoor cooking skills, by the time he has talked proudly about his upbringing, his dreams and in general charmed the hell out of the clients... well, understandably, they really like him. So when the 20-year-old daughter who has laughed at all his jokes and flashed her teeth at him all day, innocently kisses him on each cheek in nothing more than a friendly European goodnight, what is he to think? Is this a come-on? It could be, but it is likely nothing more than 'thanks for a great day and see you tomorrow.' Careful chaps, I warn them, don't misread this, you're nothing more than new friends. Too many guides have misread that and ended up being fired for 'inappropriate familiarity'. The reality is that some clients are in fact looking for sex, of course, but you have to know the difference. Warning: if you venture there, don't think that they want to take you back to the first world with them. You're probably just a passing titillation.

There's another species of khaki fever, but in this case the clients bring their partners with them. Prostitutes. High class call girls. Call them what you will, but the girls are extremely good looking and obviously used to being ferried and feted about the world. The men are almost always Russian, almost always middling drunk on vodka, almost always obnoxious, and almost always at an exclusive safari lodge just because they can be. It's a generalisation, I know, but generalisations are generally true. The lodge staff hate them, not just because they are loud and rude and demanding and without regard for other guests, but because (a far worse sin) they seem totally without respect for the environment. There is no love affair with nature.

One such man, at Serra Cafema Camp in northern Namibia, loudly related to all the horrified guests that he had hunted a polar bear from a Russian military helicopter using an AK-47 assault rifle, and went on to describe how the bear's blood had turned the snow pink. Lovely! All the while, his tall Ukrainian escort was hanging on his arm, shrieking with forced laughter, wearing high heels (which kept getting stuck in the planked flooring) and a body-hugging suit that made everyone else either envious or uncomfortable. He was an oil-Russian, he had the cash, and he was flaunting it. Their sex was noisy too, but the manager, an old hand, quickly read the situation and 'upgraded' them to the honeymoon suite down by the rapids where Rasputin's orgasmic grunts and her squeals might be drowned out by the crashing waters. Oh, those Russians!

The life of a guide may sound glamorous and exciting but it comes with that great leveller: lack of sleep. It's a very long day, waking the guests pre-dawn, driving and walking with them on activities, entertaining them at meals, doing airstrip pick-ups and drop-offs, giving out energy all day, enjoying the wine and whiskey at a splendid dinner that night, staying funny, staying sharp, getting to bed far too late... and then doing that again and again, for each set of new guests, week after week after week. Most guides are sleep deprived. After a while, you start to walk and talk like an automaton. I had times on game drive where I was so exhausted that I literally could not force words from my mouth; the most I could manage was an exhausted slur. Times when I was so bored with myself, talking about the mundanities of the life cycle of impalas, that I had to furtively pinch myself awake. Times when I inadvertently fell asleep behind my binoculars, my elbows propped up in the curve of the steering wheel. Times when I did an airstrip pick-up, fell asleep waiting for the Cessna, and was woken up by the pilot who had actually landed and taxied that noisy little bird right up to my Land Rover, covering me in dust. A time when I was so exhausted after three months of continual guiding without a single day off that as I walked rapidly back to my tent at one in the morning, desperate to squeeze in four short hours of sleep, and a pair of leopards confronted me on the raised walkway, I was so incensed at the inconvenience and potential loss of sleep time that I ran screaming at them, and scattered them to the wilderness. Diurnal creatures like humans are supposed to *sleep* at night.

Even so, it can be hard to resist 'just one for the road' in the company of an eager young lady with khaki fever. Mammalian instinct. So, when my colleague Tertius returned surprisingly soon after dinner back to the house we guides shared, we were amazed.

"We thought you were in, there, Tertius. She's lovely!" we said. "If you're not, you're just being lazy, man!"

Tertius looked at us steadily and replied, "Chinas, I've been guiding every day for the past 78 days. I'm stuffed. Right now, I'd rather have sleep than sex."

There's some weird stuff that goes on, too. As I said earlier, safari brings the genie out of the bottle, and he can be an odious fellow, so I think I'll keep this paragraph short. Suffice it to say, there was one guy all of us guides fought tooth and nail not to guide. The problem was, he kept coming back, and we had to take it in turns. He was polite and kind, and a generous tipper too. But no-one wanted to guide him. Because he would book a private vehicle, ask to be taken to any sighting where animals were reported to be mating (usually lions, which couple several times an hour), and while they were doing it, he would masturbate furtively under a game drive blanket. Let's leave it there.

So what about me, then? Well, I caught a fever early in my life, long before I became a guide. It wasn't khaki fever. It was another kind of rapture known as 'love at first sight', an enduring kind, and I have carried it with me forever. But I have been in and around the safari madness for a long time, of course. Did it ever get hold of me? It would be unusual for anyone in the safari business to have avoided it entirely.

You figure it out.

39

MISNAMES

I have been collecting these inadvertent mispronunciations for years, every one of them uttered by either a guest or a guide while on game drive. I like them so much that I tend to use them while guiding but sometimes I forget that they are actually howlers, which can elicit a strange look from the experienced and the wise. Mostly though, people are perfectly content to accept them at face value, which makes them even funnier.

BIRDS
1. Aqua duck (Namaqua dove)
2. Spare wheel goose (Spurwinged goose)
3. Black and whitesmith plover (Blacksmith plover)
4. Edible duck (Yellowbilled duck)
5. Bachelor's starling (Burchell's starling)
6. Sadly-built stork (Saddlebilled stork)
7. Fork-trunked dragon (Forktailed drongo)
8. Fog-tailed drongo (Forktailed drongo)

9. Fokken Dronk Ou (Forktailed drongo)
10. Freaking jacana (African jacana)
11. Lilac-created roofers (Lilacbreasted roller)
12. Secret ibis (Sacred ibis)
13. Grass ibis (Glossy ibis)
14. Priested barbet (Crested barbet)
15. Slutty egret (Slaty egret)
16. Crusted francolin (Crested francolin)
17. Readable wood hoopoe (Redbilled wood hoopoe)
18. Wild naked stork (Woollynecked stork)
19. Aggressive guineafowl (Crested guineafowl): sometimes under a Sickly (Sickle) bush
20. Black-chested snack eagle (Snake eagle)
21. Jenny fool (Guineafowl)
22. Tonic eagle (Tawny eagle)
23. Carp's black titty (Carp's black tit)
24. Shovel weaver (Sociable weaver)
25. Black crack (Black crake)
26. Physical flycatcher (Fiscal flycatcher)
27. Rufer-snaped lark (Rufousnaped lark)
28. Cerise-sided Silver-spotted Swerving swallow (no such bird exists. I use it when an unidentified bird flashes by, which causes guests and guides alike to frown and page though their bird identification books in puzzlement).

ANIMALS
1. Articulated giraffe (Reticulated giraffe)
2. Cylinderhead mongoose (Slender mongoose)
3. Selinda mongoose (Slender mongoose)
4. Banjo zebra (Burchell's zebra)
5. Bugger Boy (Dhaga Boy – male buffalo)
6. Honey beaver (African badger/ratel)
7. Bamboos (baboons)
8. Das rockie (Rock dassie/hyrax)

EPILOGUE

Right, so that's some of the stuff that really goes on, in the back of house, and in the back of a safari guide's mind. We exaggerate and we steal stories and we get fired and we fall in love and we get tattoos and we drive too fast and we get lost and we deal with death and (gasp!), sometimes, we even have to shoot animals. We tolerate the narrow-focused plague of the Big Five list and, too often, drink too much and get too little sleep. We contract malaria and meet amazing people and, because we have all the usual human faults, foibles and failures, sometimes we simply mess up. Sometimes, we just laugh. It's better than the alternative! These are all confessions that require no absolution. That's because we guides do a grand and willing job of showing you just how wonderful Africa is; we play a role, we create theatre, we conjure up magic and we do it on the best stage of all: the wilderness. The props are glorious and the non-speaking actors always come to the party. We love what we do. We love it! And we delight in sharing it.

But here's a final confession. Well, it's more of a connundrum, really. The wilderness has been largely tamed. Sometimes our, "Isn't this amazing?" mask slips because of an uncomfortable contradiction. It is this: wildlife tourism is great. It is great for us (jobs), it is great for wildlife (conservation of their habitats), it is great for governments (tax revenue) and it is great for safari tourists (a mind-blowing experience). It's great; but where's the edginess? Where's the wildness of the wilderness? It will always hold tremendous appeal but safari has become almost a bit too easy. Too safe, too predictable, almost *too* accessible. Is the thrill of the bush becoming tepid? There is a very real fear that the genuine magic of safari will disappear under a deluge of marketing promises and convenience: cheap air flights, virtually guaranteed game viewing, air-conditioned luxury lodges, any kind of food in any season, and high-speed internet in the camps.

As one guest commented recently as he watched hippos mouth-gaping in the Limpopo river: "Well, it's good, but it's better in Disneyland." I really, really wish he had been joking at the time. No connection, you see. He'd traded substance for surface. He'd willingly fallen in love with plastic. Still, we have to recognise that not everyone wants to be David Livingstone, that great intrepid, walking for years through Africa in futile search of the source of the Nile and dying inexorably from blackwater fever. No Google Maps and Malarone back then.

So, many safari travellers are no longer warriors. They are *worriers*. They are not necessarily present with nature, they are present with their devices. They trade wonder and awe for sound bites and video clips and check-lists. They are in a pace where healing and reconnection is *right there* but their interest is derailed by social media postings and share prices, sports scores and the self-absorbed nonsenses of moronic world leaders.

And it troubles us guides to see the actual thrill of the bush being replaced by the virtual thrill of Facebook. That's not why you're there, for goodness sake. Is it? Be in *this* moment, not that of your digital friends. Listen. Look. Most vitally, *feel!*

(Another confession: I am perfectly aware that many guides themselves fall into this trap, that their own bush experiences are defined by their shared social media presence. Plenty of guides play the nauseating game of social media one-upmanship too. They like a 'like' as much as anyone).

But I take comfort from the fact that there are still vast wild places out there, more are being accessed each year, and even if some of the wilderness has gone digital, there is still nowhere else, nothing else, that changes perspectives like an African safari can. I have witnessed it again and again: the visceral thrill of being in the presence of wildlife, of being in wild places, the reconnection with soul, the simple joy of standing in a silver pool of healing moonlight.

So, come on back: Africa Bites. Twice.

PAYING ATTENTION
(A Poem For Sunset)

You come over here and you mess with my head
(I'm thinking)
So many things that you don't leave unsaid
So many poems that are as yet un-read
Plenty to do, before I am dead.

We take a walk and you smile with the sky
So much to learn before I die
So much to write before goodbye
An abundance of time, and so much to try.

You ask and you laugh and you write it all down
An elephant passes, and as you have shown
An elephant passes, and with it you've grown
Too much of so much, and with it I drown.

You furrow your brow when a thing is unclear
Maybe, perhaps, just can't say from here
Maybe, perhaps, but the answer is near
Could be, don't know, but it's no cause to fear.

We share a firm grip on the things that should count
Yet drowning, I find out what life is about
Yet drowning, I see there are things to surmount
But struggling, I'm part of life's total amount.

We talk of our lives and it's good to recall
It's all about watching the evening light fall
It's all about noticing things which are small
The details, my friend, always hold you in thrall.

You come over here, and you mess with my head
You leave me with plans and ideas instead
You leave me with poems that are as yet unsaid
(I'm thinking)
Now I'm paying attention, and will till I'm dead.

For Westsky Dan

GLOSSARY

AA: Automobile Association. A roadside rescue company for distressed motorists

Acacia: thorny tree species, toothless versions of which occur also in Australia

Ag: expression of mild disgust (Afrikaans)

Allo-grooming: a form of mutualistic social bonding when two or more creatures clean each other simultaneously e.g. zebras, impalas

Aluta continua: the struggle continues (Portuguese)

Aloe: a family of succulent shrubs with spiny leaves that thrive mostly in arid areas

Amarula: popular milky liqueur made from the fermented juice of Marula tree fruits, best enjoyed in coffee on chilly early morning game drives

Baobab *(Adansonia digitata)*: iconic, massive tree with great spreading branches and pendulous fruit

Bakkie: small pick-up truck (Afrikaans)

Bandar-log: the monkey people of Rudyard Kipling's *The Jungle Book* (Hindi)

Biltong: traditional dried cured meat vastly under-appreciated by many safari travellers (Afrikaans)

Bokmakierie: strikingly coloured bush shrike with a marvellous ringing call (Afrikaans – onomatopoeic)

Boma: traditionally a communal meeting place, usually within a stockade, a concept that safari lodges have adapted as a safe alfresco dining space for the evening meal (kiSwahili)

Braai: the proper term for barbecue. Fresh meat grilled over hot coals. Salads also available but largely ignored (Afrikaans)

Bru: affectionate term for a brother/friend (Afrikaans; short for *broeder*)

Bunting: small seed/insect eating bird, sometimes brightly coloured, always numerous

Bushveld: semi-arid thorn tree savannah, highly suited to a wide variety of wildlife (English/Afrikaans)

Cecil the Lion: a well-known male lion from Hwange National Park that was illegally and controversially bow-hunted in 2015, causing a furore in conservation circles

China: china plate = mate = friend (colloquial, South African English, originally from Cockney rhyming slang)

Chippy: what New Zealanders call carpenters

Crocuta crocuta: Latinised zoological name for the Spotted hyena

Croton megalobotrys: widespread large-leafed tree occurring on island fringes of the Okavango delta

Cuca shops: small rural shop constructed of corrugated iron and wood that sells warm beer in quarts, single cigarettes and other essentials (Portuguese)

Dagga: marijuana. Widely enjoyed across sub-Saharan Africa with little legal repercussion (isiZulu)

Dhaga Boy: old male buffalo that likes to wallow in comforting mud ('dhaga' = mud in isiZulu)

Damara-Nama: the shared language of the Damara and Nama peoples of Namibia

Dassie: originally from the Dutch 'dassen', meaning rabbit. A cliff and tree dwelling rodent (Afrikaans)

Donga: a rain and wind eroded ravine system, dry, except in the rainy season (isiZulu)

Dunedin Star: a British ship wrecked on the Skeleton Coast of Namibia in 1942. An overland rescue mission to fetch beach survivors took only a single hand-pump. Countless punctures slowed the mission down considerably

Eland: the largest of all the African antelopes (Dutch)

ETA: estimated time of arrival

Euphorbia: a family of thorny succulent trees mostly found in arid areas of Africa

Flehmen-face: a behaviour in some mammals (e.g. horses, antelopes and cats) in which the animal tests the mating readiness of a potential partner by inhaling with the mouth open and upper lip curled in order to facilitate exposure of the vomeronasal organ to a scent or pheromone.

FNG's: fucking new guys

Francois Pienaar: legendary World Cup-winning South Africa rugby captain from 1993 to 1996

Gaijin: foreigners (Japanese)

Gemsbok: or Southern oryx. A large antelope that prefers near-desert environmental conditions (Afrikaans)

Genny: abbreviation for generator. The classic lodge genny was the old diesel Lister

Goen: the largest of the multi-coloured marbles (Afrikaans)

Grewia: a common shrub with several species, known as a raisin bush for its edible fruit

Guarri bushes *(Euclea divinorum)*: common small shrub

Harry Wolhuter: famous South African game ranger in the Kruger National Park who in 1903 was mauled by a lion, but which he killed using his sheath knife

Hamerkop: a medium-sized brown egret that sports a hammer-shaped crest on its head, hence hammer-head (Afrikaans)

Hilux: Toyota Hilux, a much favoured, reliable *bakkie* used extensively across Africa in preference to other brands because it never breaks down. Often used to pull stuck Land Rovers out of thick mud and deep sand

Himba: correctly, OvaHimba. A migratory pastoral tribe of northern Namibia/southern Angola

Honshu: the largest island in the Japanese archipelago

Horbors: plenty, many (Rhodesian slang)

Hou noord en fok voort: head north, and just keep fucking going (Afrikaans)

Hush Puppys: cheap plastic town shoes with soft soles, popular in South Africa in the 70's/80's but still worn alarmingly often to this day

iMkuze (Game Reserve): a KZN wildlife reserve

Isandhlwana: a battle fought on the afternoon of a solar eclipse (22 January 1879) where the Zulu *impis* (regiments) annihilated a British force of more than 800 men

isiZulu: the language of the Zulu people

Ja: yes. Used universally by all people across South Africa (Afrikaans)

Jussus: exclamation of amazement/frustration; literally, Jesus (Afrikaans)

Kak: shit (Afrikaans)

Kasane: a small town in the north-eastern corner of Botswana, on the Chobe river

Khakis: ubiquitous hard-wearing cotton uniform clothing worn by rangers/guides and certain enthusiastic safari clients

Khoekhoe: indigenous nomadic pastoralist peoples of south-western Africa

Kobas: a squat mountain tree typical of high rocky places in Namibia

Korhaan: long-legged ground bird with a distinctive frog-like call (Afrikaans)

Koppie: small bouldery hill (Afrikaans)

Klipspringer: small goat-like antelopes that live in pairs on *koppies* (Afrikaans)

KNP: Kruger National Park, often known simply as 'The Kruger'

Kraal: enclosure for livestock in an African homestead (Afrikaans)

KZN: KwaZulu-Natal. The most important of the nine provinces of South Africa

Landy: abbreviation of Land Rover, the legendary safari vehicle of Africa

Lapa: shaded communal open-sided gathering place for meetings and meals (Sotho)

Lassi: a flavoured drink made from yoghurt or buttermilk (Hindi)

Leguaan: a large monitor lizard, usually associated with water (Afrikaans)

Lekker: great/nice (Afrikaans, but widely used by all races in South Africa)

Lekgoa: a white person. Derogatory (Setswana)

Lowveld: low lying bush savannah in north-eastern South Africa (English/Afrikaans)

Magtig: Almighty God! An expression of surprise (Afrikaans)

Malarone: anti-malarial prophylactic

Manne: men (Afrikaans)

Marie biscuits: ever popular South African tea-time snack

Marthambles: a fictitious disease invented by English quacks in the early eighteenth century which they claimed could be cured only by their own special concoctions

Maun: an uninspiring town on the edge of the Okavango Delta that supplies and services the lodges of the Swamps

Mangosteen *(Garcinia livingstonia)*: a common bushveld tree with upright branches that resemble the hairstyle of Don King

Meneer: Sir. A term of respect (Afrikaans)

Mlungus: white people. Commonly used, not necessarily respectful (Bantu languages)

Mombo: a lodge in the heart of the Okavango delta

Mopane *(Colophospermum mopane)*: an indigenous tree in arid areas

Nama: a tribal grouping, mostly in south/central Namibia

NGO: privately funded non-governmental organisation, typically run by well-meaning and sometimes effective enthusiasts whose principles may not be as well aligned with national policy as the government would like them to be

Nyala: medium-sized antelope native to riverine bush in the eastern parts of southern Africa (Tsonga)

Okes: guys (Afrikaans)

Onsen: hot spring, for bathing (Japanese)

Ou maat: old friend (Afrikaans)

Panga: large broad-bladed machete/bush knife (kiSwahili)

Paraffin: lantern fuel (kerosene)

PB: personal best. Usually used to describe one's best athletic performance

Platteland: the treeless flatlands of the interior plateau of southern Africa (Afrikaans)

Pietermaritzburg: capital city of the province of KwaZulu-Natal. Once known as the Garden City, but now in decline (Afrikaans)

QEP: Queen Elizabeth Park, HQ of Ezemvelo KZN Wildlife, the public body that runs the game reserves of KZN province in South Africa

Sabi Sand Game Reserve: a vast private game reserve consortium west of and contiguous with the Kruger National Park

Sies: expression of utmost disgust (Afrikaans)

Skabenga: a villainous scoundrel or miscreant. Often used as an affectionate insult (isiZulu)

SLR: single lens reflex camera. A camera in which the lens that forms the image on the film also provides the image in the viewfinder

Smarties: South African version of MnM'z, sugar-coated chocolate buttons in a range of bright colours. A basic food group for many first world children

Stywe pap: the basic carbohydrate for most Africans, derived from milled maize. Eaten as a stiff porridge (Afrikaans)

Soutie (Soutpiel): derogatory description of an English-speaking South African, usually from KZN. Derived from the perception that such people have divided loyalties, with one foot in England, another in South Africa, with their penis hanging in the briny ocean. Literally, 'salt-penis' (Afrikaans)

Spoor: tracks and traces indicating the passage of animals. Hence "following spoor", or tracking, to locate an animal (Afrikaans)

Sumimasen: excuse me, or sorry (Japanese)

Tjommie: chum/friend (Afrikaans)

Two-spoor tracks: rough, non-maintained roads in the bush with a middle-hump which the wheels and undercarriage of a vehicle (usually) do not touch

USP: advertising jargon for unique selling point, a competitive differentiator

Veld: open grassland in southern Africa (Afrikaans)

Veldskoene: leather shoes traditionally made from antelope hide (Afrikaans, lit. bush shoes)

Waterpomp plier: slip-joint pliers universally and generally successfully employed to fix almost anything in the bush (Afrikaans/English)

Witblitz: moonshine (Afrikaans)

WTM: World Travel Market, an annual tourism bunfight (trade show) in London

Zululand: now KwaZulu, the area north of the Thukela river in KwaZulu-Natal province in South Africa, and the traditional homeland of the Zulu nation

.375: the calibre of a rifle commonly carried by guides when walking on safari

ABOUT THE AUTHOR

Lloyd Camp is a safari itinerary specialist, guide and guide trainer who grew up in South Africa and who has been leading wildlife trips into the wilderness areas of Namibia, Zimbabwe, Zambia, Botswana, Mozambique, Rwanda, Kenya, Tanzania, Uganda and South Africa since 1992.

He started his career in the South African Lowveld before managing lodges and guiding in the Okavango Delta and Linyanti regions of Botswana. Later he moved to Namibia where he established a training school for a prominent safari company and earned his reputation for leading bespoke safaris across the continent, including walking safaris, as well as for running guide training courses in several countries, focusing on bringing local people into the safari industry.

Lloyd and his wife, Sue, live in Richmond, south-west London.

In his spare time he likes to climb mountains, run marathons, paddle rivers, race his bicycle and go for very long walks. But not at night. At night, he reads. Everything he can get his hands on. Unless he's watching sports on TV.